Gail Jones

SYDNEY STUDIES IN AUSTRALIAN LITERATURE

Robert Dixon, Series Editor

The Sydney Studies in Australian Literature series publishes original, peer-reviewed research in the field of Australian literary studies. It offers engagingly written evaluations of the nature and importance of Australian literature, and aims to reinvigorate its study both locally and internationally.

Alex Miller: The Ruin of Time
Robert Dixon

Australian Books and Authors in the American Marketplace 1840s–1940s
David Carter and Roger Osborne

Christina Stead and the Matter of America
Fiona Morrison

Colonial Australian Fiction: Character Types, Social Formations and the Colonial Economy
Ken Gelder and Rachael Weaver

Contemporary Australian Literature: A World Not Yet Dead
Nicholas Birns

Elizabeth Harrower: Critical Essays
Ed. Elizabeth McMahon and Brigitta Olubas

Fallen Among Reformers: Miles Franklin, Modernity, and the New Woman
Janet Lee

The Fiction of Tim Winton: Earthed and Sacred
Lyn McCredden

Gail Jones: Word, Image, Ethics
Tanya Dalziell

Gerald Murnane: Another World in This One
Ed. Anthony Uhlmann

Richard Flanagan: Critical Essays
Ed. Robert Dixon

Shirley Hazzard: New Critical Essays
Ed. Brigitta Olubas

Gail Jones

Word, Image, Ethics

Tanya Dalziell

SYDNEY UNIVERSITY PRESS

First published by Sydney University Press

© Tanya Dalziell 2020
© Sydney University Press 2020

Reproduction and communication for other purposes

Except as permitted under the Act, no part of this edition may be reproduced, stored in a retrieval system, or communicated in any form or by any means without prior written permission. All requests for reproduction or communication should be made to Sydney University Press at the address below:

Sydney University Press
Fisher Library F03
University of Sydney NSW 2006
AUSTRALIA
sup.info@sydney.edu.au
sydneyuniversitypress.com.au

A catalogue record for this book is available from the National Library of Australia.

ISBN 9781743326978 paperback
ISBN 9781743327012 epub
ISBN 9781743327029 mobi
ISBN 9781743327036 pdf

Cover image: Heike Steinweg Photography

For Eladia, Caleb & Jordi

Contents

Acknowledgements ix

Introduction 1
1 Weather 23
2 Time 49
3 Reading and Writing 79
4 Image 105
5 Modernity 141
Conclusions 169

Works Cited 173
Index 181

Acknowledgements

I would like to thank Robert Dixon, the SUP series editor. Robert's scholarship on Gail Jones' novels is an inspiration and his intelligent engagement with this volume has been invaluable. I wish to acknowledge and thank the Honours students with whom I have discussed Gail Jones' writing over several years. Their insights and questions have helped shape my thinking and reading. I am grateful for the collegiate spirit and solidarity that distinguishes our English and Literary Studies group at the University of Western Australia. Special thanks to Paul Genoni for his friendship, erudition and good humour, and to Victoria Burrows for her camaraderie. As always, Margot and Kevin Dalziell have been unfailingly supportive. My deepest, affectionate thanks are owed to Jamie Hamilton and Eladia, Caleb and Jordi Hamilton-Dalziell.

Introduction

The opening story of Gail Jones' earliest short-story collection, *The House of Breathing* (1992), tells of a young girl from a small Siberian village who attends a Moscow cinema for the first time. The year is 1920, the film is a comedy, and the girl is utterly terrified by what she sees:

> Human beings are visually torn to pieces, the heads thrown one way, the bodies another. Faces loom large or contract to tiny circles. There are severed heads, multiple dismemberments, and horrible discontinuities.[1]

The girl's fear derives from her unfamiliarity with cinematic conventions. She interprets close-ups as amputations; the film world is awry. She flees from the cinema, and much later finds comfort in the encircling embrace of her babushka. But what she relates of her astonishing experience is unexpected. Instead of recounting the horror she has seen, the girl "dwelled, in concentration, on a single detail: there had been a cone of bright light, a white passageway of floating motes, delicate, enchanting, apparently transcendental, which might, after all, have somehow mystically signified the transit of angels" (18–19). She tells of her affective transportation by light, of metaphysical visions reframed in terms of mechanical reproduction.

While it is unwise to place retrospective over-importance on a single story – particularly one so conveniently positioned at the very beginning of a writing career now spanning over twenty-five years – it is nevertheless compelling in that it speaks of what preoccupies much of Jones' writing. The story is premised on an intelligent, exceptional female protagonist who is given to serious and passionate inner excursion; conditions of estrangement; and a fascination with technologies of modernity. (The title – "Modernity" – almost too neatly anticipates an abiding interest of Jones' texts.) It allows for the possibility of extra-linguistic visions and

---

[1] Gail Jones, "Modernity", *The House of Breathing* (Fremantle: Fremantle Arts Centre Press, 1992), 11. All subsequent references are to this edition and appear in parentheses in the text.

aesthetic affirmations to traverse forms of loss and damage, while also foregrounding acts of representation through the cinematic nightmare of gruesome partition and the narrative in which the girl's illumination is told.

Not only is the girl a first-time movie goer, a status that affords her especial insight into the strangeness and wonder of cinema, like so many of Jones' protagonists, the young girl of "Modernity" is also a writer of sorts. She is said to have sent her father a letter detailing the shocking sight she had witnessed on screen, a personal act that supplements "the history of representation" (11). Jones herself has fielded the closely related question that authors are inevitably asked: "Why do you write?" Her response is redolent of the concerns of "Modernity": "To find cogency, peace, quiet, and joy; to practise radical attention to the world, to be an activist through words, and to forge solidarity through imagination."[2]

As an essayist and an academic (as well as a writer of short and long fiction, and an occasional book reviewer), Jones has had much to say about how and why imaginative writing might matter. In an interview she gave on being presented with the Sydney PEN award in 2011 for her active support of the network's charter, Jones said: "I've always thought literature might function as a mode of solidarity inasmuch as we're obliged to imagine the lives of others; this is the ethical capacity of writing that PEN vouchsafes in its internationalist charter and spirit."[3] Jones is circumspect about these ambitions: "I know better than to overestimate the role of the literary in political change."[4] Yet, she also insists on literature's ethical facility, which involves "an admission of uncertainty, a calculation of difficulty, and awareness that justice – and human relations – ... require commitment to some state of thinking that radically oscillates across time, between past and future and is therefore a condition of hope, rather than of certainty."[5]

Jones has expressly linked her thinking about ethics, writing and reading in part to the work of the philosopher Martha Nussbaum, whose advocacy of poetic justice rests, in Jones' words, "on the belief in rational emotions as the premise for a judicious literary intelligence" and is "one part, one small part, of the public discourse".[6] While the ethical literary tradition in which Jones has located her work is not without its detractors,[7] Nussbaum privileges what sympathetic commentators

---

2   Gail Jones, "Open Page", *Australian Book Review* no. 329 (March 2011): 68.
3   Gail Jones, "Supporting justice and the power of the individual voice", interviewed by Anon., *Sydney PEN Magazine*, November 2011, 5.
4   Gail Jones, "Surviving a Bootprint on the Page", *The Australian Literary Review*, 2 May, 2007, 25.
5   Gail Jones, "Speaking Shadows: Justice and the poetic", in *Just Words?: Australian Authors Writing for Justice*, ed. Bernadette Brennan (St. Lucia: University of Queensland Press, 2008), 86.
6   Jones, "Surviving a Bootprint", 25.
7   Dorothy Hales, for instance, has asked why it is that (in her understanding) "literary critics and theorists have drawn their ideas about ethics from Emmanuel Levinas, Jacques Derrida, Michel Foucault, Giorgio Agamben, and Alain Badiou, but have felt little or no need to consult past or present moral philosophers". Dorothy Hales, "Aesthetics and the New Ethics: theorizing the novel in the twenty-first century", *PMLA* 124 no. 3 (2009): 896. It is a conversation Mark Sanders sought to start with his essay "Introduction: ethics and interdisciplinarity in philosophy

have nominated "a different sort of eye, attentive to different sorts of things"; not a thesis, as in the case of a "straight" philosophical treatise, but rather a "subjunctive mood" that "deals in possibilities, ifs, conditions. Its form is interrogative".[8] Ethics, in the literary sense that Nussbaum propounds, is therefore vastly different from the foundational premises of moral philosophy, with its universal sweep and propensity to fix moral guidelines in advance of specific events or contexts.[9] Along with other literary theorists and philosophers, including Derek Attridge and David Palumbo-Liu,[10] Nussbaum is interested in the potential of literature to approach, enact and interrogate the ethical. For Nussbaum, "ethical theorizing proceeds by way of a reflective dialogue between the intuitions and beliefs of the interlocutor, or reader, and a series of complex ethical conceptions, presented for exploration".[11] Literature is a constitutive part of this dialogue.

Nussbaum develops the claims she makes for this ethical force of literature by working from the assumption that "the novel itself is a moral achievement, and the well-lived life is a work of literary art".[12] Literature is accorded this role because, according to Nussbaum, it "searches for patterns of possibility – of choice and circumstance, and the interaction between choice and circumstance – that turn up in human lives with such persistence that they must be regarded as *our*

---

and literary theory", *Diacritics* 32 no. 3-4 (2002): 2-16. Even between that small selection of philosophers Hales singles out as the favoured few of literary scholars, there is considerable debate over what constitutes ethics, let alone literary ethics. For one critical account, which extends beyond Hales' list, see Robert Eaglestone, *Ethical Criticism: Reading after Levinas* (Edinburgh: Edinburgh University Press, 1997). Grounding Eaglestone's thesis is the work of Emmanuel Levinas, in particular *Humanism of the Other*, trans. Nidra Poller (Urbana: University of Illinois Press, 2006) and *Otherwise Than Being; or, Beyond Essence*, trans. Alphonso Lingis (Pittsburgh: Duquesne University Press, 1998).

8   Cora Diamond, "Martha Nussbaum and the need for novels", in *Renegotiating Ethics in Literature, Philosophy and Theory*, eds. Jane Adamson, Richard Freadman and David Parker (Cambridge: Cambridge University Press, 1998), 49. Curiously, Nussbaum's claims about literature and ethics largely ignore cognate debates that have taken place within literary theory, particularly poststructuralist or deconstructionist thinking. Simon Critchley is not alone when he suggests that "deconstruction should be understood as an ethical demand", not least on the basis of its efforts to call into question ethics itself. Simon Critchley, *The Ethics of Deconstruction: Derrida and Levinas* (Oxford: Blackwell, 1992), 1.

9   These universalist claims of moral philosophy have troubled theorists and critics trained to privilege pragmatism – Jean-François Lyotard's work is especially influential in this regard – as well as difference, pluralism, particularity and anti-foundationalism. See Jean-François Lyotard and Jean-Loup Thebaud, *Just Gaming*, trans. Brian Massumi and Samuel Weber (Minneapolis: University of Minnesota Press, 1985). For these scholars, the absolute criteria that underpin ethics, which lie beyond question, are not indisputable truths that sensibly ground systems of thought, wisely guide our moral judgements and generally maintain social order. Rather, they are deeply troubling means by which relations of power are organised ideologically.

10 Derek Attridge, *The Singularity of Literature* (London: Routledge, 2004); David Palumbo-Liu, *The Deliverance of Others: Reading in a Global Age* (Durham: Duke University Press, 2012).

11 Martha C. Nussbaum, *The Fragility of Goodness: Luck and Ethics in Greek Tragedy and Philosophy* (Cambridge: Cambridge University Press, 1986), 10.

12 Martha C. Nussbaum, *Love's Knowledge: Essays on Philosophy and Literature* (Oxford: Oxford University Press, 1990), 148.

possibilities".[13] In other words, literature does not just present ethical difficulties but also offers ways to work through a particular set of issues heuristically. And it does so not with the aim of reaching some fixed answer, but rather as an open-ended enquiry. It is the condition of hope, this ethical curiosity and urgency in Jones' writing, that this book traces.

To date, Jones is the author of two short-story collections (*The House of Breathing* and *Fetish Lives* (1997)); a slim book on Jane Campion's film *The Piano* (1993) (*The Piano* (2007)); and many essays (including ficto-critical pieces) on topics that have the Australian body politic in their sights.[14] Her contributions to collections such as *Just Words?: Australian Authors Writing for Justice* (2008) and *A Country Too Far* (2013), a volume responding creatively to the controversial asylum-seeker policies of successive Australian governments, insist on the complicated relationships texts have with the contexts in which they are written and read, and emphasise the political, as well as aesthetic and personal, registers of Jones' literary commitment. A concern with the persisting legacies of British colonialism in Australia is especially evident across her writing. Jones' essays are notable for their respectful meditations on the resilience and resistance of Indigenous people and cultures, and the ethics of representation non-Indigenous writers in postcolonial Australia are faced with in the knowledge and context of a long and troubling colonial history. It is a history that has seen Aboriginal people, kin and land subject to murderous displacement, appropriation and assimilation, and one that has indelibly implicated Jones herself.

In many of her essays, Jones writes in the first-person point of view and makes specific reference to her childhood as a way of suggesting this involvement. In her fiction, childhood carries a special significance. Children are often afforded a unique kind of perception, and childhood memories are never far from the minds of her adult characters.[15] While such an autobiographical gesture in the essays might be taken as an explanation for Jones' writing interests, Jones insists that such memories, however uneasy and uncomfortable, are integral to the ethics she desires for literature – its responsibilities to reflect critically on private memories and experiences, which speak to larger histories:

---

13   Nussbaum, *Love's Knowledge*, 171. Nussbaum singles out the novels of Henry James as exemplary of the literature she is talking about. It is perhaps no coincidence that Alice Black in Jones' *Dreams of Speaking* (2006) purposefully purchases a novel by James.
14   Dominique Hecq has also noted that "One of the most remarkable features of Jones' work is its willingness to integrate many different discourses from areas such as philosophy, science, ethnography, psychoanalysis, feminism, narratology, narrative and the lyric. Yet Jones' work is memorable not for its polygeneric quality but precisely for not confining itself to mixing or juxtaposing antipodal modes and registers." Dominique Hecq, "Autofrictions: the fictopoet, the critic and the teacher", *Cultural Studies Review* 11 no. 2 (2005): 183.
15   Fiona Duthie has devoted an essay to the representation of the child in Jones' writing. See Fiona Duthie, "From Innocent to Evil: the representation of the child in the works of Gail Jones", *Westerly* 58 no. 1 (2013): 126–47.

> Since we live backwards as well as forwards, matters of conscience essentially require this revision; to be self-critical is to be circumspect, to learn what might stand in the way of right or wrong actions and thinking. Writerly elaboration – naming the past, speaking of it, offering an account – is one of our forms of negotiation.[16]

Jones emphasises this point in "Speaking Shadows: Justice and the Poetics", an essay that begins with a meditation on the poetry of Paul Celan[17] and leads to reflections on the ethical demands made by Indigenous people's testimonies comprising *Bringing Them Home: Report of the National Inquiry into the Separation of Aboriginal and Torres Strait Islander Children from Their Families* (1997). The report publicly brought to non-Indigenous attention the policies and practices that saw Aboriginal children forcibly removed from their families, and it provided Indigenous people with an opportunity to tell of their ongoing suffering. Jones writes:

> Ethical and moral laws are not mysteriously inscribed upon the singular heart; they occur in conceptions of public action and in social contracts. Value is in exchange, in dialogue, in complicated forms of reciprocity and redistribution. Much as we might admire what is often described as the individual "voice" of a writer, it is their participation in cultural value, their more generalised contribution to the richly strange economies of imagination, that finally matters.[18]

This "multidimensional memory" is at work across Jones' writing,[19] and its ethical force is apparent in her essay titled "Skulls, Fontanelles and the Spaces Between". Jones begins the essay by recalling a childhood experience, at the age of ten, at a private museum to the east of the mining town of Kalgoorlie in Western Australia. Here, among the "snakes and foetuses drifting spookily in formaldehyde", was a back room devoted to skulls, where her remembered precocity is also on display:

---

16   Jones, "Surviving a Bootprint", 24.
17   Jones' interest in Celan's poetry is an abiding one. The title, and ethical imperative, of Jones' essay speaks to Celan's ethical project of *Schatten Sprach*, his language of shadows, which is founded on loss. And a line from a poem in his volume *Die Niemandrose* (1963) – "Grow more heavy. Be more light" – serves as the epigraph to her most recent novel, *The Death of Noah Glass* (2018). Beth Hawkins interprets this poetic line suggestively: "Lightness suggests limitless possibility, but brings with it a great burden: to create meaning in the face of emptiness." Beth Watkins, *Reluctant Theologians: Franz Kafka, Paul Celan, Edmond Jabès* (New York: Fordham University Press, 2002), 115. It is an idea also suggested by the epigraph to *Dreams of Speaking*. There Jones quotes the Portuguese modernist Fernando Pessoa: "Let us sculpt hopeless silence in all our dreams of speaking." Fernando Pessoa, *The Book of Disquiet*, trans. Richard Zenith (London: Penguin, 2015), 348. All of Jones' writing grapples with this ethical demand.
18   Jones, "Speaking Shadows", 82.
19   This phrase is Michael Rothberg's. Rothberg is interested in how the Holocaust has enabled the telling of other traumatic histories while simultaneously being claimed as singular. His is a comparative, rather than competitive, study of memory, loss and trauma. "Multidirectional memory," he writes, "is often the very grounds on which people construct and act upon visions of justice." Michael Rothberg, *Multidirectional Memory: Remembering the Holocaust in the Age of Decolonization* (Stanford: Stanford University Press, 2009), 19.

> These were lined up, in a serried gradation, from the largest to the tiniest: horses, camels, kangaroos, wallabies down to possums, rats and dozens of mice. Somewhere in this line were two human skulls – "a coupla natives," said the fettler's adult son – and these rested there, misconstrued and distinctly anomalous, with a kind of terrible conspicuousness. Even as a child I sensed the possibility of atrocity and was halted, perplexed.[20]

What follows is a sophisticated consideration of what Jones says she intuited as a child: the physical and epistemological violence entailed in the fetishistic colonial practice of Indigenous skull collecting. More than telling of this history, the essay consciously sets out to enact "a language (a tone, a poetics) to express the ethical imperatives of mourning".[21] The essay provides an unsettling juxtaposition between the vulnerable fontanelles of infants and stockpiled crania as it shifts between times and subject positions, personal recall and scholarly theorising, and circles around Fanny Balbuk, a Noongar woman made posthumous while alive by scientific racism and to whom the essay is dedicated in remembrance.

In another essay, "The Legend of Jandamarra", Jones reflects on a performance in Bunuba country, Windjana Gorge in the Kimberley region of Western Australia; a staging "*in situ* and *in language*" of *Jandamarra* (2008), "a play honouring the life of the Bunuba lawman and warrior who led a battle of resistance against colonial settlers from 1894 to 1897". Accompanying her on the journey are her mother and brother, and their travel is also a return to childhood: "small Kimberly doves begin the throb of their early morning call. No sound reminds me of my childhood more than this. *Ud dood dood* is the indigenous name." Jones understands the play to be a testament to "the persistence and vitality of Indigenous history" and an act of munificence: "it is through the generosity of Kimberley people that it is to be shared and reanimated." As Jones relates it, her response to the performance is intellectual as well as somatic: "My brother says it makes the hairs on the back of his neck stand up and I understand what he means." And it involves an awesome silence in the face of traumatic history – "the repeated vision of Bunuba people yoked in neck chains" – and deep time: "Windjana Gorge is a rock formation of ancient reef from the Devonian age, over 300 million years old." When the production finishes, Jones says that "We can't really speak." It is only later that words can begin to give shape to the experience. Yet, the present tense in which the essay is written suggests both its affective intensity and immediacy, which is also eternal as its concluding image submits: "the fork-tailed kites that circle and circle, floating above in silence, as they have done forever."[22]

If Jones repeatedly turns to autobiographical details in her essays, then it is a gesture that encourages complicated thinking about history, meaning, memory

---

20 Gail Jones, "Skulls, Fontanelles and the Spaces Between", *The UTS Review* 1 no. 2 (1995): 170.
21 Jones, "Skulls", 178.
22 Gail Jones, "The Legend of Jandamarra", *The Monthly* October, 2011, 14–15.

and time. In "A Dreaming, A Sauntering: Re-imagining Critical Paradigms", Jones writes again of her childhood on an isolated former quarantine station located just outside of Broome in the north of Western Australia. She tells of a recollected time that involved both physical emancipation and existential anxiety; the space she dwelled in was both inviting of "imaginative excursions" and "without markers of stable meaning".[23] Jones also relates walking across the ocean floor at low tide with her father and brothers to see an otherwise submerged wreck of a Japanese bomber plane that had been shot down during the Second World War. She then relates dreaming of finding drifting bones that did not *"fully figure"* the pilot Jones had half-imagined, with the help of Hollywood, to be still skeletally present and intact in the cockpit.[24] Later in the same essay, Jones writes that her father had recently informed her that what they had come across during that ocean-bed walk was not a Japanese aeroplane at all but rather a Dutch amphibious craft that had been carrying refugees. This correction of her memory leads Jones to reflect on oneiric knowledge and its "ingenious symbology".[25] It also invites reflection on the limitations of dream-logic as a "viable heuristic and conceptual model" with the principal reservation relating "to the loss of the contextual and the corporeal".[26] The story is sad and compelling, and it is told by Jones in her essay's introduction to do more than relate personal experience and memory. Jones claims that:

> My story furnishes an epistemological model and a critical attitude. This is, I trust, no narcissistic elaboration, it is a wish to narrativise matters which seem to me intrinsic to all writing practices: the negotiation of lost histories, the power of idealisation and the wish, even if unconscious, to embrace or to incorporate the body of another.[27]

This "epistemological model and a critical attitude," is also active in the short-story collections and the seven novels Jones has written to date. These texts are attuned to the world beyond their pages in highly crafted ways, and in turn they have been nationally and internationally recognised. Her work has been shortlisted multiple times for the Miles Franklin Literary Award, Australia's most prestigious literature prize, as well as for the Dublin IMPAC and the *Prix Femina Étranger*. It has also been longlisted for the Man Booker Prize and the Orange Prize. Jones is the

---

23 Gail Jones, "A Dreaming, A Sauntering: re-imagining critical paradigms", *JASAL: Journal of the Association for the Study of Australian Literature* 5 (2006): 12.
24 Jones, "A Dreaming", 12.
25 Jones, "A Dreaming", 17.
26 Jones, "A Dreaming", 20. It is a scene of destruction that finds its fictional rendition in the later novel, *Sorry*, "Sixteen Dutch refugee planes were sunk in the bay and six military planes were destroyed at the airport. … the refugees trapped in the planes were bombarded as they leapt into the water, or burned to death as their planes exploded." Gail Jones, *Sorry* (North Sydney: Vintage, 2007), 132. All subsequent references are to this edition and appear in parentheses in the text.
27 Jones, "A Dreaming", 12–13.

recipient of honours including the Prime Minister's Literary Award for Fiction, the WA Premier's Award for Fiction, the Nita B. Kibble Award, the Steele Rudd Award, *The Age* Book of the Year Award, the Adelaide Festival Award, the SA Premier's Award, and the ALS Gold Medal. Her texts have been translated into many languages – Italian, German, French, Dutch, Portuguese, Spanish, Hebrew, Mandarin, Polish, Croatian and Czech – suggesting their wide reach and interest.

The House of Breathing, the first of Jones' collections, comprises fourteen short stories. While they globe-trot and range across diverse subjects – the invasion of East Timor and its colonial history, the "imbecile dwarf" who is imagined to save Sigmund Freud's life, the death of Mary Wollstonecraft, cross-cultural misunderstanding in "Touching Tiananmen" – the stories are beaded together by dreams, fleeting moments and metaphors. The prose is often poetic as well as playful, as suggested by the short story "The Word 'Ruby'": "A capacious word, cadenced, consonantal – oriental, somehow, and possibly Aladdinish, summoning tessellated window lattices, incense burners of brass filigree, tasselled velvet robes, anti-gravitational, speed-unlimited carpets, sunsets of pure peach over spiky minarets, dome on breast-shaped dome for mile after Middle Eastern mile."[28] And the volume's abiding interest lies with the inner life. "These Eyes", for example, follows the movements of its protagonist's mind, which are prompted by the sight of a fellow passenger reading on a suburban train the exemplary tale about suffering, *King Lear*. The narrative traces the arc of the play and includes an erotic fantasy of a lover reading, the memory of weeping at a cinematic adaptation of Shakespeare's play, and the recollection of a young girl blinded in a childhood accident. It is a story about how certain texts can enter a life and how reading "is in part the process of acquiring the resources of interpretive circumspection and complication".[29]

Fetish Lives (1997), the second of Jones' short-story volumes, is in dialogue with the literary history that sets in motion the protagonist's thoughts in "These Eyes". The collection re-visions not only the lives, and deaths, of now famous writers and artists – a shared concern of *The House of Breathing* – but also their art. Most of these stories are creative biographies; each takes a moment from the known life of its subject (Anton Chekhov, Walt Whitman, Virginia Woolf, Marcel Proust, Mata Hari, Madame Tussaud, Elvis Presley, Eleanor Marx) and imagines what might have been; they also fashion creatively the afterlives of their subjects, such that an Elvis impersonator in "Heartbreak Hotel" dons not only a glitzy, sequinned jumpsuit but is also illuminated by suggestive sibilance, with twinkling mirrored lights sliding "along the walls in slow slinky circles, slow as a croony 'Love Me Tender,' slow as a sexy expectation, slow as a sax on a slow 78".[30] Many stories in the

---

28 Gail Jones, "The Word 'Ruby'", *The House of Breathing* (Fremantle: Fremantle Arts Centre Press, 1992), 71.
29 Gail Jones, "Imaginative Excursions: About *The House of Breathing*", interviewed by Peter Holland and Pippa Tandy, *Fremantle Arts Review* 7 no. 12–8 no. 1 (1992–3): 5.
30 Gail Jones, "Heartbreak Hotel", *Fetish Lives* (Fremantle: Fremantle Arts Centre Press, 1997), 116.

collection rest on the transformative, creative power of idiosyncratic reading. The poetry of Walt Whitman is a revelation to the schoolgirl who lives "not quite [at] the centre of anything" in the short story "Touch (The Births of Walt Whitman)".[31] While her teacher "has made it clear this man is a gasbag and mad, she feels the ineffable intake of a tremendous breath. Her lungs bloom open and her heart is rosy and turbulent. This is the reminder of life untold" (132). It is this conceit that links together Jones' two volumes of short stories, and the novels that follow: literature is a "house of breathing", life-giving and constitutive of the cusp between inner and external worlds.

The first of these novels, *Black Mirror* (2002), continues Jones' concentration on imaginative biography. It tells the interlaced stories of a would-be biographer, Anna Griffin, and a dying, Paris-based Surrealist painter, Victoria Morrell. Each grew up, some decades apart, in a small, Western Australian gold-mining town founded on Indigenous displacement and diminishment. *Sixty Lights* (2004), Jones' second novel, has a voice in the night call out the name "Lucy", announcing from its first line the book's orphaned protagonist who travels from colonial Australia to England and another outpost of empire, India, during the mid-nineteenth century.[32] This introductory word, with its connotation of light flashed in the dark, also anticipates the novel's presiding preoccupation with the possibilities of the newly emergent art-science of photography, which Lucy passionately pursues.

Dreams of Speaking (2006) extends the interest of *Sixty Lights* in modern technologies and turns on the friendship of Alice Black and Mr Sakamoto. Alice is an Australian academic who moves to Paris to write a book on the poetics of modernity; Mr Sakamoto is an atomic bomb survivor who is researching the life of the telephone inventor, Alexander Graham Bell. Their friendship is accelerated over their shared love of near-obsolescent machineries, and revolves around private griefs. *Sorry* (2007), Jones' fourth novel, centres on the wartime, mid-twentieth century Australian childhood of Perdita Keene who develops a deep friendship with Mary, a Walmajarri girl forced to work for the Keene family and who is imprisoned for a violent act Perdita later remembers committing. The novel also makes a deliberate literary intervention in its moment of writing and initial reception: the refusal of the then Federal Government to admit to, and apologise for, the ongoing wrongs done to Aboriginal people, land and culture in the name of settler colonialism.[33] Of all Jones' texts, *Sorry* has attracted the most scholarly and

---

31 Gail Jones, "Touch (The Births of Walt Whitman)", *Fetish Lives* (Fremantle: Fremantle Arts Centre Press, 1997), 131. All subsequent references are to this edition and appear in parentheses in the text.
32 Gail Jones, *Sixty Lights* (London: Harvill Press, 2004), 3.
33 In February 2008, an apology was finally given by the Parliament of Australia. Subsequent to that historic moment, the Parliament has rejected reforms demanded by the Uluru Statement from the Heart, an Indigenous consensus position on the need for constitutional recognition of Aboriginal Australians. Uluru Statement From the Heart, Final Report of the Referendum Council, 30 June 2017, https://www.referendumcouncil.org.au/sites/default/files/report_attachments/Referendum_Council_Final_Report.pdf

popular attention,[34] largely because of its efforts to think through the meanings and implications of (not) apologising, which speak to concerns beyond its pages.[35] In an essay that coincided with the publication of *Sorry*, Jones reflected on the novel's ethical vision and political concern:

> The book has a political-allegorical aspect, as one would expect, claiming such a title, but it is not centrally concerned with representing the stolen generations. As a non-indigenous Australian, it would be presumptuous of me to do so and it would risk appropriation of others' painful experience. Nevertheless, *Sorry* deals with culpability and the refusal to say sorry, the characteristics, as we now know, of a certain type of (persisting) dispossession.[36]

Allegory, Jones suggests, allows for the making of new meanings and insights without laying claim to the experiences of others. In telling of Perdita's regret at not-saying-sorry to Mary for her forgotten part in a violent event that refuses to remain in the past, the novel exposes culpability. It also imagines the damage of complicated denial, which addresses broader preoccupations in contemporary Australian society.

If *Dreams of Speaking* and *Sorry* have friendships at their centres, Jones' fifth novel, *Five Bells* (2011), involves four characters who are largely strangers to each other in multicultural Sydney.[37] Taking its literary cue from the modernist literary tradition it consciously references (James Joyce's short story "The Dead" (1914) is very much on one character's mind), the novel traces shifting thoughts on one sunny summer day. The characters come into brief contact only, as past lovers awkwardly reunite over lunch at Circular Quay and others are possible witnesses to the disappearance of a young girl. Their shared thinking about time and loss encircles them.

---

[34] As Liliana Zavaglia has noted, *Sorry* "intervened in the contemporary political sphere in an attempt to correct the Howard Government's refusal to apologise in 1997". Liliana Zavaglia, *White Apology and Apologia: Australian novels of reconciliation* (Amherst: Cambria, 2016), 147. Dolores Herrero has made a similar observation in her treatment of the text as a trauma narrative. See Dolores Herrero, "The Australian apology and postcolonial defamiliarization: Gail Jones' *Sorry*", *Journal of Postcolonial Writing* 47 no. 3 (2011): 283–95.

[35] For an overview of the role Australian fiction has had in imagining the apology, see Sue Kossew, "Saying Sorry: the politics of apology and reconciliation in recent Australian fiction", in *Locating Postcolonial Narrative Genres*, eds. Walter Goebel and Saskia Schablo (New York: Routledge, 2011), 171–83. For accounts of the wider debates over saying sorry see, among other essays, Lyn McCredden, "Saying Sorry: the Apology", in *Telling Stories: Australian Life and Literature 1935–2012*, eds. Tanya Dalziell and Paul Genoni (Clayton: Monash University Press, 2013), 559–65 and John Frow, "The Politics of Stolen Time", *Australian Humanities Review* 9 (1998): http://australianhumanitiesreview.org/1998/02/01/a-politics-of-stolen-time/.

[36] Jones, "Surviving a Bootprint", 24.

[37] Susan Midalia has noted that *Five Bells* "is a celebration of multicultural Australia". Susan Midalia, "The Idea of Place: reading for pleasure and the workings of power", *English in Australia* 47 no. 3 (2012): 46.

A Guide to Berlin (2015) leaves behind the sun of Sydney and concentrates on Cass Turner, a young Australian woman who travels to Berlin in mid-winter with intentions to write. She unexpectedly finds herself part of a group that is drawn together because of its members' common literary hero, Vladimir Nabokov. Their meetings involve the telling of buried shames and memories, and culminate in a calamitous event that prompts a questioning of the purpose and value of literature, and the obligations the characters have to each other.

And Jones' most recent novel, *The Death of Noah Glass* (2018), foregrounds Cass' reflection in *A Guide to Berlin* that "So much depends … on correctly determining the genre".[38] In mourning for their Australian art-historian father who comes to be unexpectedly implicated in an Italian art heist, Evie Glass and her brother, Martin, recognise that the scenario in which they find themselves is "crazy, it's like a *giallo* … Italian detective stories. Yellow covers. Hard-boiled, nuggety crims, dodgy perps, that kind of thing. Something grisly and revolting in the backstreets of Naples."[39] Martin travels to Palermo to see what he can learn about his father's movements and intentions, while Evie remains in Sydney. Yet, rather than knowledge made definite, hidden motivations exposed and explained, and the momentary disruption of order restored, as detective narratives can reassuringly instate, the novel insists, in the end, on uncertainty. While Jones' writing is a space for the imagining and meeting of others, it also retains the enigma of experience and admits that the self involves an opacity that resists conclusive explanation or representation.

What such short summaries of Jones' texts fail to disclose is not only the complexities these texts entertain, but also how they go about representing them. The form and style of Jones' texts are abiding subjects in the pages that follow, but as a prelude to that discussion it is fair to say that they are not straightforward; they have an enthusiastic disregard for linearity. Their interest lies instead with discontinuity, and they proceed paratactically. "She is about to die, this Mary Wollstonecraft," writes Jones at the near-beginning of *The House of Breathing* short story "On the Piteous Death of Mary Wollstonecraft".[40] What follows is not the telling of the titular character's painful, prolonged demise from childbirth complications but rather the relating of a blissful sexual tryst some years earlier in the low grass of Neuilly. This story moves back and forth in time; the proleptic gesture of narrating an event at a point earlier than its chronological place in the story, a telling before time, is apparent in many of Jones' narratives and can be read as a sign of narrative joy as well as ethical thinking. Jones herself has written of the delight she derives from texts of narrative daring. Singling out Michael Ondaatje's novel *In the Skin of a Lion* (1987), Jones asks:

---

38 Gail Jones, *A Guide to Berlin* (North Sydney: Vintage, 2015), 125.
39 Gail Jones, *The Death of Noah Glass* (Melbourne: Text, 2018), 28. All subsequent references are to this edition and appear in parentheses in the text.
40 Gail Jones, "On the Piteous Death of Mary Wollstonecraft", *The House of Breathing* (Fremantle: Fremantle Arts Centre Press, 1992), 105.

> What do I love about this novel? First, the complex audacity of its form. It is a strange, quiet book, full of elisions and gaps, ruptures and repetitions. Yet the riddling structure is a wonderful provocation; there is a constantly surprising quality to its modernist manoeuvres and one pieces together the plot so that the ending works as a revelation. … It is not without flaws – no novel is – but it remains for me exemplary of the integrity of narrative risk.[41]

Jones' affectionate determination that Ondaatje's novel is "a strange, quiet book, full of elisions and gaps, ruptures and repetitions", and indeed her identification of the "surprising quality to its modernist manoeuvres", are features readily apparent in her own work. Further, Jones' acknowledgement of the "flaws" of Ondaatje's novel is, counterintuitively, a tribute and a quality that her narratives value. In *Sixty Lights*, Lucy Strange's photographic aesthetics are deliberately and contrarily wedded to the maculate. As with much of Jones' writing, and unlike the men of the London Society of Photographers in the novel who insist on flawless photographic images, Lucy's interests lie with what such dictates would determine to be faults – the stained, the spotted, the marked and the shadowed. This aesthetic in Jones' writing is ethically charged and demands an artful narrative form. *Black Mirror*, for example, commences with a diptych – an image of Anna Griffin in inclement weather and her biographical subject, Victoria Morrell, staring out from a window watching her approach – which brings to mind Virginia Woolf's idea that "[b]iography will enlarge its scope by hanging up looking glasses at odd corners".[42] (This inference is not as arbitrary as it might first appear. It is with Woolf, as a metonym for modernism and its commitment to thinking about narrative form and language beyond the stringencies of realism, that Jones' work has a deep affinity.[43] Another modernist writer with whom Jones' work is interlaced is Walter Benjamin, always querying after "what one is entitled to ask from a work of art".)[44]

---

41 Gail Jones, "My Favourite Novel: Swooning to Ondaatje's roar", *The Australian*, 6 August 2011, 18.
42 Virginia Woolf, "The Art of Biography", *The Essays of Virginia* Woolf, vol. 6, 1933–41, ed. Stuart N. Clarke (1939; London: Hogarth Press, 2011), 186.
43 This is but one understanding of modernism. As Jones herself has acknowledged when writing of the "ambivalent modernism" of Patrick White and recalling the postwar meditations on modernism by Theodor Adorno, "Modernism he [Adorno] claimed was governed by 'occultism,' by a regressive form of deranged thinking in which a kind of banal supernaturalism offered emotional recompense for the shattered real. If the war had destroyed reason, if history was represented in camps, ruins, death and displacement, there were forms of delusional certainty that might offer another kind of authority, in this case unimpeachable because finally inscrutable." Gail Jones, "Desperate, Marvellous, Shuttling: White's Ambivalent Modernism", in *Patrick White Beyond the Grave: New Critical Perspectives*, eds. Ian Henderson and Anouk Lang (New York: Anthem Press, 2015), 155. Elsewhere, Jones identifies a familiar modernist trope present in White's writing: "the singular project of someone for whom art offered questions, not answers, and an anguishing search for resolution in the irresolute business of being." Gail Jones, "Introduction", in Patrick White, *The Cockatoos* (Melbourne: Text, 2019), viii.
44 Walter Benjamin, "The Work of Art in the Age of Mechanical Reproduction", in *Illuminations*, trans. Harry Zorn, ed. Hannah Arendt (1968; London: Pimlico 1999), 227.

While Anna struggles with the conventions of her chosen form, the novel itself points to what might be told if reflective surfaces are placed in unexpected recesses as it moves across memory and dream, recollection and the present tense of the women's encounter, and insists on the withholding of certain stories.

A heightened interest in language is another notable feature of Jones' writing. This observation might seem banal – the very stuff of Jones' writing is language, after all. In the worlds of Jones' stories, however, words (and reading) matter a great deal, with a frequent complaint in newspaper reviews of Jones' writing being that a dictionary is often required to understand its vocabulary. It is a point demonstrated by the lover in Jones' short story "The Astronomer Tells of Her Love". In that first-person narrative in *The House of Breathing*, the protagonist calls on the language of her profession (she has a special interest in sunspots) to speak of her desire. Unimpressed, her lover responds unpoetically by rolling over in bed and turning his face to the bedroom wall. Despite the linguistic fatigue of the astronomer's lover, words in Jones' texts are to delight in as well as to apprehend; they conjoin sound and sense, the intellect and the sensual. Without wishing to push the analogy too far, like thick paint in some art, words are rendered perceptible in Jones' writing. Martin Glass, the artist in *The Death of Noah Glass*, articulates this idea expressly when he reflects on "the almost erotic moment when paint squeezed out, depositing the sludge of its glossy impasto onto the palette" (56). Or, more accurately, the poetic way in which Martin's thoughts are conveyed, with an emphasis on rhythm and sound, draws attention to the words' aesthetics, as well as their sexual implications. (Correspondingly, elsewhere in the narrative his sister, Evie, pauses before the Italian word *tiglio* and admits "She adored this word. It could have been a seduction" (202).) The suitably tactile metaphor of "texture" is one Jones has used to convey her thinking about language in her work. Speaking with Maria del Pilar Royo Grasa, Jones has acknowledged that:

> I am attracted to poetry, and as a novelist I read a lot of poetry. What I love about poetry is its quality of intensification and condensation, and the fact that it gives a privilege to metaphor. When I write prose, I am not thinking so much about the forward movement of the story, about the unfolding of the plot. I am thinking more about the texture of the language because it is a more complicated kind of aesthetic compulsion.[45]

What words are doing in Jones' writing is far more than transmitting a story, whether it be emphasising aesthetic interest and pleasure, making visible the relations of power in which they circulate, or insisting on the narratives' own realities. In "Eleanor Reads Emma" in *Fetish Lives*, a short story that re-imagines Eleanor Marx translating Gustave Flaubert's *Madame Bovary* (1856), Eleanor is

---

[45] Maria del Pilar Royo Grasa, "In Conversation with Gail Jones", *JASAL: Journal of the Association for the Study of Australian Literature* 12 no. 3 (2013): 1.

said to be compelled by "[f]ine words", and the narrative gladly submits to its protagonist's inclination away from practical vocabularies. It sends her off on a "word-fuelled transportation (she thinks of herself elongated, uninhibited, leaning into an invisible dark wind-tunnel)".[46] This hesitation before literalism takes on a twinned political and romantic charge in *Five Bells*. Remembering her "re-education" in a prison camp as part of China's Cultural Revolution, Pei Xing also recalls how her attraction to Xun, a fellow prisoner who would later become her husband, is aroused by his refusal to speak in Maoist slogans. The poetic description of this recollection sympathises with Xun's protest against the ventriloquism of words made dead under the weight of propaganda: "He talked, Pei Xing thought, as if words mattered, as if they might be relied upon to untie the tongue into praise songs to the world, to describe falling snow, perhaps, or the shifts in fluid light on the surface of the Huangpo River at the very moment at which a migratory flock of birds ascends."[47] These are words of which readers are asked to take notice – language is held up as consequential – and this is also the case in *A Guide to Berlin*. The soft-falling snow that so delights Cass in that novel finds its equal in the slow gathering of words. Words are shared between the characters for their aesthetic pleasure and the dense networks of private meanings and histories they carry – words such as ferrule, lemniscate, ensellure, *meerschaum*. To know that ensellure refers to the concave curve formed by the spine (a lumbar incurvination – an almost equally compelling phrase) is one thing; to remember or to learn that Nabokov gave this very word to Humbert Humbert to detail his initial encounter with Rita in *Lolita* (1955) is another. That words might also offer readers a chance to listen, to savour and feel – to be alert to their resonances and shapes – is yet another possibility.

Such an invitation is taken up in *The House of Breathing*'s "Babies". This short story sees the narrator tell of her mad, pregnant sister who is marked by linguistic fecundity. It is this feature, and perhaps her sexual activities out-of-wedlock, that has her nominated "a lunatic" by her repressed mother and committed to an asylum, with her baby removed from her care.[48] Yet, for her part-comprehending sister who is the story's narrator, the very sounds of the words her sister utters call forth hitherto unknown desires: "Again and again came a torrent of articulate and sensational gibberish, words of such immediate and bodily power, such sensual investment, that I was giddy with the possibilities of a secret life … I thought for the first time of lovers and nakedness" (98). Words are marked by plenitude in Jones' writing.

Yet, at the same time, Jones' narratives fashion their ethics in part through a thinking with grief in ways that can confound language. Loss (in a multitude of configurations) is an abiding concern of Jones' texts, and its force lies with the

---

46 Gail Jones, "Eleanor Reads Emma", *Fetish Lives* (Fremantle: Fremantle Arts Centre Press, 1997), 48. All subsequent references are to this edition and appear in parentheses in the text.
47 Gail Jones, *Five Bells* (London: Harvill Secker, 2011), 159. All subsequent references are to this edition and appear in parentheses in the text.
48 Gail Jones, "Babies", *The House of Breathing* (Fremantle: Fremantle Arts Centre Press, 1992), 95. All subsequent references are to this edition and appear in parentheses in the text.

questions it poses about the integrity of the self; how differences to, and connections with, others might be conceived, forged and respected; and the aesthetic and political roles representational forms have in their telling. Losses also come with a question that Jones poses in an essay she has expressly written on grief. Jones wonders: "for all that goes under, what is it that rises up?"[49] This searching preoccupies Jones' writing, and the way it is imagined sets it apart from some recent philosophical thinking on loss and grief. While admiring of the negotiation with absence that the writing of Maurice Blanchot enacts, for instance, Jones is also rightly cautious about its aloofness:

> I wonder if there is not a kind of cruelty of the imagination at work here, that somehow avoids the heart-of-the-matter (there is no mention of affect, of weeping, of the so-typical distresses that undo and disarticulate) to produce such a tranquil and magisterial dissociation of image and object. This is a suspicion, I suppose, of both style and method; affectless style marks an almost ethical deficiency, a refusal of humane discomposure. Blanchot has death where he wants it: it is perfectly philosophical.[50]

With its attention to experiences of loss and trauma, Jones' writing is also very much concerned with what might emerge from those experiences, and how words and narratives might approximate extra-linguistic feeling. There is its attendant call, too, to materialise seemingly disembodied analysis.

Jones' works therefore invite extended attention to the patterns, tropes and themes that play out across them. The apology not given in *Sorry*, for example, is returned to in *Five Bells*. In this latter novel, non-Aboriginal characters briefly discuss the 2008 National Apology to the Stolen Generations, which inaugurated formal political recognition of the devastation wrought by British colonialism on Aboriginal people and cultures. They also carry the hope that this apology "will change everything. It will alter history" (111). In that same novel, different apologies and acts of forgiveness are explored as two characters with a shared past meet unexpectedly in Australia and reckon with atrocities committed years before in the name of China's Cultural Revolution.

Echoing the travelling of ideas across Jones' writing, her protagonists are afforded a notable physical mobility, which is simultaneously subject to scrutiny in the novels. Jones' characters routinely cross national borders with ease, and their experiences are presented as a form of "radical encounter".[51] Yet even as Jones'

---

49   Gail Jones, "Without Stars: a small essay on grief", *HEAT* 7 (1998): 141.
50   Jones, "Without Stars", 146. Blanchot seems to think that the way to speak of "impossible necessary death" is "soberly". Maurice Blanchot, *The Writing of the Disaster*, trans. Ann Smock (University of Nebraska Press, 1986), 67. It is an attitude that Woolf might think of as "Unwarmed by imagination". Virginia Woolf, *The Waves* (1931; London: Penguin, 1992), 25.
51   Gail Jones, "The Pleasure of Language Itself: An Interview with Gail Jones", interviewed by Robert Wood, *Los Angeles Review of Books*, 4 May 2018, https://blog.lareviewofbooks.org/interviews/pleasure-language-interview-gail-jones/

characters find themselves in Berlin, Tokyo, Paris, Bombay, London, Palermo and Shanghai (in memory), two Australian cities, located on different edges of the country, are specially encoded places in her narratives. Some commentators have been keen to make direct links between Jones' lyrical celebration of Sydney's Circular Quay and Opera House in *Five Bells* and her move to that city (and a professorial position at Western Sydney University) from Perth, where she had lived and worked most of her adult life.[52] In a more recent piece meditating on the inner-city Sydney suburb of Glebe, Jones puts to her advantage her shift across the continent, claiming the "obstinacy of an outsider" to criss-cross, flâneuse-like, both the physical design of the suburb and its otherwise unremarked histories and inhabitants.[53] If Sydney is lovingly described in *Five Bells*, then Perth is a place initially imagined in *Dreams of Speaking* in less than complimentary terms. It is "not even a city by most estimations" and is rendered "pragmatic, secular, dun-coloured, dull".[54] In *The Death of Noah Glass*, which partly takes place in Sydney, Noah Glass returns to Perth, the city of his birth, to attend his estranged father's funeral. While "[c]aught in a confusion of remembering and forgetting" (133), he thinks of the city as not only a "town that has seen better days" with "dehydrated streets" (133), but also one seemingly stuck in the past: Noah's hotel room meaningfully sports "an orange nylon bedspread", "garish primrose decor" (133) and "a hideous light fixture of seventies vintage" (134). For an art scholar who has a lifelong commitment to the Renaissance paintings of Piero della Francesca and is experiencing complicated grief, Perth is clearly an aesthetic affront, not to mention stalled in time. Yet, for Alice Black in *Dreams of Speaking*, the Swan River that runs through that city offers her existential promise. Her longing from Paris for that freedom is suggestive of the affective charge Australian places hold for Jones' characters and how they are imaginative sites that shape Jones' writerly orientation.

Gail Jones: Word, Image, Ethics starts from the premise that attention to these designs and recurrences opens up thinking about the ethical work Jones' writing enacts. The intention, however, is not to flatten out the specificities of Jones' texts, or indeed to seek consistency in them. There is no expectation that this body of writing *should* form a coherent whole simply because it is written by an individual author. Instead, Jones' thoughts on the suggestiveness of the fragment as an

---

52   James Bradley, "On *Five Bells*", *Griffith Review* (2011): https://griffithreview.com/five-bells-gail-jones/
53   Gail Jones, "Turnings and Over-turnings in Glebe", *Sydney Review of Books*, 9 February 2018, https://sydneyreviewofbooks.com/turnings-and-over-turnings-in-glebe/ In her review of David Wish-Wilson's book on *Perth* (2013), Jones concedes that what recommends her former home city, at least as Wish-Wilson presents it in his book, "is the great generosity, inclusiveness and idiosyncrasy of its vision". Gail Jones, "Celebrating our far western city of contradictions: CITIES", *The Age*, 1 March 2014, 31.
54   Gail Jones, *Dreams of Speaking* (North Sydney: Vintage, 2006), 4. All subsequent references are to this edition and appear in parentheses in the text.

organising principle give shape to the structure of this book and its engagement with her writing:

> What might it mean to take the fragment or the trace as a paradigm of knowledge and to assume that assemblage, not reconstitution, is our critical task? In this model it is the manufacture of intelligible design – rather than, say, the explanation of facts – that generates and constitutes our understanding.[55]

Like Alice Black's project in *Dreams of Speaking*, "a list of categories" or fragments informs the assemblage of this book and its attempts at "intelligible design" and "understanding" (27). In an effort to sketch out for herself the interests of the monograph she is preparing to write, Alice turns to expressive associations:

> *electrics, mechanics, communication, transportation*
> Then:
> *spiritualisation, secularisation, sexualisation*
> And:
> *gigantism, miniaturisation, division, replication*
> *vision, sensation, cognition, precognition*
> *tragic, comic, nostalgic, melodramatic* (27)

It is with "this slightest of codes, arbitrarily jotted" that Alice begins to "elaborate her poetics of modernity" (27). *Gail Jones: Word, Image, Ethics* has its own structuring codes for approaching Jones' writing, although they are not altogether arbitrary and they are stubbornly porous. The chapters turn on tropes – "Weather", "Time", "Reading and Writing", "Image" and "Modernity" – to foreground particular interests that re-emerge in Jones' narratives and to provide a focus for apprehending these texts' ethical querying. It is a focus that is necessarily blurred, therefore, as ideas and texts dealing "in possibilities, ifs, conditions" are purposefully revisited with different emphases and interpretations. The logic is one of loops, a meeting of ideas as they are fashioned and re-formed within and across Jones' texts, rather than the prosecution of a definitive thesis.

Admittedly, other selections and approaches might have forwarded quite contrary readings of Jones' *oeuvre*. Each of Jones' texts could have been presented in its historical turn, for example. Such a method might have allowed for more in-depth engagement with particular essays and stories, and responses to them (rather than the method attempted here, which is to identify and follow specific ideas that thread through Jones' writing, with scholarly contexts and debates forming an amicable conversation in their undertow). Perhaps the outcome might have been more satisfying if other tropes had been pursued to come to radically dissimilar interpretations. And it is true that the weather might be an unlikely

---

55   Jones, "A Dreaming", 13.

entry point for thinking about Jones' writing, particularly in the knowledge that so much of the scholarship on it to date has thoughtfully turned not on meteorological concerns at all.

Most of the critical work on Jones' writing has focused on individual novels, with the short stories and essays receiving considerably less attention. Lyn Jacobs' sophisticated essay on the representation of photography in Jones' writing, and Norman Saadi Nikro's thinking about parataxis in the novels, are notable exceptions. Nikro is interested in duration and the "suspension of the instrumentalization of time" across Jones' texts.[56] And Jacobs traces the motif of photography throughout Jones' work, drawing from photography theorists including Roland Barthes and Eduardo Cadava whom Jones expressly references in her work, to suggest that in Jones' narrative worlds "photography is less a sign of loss or identification and more a point of access, an emblem of potential".[57]

Jacobs' alertness to the presence of these theoretical intertexts in Jones' writing is also taken up by other scholars, among them Kate Mitchell, who shares Jacobs' focus on photography but retrains it to read *Sixty Lights* as a "neo-Victorian fiction" that posits "the persistence of the past as embodied memory".[58] Mitchell situates her reading of *Sixty Lights* within the burgeoning field of Neo-Victorian studies that marks "a departure from much scholarship on contemporary historical fiction which has ... focused upon the ways such fiction problematises the representation of the past and foregrounds the difficulty of attaining historical knowledge".[59] She harnesses the insights of Neo-Victorian studies, concerned to identify "the ways in which fiction *can* lay claim to the past, provisionally and partially, rather than the ways that it can not",[60] to suggest *Sixty Lights* retrieves the Victorian past by means of the affirmative register of the photograph.

Having written a number of essay on Jones' novels, Robert Dixon has a special interest in how each narrative he considers might be interpreted as actively staging certain theorisations because they "are often ways of thinking through in fictional form the theoretical issues that preoccupy [Jones'] essays".[61] In his reading of *Five Bells*, Dixon suggests that the 1950s Situationist Internationalist Movement, fronted by Guy Debord and at the vanguard of psychogeography, is a touchstone for understanding that novel's interest in forging connections in an otherwise alienating urban space.[62] In his most recent essay on *The Death of Noah Glass*,

---

56   Norman Saadi Nikro, "Paratactic Stammers: temporality in the novels of Gail Jones", *JASAL: Journal of the Association for the Study of Australian Literature* 16 no. 1 (2016): 1.
57   Lyn Jacobs, "Gail Jones's 'light writing': Memory and the Photo-graph", *JASAL: Journal of the Association for the Study of Australian Literature* 5 (2006): 192.
58   Kate Mitchell, "Ghostly Histories and Embodied Memories: Photography, Spectrality and Historical Fiction in Afterimage and Sixty Lights", *Neo-Victorian Studies* 1 no. 1 (2008): 99.
59   Kate Mitchell, *History and Cultural Memory in Neo-Victorian Fiction: Victorian Afterimages* (London: Palgrave, 2010), 3.
60   Mitchell, *History and Cultural Memory*, 3.
61   Robert Dixon, "Invitation to the Voyage: Reading Gail Jones's *Five Bells*", *JASAL: Journal of the Association for the Study of Australian Literature* 12, no. 3 (2012): 1.

Dixon draws attention to how Jones' novel can be read as concerned "with the image-text dialectic, but in such a way that the novel form itself – its narrative structure, its characters and settings, its intermedial allusions and its complex temporality – becomes a device for actively staging such theorisations".[63]

Other critics have insightfully recognised the importance of the wide-ranging literary allusions in Jones' texts. At times, these references are as oblique as an uncommented-upon line of poetry that forms part of a character's thoughts; a whisper that remembers the novels of Toni Morrison; or the music of a didgeridoo described in terms that recall Virginia Woolf's rendering of the sound of time in *Mrs Dalloway* (1925). (The blue of the hydrangeas that Sally Seton writes of in that novel also appears throughout Jones' novels.) At other moments, they are made overt (at least to readers who share some of Jones' literary reference points). The title of *Five Bells* acknowledges that novel's most obvious intertext, Kenneth Slessor's elegy "Five Bells" (1939), which memorialises the death of Joe Lynch, Slessor's friend who drowned at Circular Quay. Jones' novel shares with Slessor's poem a Sydney setting, a preoccupation with memory and time, and a recognition of the limits of language in memorialising the dead. Lines of this poem are correspondingly threaded through *Five Bells* and, as Leigh Dale has carefully detailed, Jones "explicitly reiterates and replays Slessor's poem, most obviously in the dramatic and terrible passage, late in her novel, in which the key male character dies in the manner of Joe Lynch [… and] thereby replays that moment of lost connection that is so powerfully expressed in Slessor's poem".[64] Stella Keene's infatuation with Shakespeare in *Sorry* is mirrored, albeit more critically, by that novel's sustained engagement with Shakespeare's writing and its legacies, which Russell West-Pavlov, Valérie-Anne Belleflamme and Pilar Royo Grasa have discussed in detail,[65] and which Liliana Zavaglia interprets not as "an outworking of academic valorisation" but rather as "a symptom of a mental disordering – which, although it provides some measure of comfort, cannot provide sustenance" within the world of the novel.[66] And the writing of Nabokov clearly shapes *A Guide to Berlin*, with the title of that novel recalling his short story of the same name. The broader point to make about this community of stories, which Jones' writing promotes and firmly situates itself within, is that it is a claim made for the capacity

---

62   Dixon, "Invitation to the Voyage", 3–7.
63   Robert Dixon, "Figures in Geometry: *The Death of Noah Glass* by Gail Jones", *Sydney Review of Books*, 7 September 2018, https://sydneyreviewofbooks.com/death-noah-glass-jones/
64   Leigh Dale, "No more boomerang? 'Nigger's Leap' and 'Five Bells'", *Journal of Australian Studies* 37 no. 1 (2013): 54.
65   Russell West-Pavlov, "Shakespeare Among the Nyoongar: post-colonial texts, colonial intertexts and their imbrications – *Macbeth* in Gail Jones' *Sorry*", *ZAA* 63 no. 4 (2015): 391–410; Valérie-Anne Belleflamme, "'Shakespeare was wrong': counter-discursive intertextuality in Gail Jones' *Sorry*", *Journal of Postcolonial Writing* 51 no. 6 (2015): 661–71; Maria Pilar Royo Grasa, "Looking for Othello's Pearl in Gail Jones's *Sorry* (2007): Symbolic and Intertextual Questioning of the Notion of 'Settler Envy'", *Journal of Postcolonial Writing* 54 (2018): 200–13.
66   Zavaglia, *White Apology*, 163.

of narrative to discern patterns and connections in contingency, and to credit them ethical and aesthetic value.

As many critics have done, *Gail Jones: Word, Image, Ethics* takes a cue for its approach to her work from Jones herself. The prompt is a model of reading Jones privileges and enacts in her monograph on Jane Campion's film *The Piano*. With its violence, unabashed representation of female sexual desire, a complex mother–daughter relationship and distinctive, watery cinematic vision, all rolled into an imagined colonial setting, *The Piano* has attracted much popular and academic attention. Jones is alert to the debates and affective registers the film has elicited:

> This is a movie much written about – sometimes in depressingly reductive and schematic ways – yet it carries an aesthetically distinctive poetics, even as it rehearses familiar genres with mostly familiar movie stars. Famously, too, *The Piano* inspires adoration, sometimes to the point of gushy devotion … Its popular success … has in many ways occluded the formal qualities of the movie, and presented it, predictably, in more market-driven terms: the virtuosity of the stars, the sexual plot, the dank exoticism of darkest New Zealand. Early reviewers sometimes offered appalled condemnation.[67]

Jones' interpretations of the film have little interest in passing judgement on it, preferring instead to participate seriously in its politics and poetics. Further, they also subtly signal an awareness of the oftentimes imperceptible demands brought to bear on reading practices that emerge out of scholarly study. Elsewhere, Jones has highlighted in meaningful parentheses and italics what she sees as the tendency of academic discourse to repeat its own logic and to strive for impersonality:

> *(We tend to discount not only melodrama but the broad resources of the rhapsodic. In high theorising we aim for tonal equanimity, for a tone hieratic, magisterial, and remotely impersonal. So academic prose is marked, for the most part, by a repressive absence of the lyrical. By wide-awake realisms. By studious passionlessness. By loss of affirmation.)*[68]

Jones' words were published some twenty-five years ago; the concerns they articulate continue to have currency today as literary scholars find themselves in a long moment that, in some quarters at least, is said to be post-theory.[69] If the second

---

67 Gail Jones, *The Piano* (Sydney: Currency Press, 2001), 4–5. All subsequent references are to this edition and appear in parentheses in the text.
68 Jones, "Skulls", 175. In line with these thoughts, Jones applauds Roland Barthes for explicitly departing from his contemporaries' "fashionable psychoanalysis of seeing". Gail Jones, "The Heart Beating Across the Room (On Possessing Someone Else's Photographs)", *Australian Book Review* 173 (August 1995): 38.
69 For example, see Jane Elliot and Derek Attridge, eds. *Theory After Theory* (London: Routledge, 2011).

half of the twentieth century saw the rise of literary theory, today some scholars are questioning not only its tone but also what it might have unintentionally set in train. Being after theory (if that is indeed where things are) does not suggest that there is no longer a need to identify and interrogate the assumptions underpinning critical analysis. Rather, it prompts thinking about how certain forms of theory have come to assume influence and authority (even as they often set out to appraise such power) and what assumptions this ascendency has rested on, and privileged. It also offers practices that might flow from this moment.[70] Jones' current project-in-progress on world literatures, undertaken with colleagues at Western Sydney University, might be seen as part of a larger shift in recent thinking about where literary scholarship comes from (intellectually and geographically) and where and how it lands. It also seeks to explore how creative and critical discourses might be brought into more active conversation as forms of interrogative thinking. These preoccupations are also apparent in the style of Jones' earlier engagement with Campion's *The Piano*.

Jones is certainly not discounting in her book on *The Piano* or elsewhere what theories of reading bring to interpretive practice. Many of her essays, which engage energetically with philosophers and writers who constitute the theoretical canon of the late twentieth and early twenty-first centuries, underscore an appreciation of, and indebtedness to, their intellectual verve and value. What troubles Jones in that prescient, earlier essay is how interpretive practices can sidestep the personal and the lyrical, and become ossified and non-reflexively employed. Jones makes this concern clear in her monograph on *The Piano*. Some way into her discussion of the film, Jones pauses to observe the manner in which *The Piano* has been insistently read. The moment in question sees a male character sever the finger of his wife, the wilfully mute heroine, Ada. Jones writes of the commentary on this shocking cinematic moment: "There exists a vast number of articles on *The Piano* that speak of Stewart's 'castration' of Ada in hacking off her finger. But this seems too vulgar-Freudian and reductive for the density of what has occurred" (59). Jones' intervention comes as a relief, not from the violence of Stewart's action – which surely continues to distress, no matter how many times Campion's film is viewed – but rather from the habits of interpretation.

Jones' call is to attend to the complexities of textual worlds carefully and attentively; she enacts this approach by setting herself up in the first pages of her study as an impersonator of a viewer. Like the young girl in the short story "Modernity", she proposes to see "the movie for the very first time" (5). In this capacity, Jones determines that she will "assess" *The Piano*'s "unearthly and

---

70 Wai Chee Dimock, for example, asks: "What associative forms might come from … any theory that does not aspire to full occupancy in the analytic field, that settles for a low threshold in plausibility and admissibility? What could be said for a critical practice that does not even try to clinch the case?" Wai Chee Dimock, "Weak Theory: Henry James, Colm Tóibín, and W. B. Yeats", *Critical Inquiry* 39 no. 4 (2013): 736.

controversial visions, its attractive powers, and its capacity to alienate and to entrance" (5). The rest of that analysis proceeds accordingly. Importantly, though, the conceit of seeing the film as if "for the first time" does not rest on naive reading. Jones conducts the "impersonation" as a bold conceptual move (and certainly not in the service of fraud or entertainment as impersonation might be understood). It is a standpoint that issues a challenge to received ideas and promises to look afresh at its chosen subject.

In this spirit, Jones' works are read very closely in the pages that follow. This practice, which turns on what Roland Barthes has nominated the "ethic of both pleasure and intellectual vigilance",[71] is intended to afford ample consideration to the texts, which oftentimes pose challenges to the broader social and political contexts in which they circulate. The weather is one prompt for this thinking and looking, which is also personified by Jones' Eleanor Marx. Freshly enamoured with Flaubert's realism, Eleanor surveys her room "with novelistic vision" and sees tiny objects "newly exact and radiantly meaningful" (50). Notwithstanding the sober warning that Eleanor (like Emma Bovary) comes to a self-inflicted poisoned end, and while there is no promise that what emerges in this book is radiantly meaningful or newly exact, or even comes close, the hope is that Jones' writing and its ethics are met attentively to further future conversations, which can be anticipated to extend alongside Jones' ongoing writerly career.

---

71 Roland Barthes, *The Grain of the Voice: Interviews 1962-1980*, trans. Linda Coverdale (Berkeley: University of California Press, 1991), 175.

1
Weather

At more or less the centre of *A Guide to Berlin*, the book's protagonist tells her lover: "I've become rather obsessed with the weather."[1] It is a fixation that even the most inattentive of readers could not have missed. From the very first pages of the novel, Cass Turner has the weather on her mind. Travelling by train through Berlin, where she is newly arrived from summery Sydney, Cass conceives of the city and its history in decidedly inclement terms:

> Before the snow truly began, the city was a desolatingly ash-grey, and bitterly cold. It felt stiff and dead … The white sky was menacing. The plates of ice on the Spree, uneven and jagged, resembled a spray of shattered glass after a wartime bombing … It was hard to imagine the icy water thawed and re-sealing, or the sky returning to a lively blue. (3)

Soon enough, the weather anticipated through a grimy S-Bahn window finds its way into Cass' leaky boots; she seems wholly unprepared for a northern hemisphere winter. It makes her body radically unfamiliar, with her "marble blue feet" transformed into "hard foreign appendages" that "stung appallingly" (128–9). And yet despite, or perhaps because of, this discombobulation and severe discomfort, Cass comes to love the snow inordinately. At the first snowfall, she "forgave Berlin its cruel winter" and experiences something approaching transcendence: "She might have been dissolving into airy whiteness. She might have been experiencing transfiguration" (102). By her own admission, Cass is highly attuned to changes in the weather, "finding it soaking inside her, altering her moods" (103). Her inner life is curiously responsive to her outer environment, which itself is the image of inward feelings. Her imagination seems to let the snow in.

---

[1] Gail Jones, *A Guide to Berlin* (North Sydney: Vintage, 2015), 138. All subsequent references are to this edition and appear in parentheses in the text.

Cass is not the only one of Gail Jones' characters to entertain a fascination with snow or to be affected by matters meteorological. Stella Keene, unhappily exiled to a remote, outback town in wartime Western Australia in *Sorry*, dreams of snow falling in the desert, "[a]s if beneath a plastic dome".[2] In *Five Bells*, despite the summer warmth and light of Sydney that infuse the single day across which the story takes place, images of snow, lifted from literature, form connective patterns between two (of four) main characters whose paths intersect three times during the day: Catherine Healy's grief for her brother calls forth "the intimate presence of snow" concluding James Joyce's short story "The Dead" (1914); Pei Xing recollects "a section of *Doctor Zhivago* that is full of snow", which her father had meticulously translated.[3] Catherine furthers the imagined connection by calling on snowflakes to metaphorically denote their shared, but different, diasporic histories: "Perhaps the woman had been born in Australia … or any of a hundred thousand other places Chinese immigrants now lived. Like the Irish, dispersed. Flung like snowflakes in a flurry, like particles motioning through water" (169).

Alice Black in *Dreams of Speaking* also experiences snow. She encounters it in Paris and attributes it special significance. She imagines snow as something radically other to those electrical and mechanical things of modernity that otherwise preoccupy her: "Alice opened her mouth and caught snowflakes on her tongue as they passed. There was this insubstantiality to the natural things in the word, of which snow was exemplary."[4] She is also affected by the "fickle wind" in her home city of Perth (5). This wind does more than propel Alice along the Swan River on her windsurfing board; it offers her revelation: "Sometimes the wind off the river was so strong and the air so alive she felt she was surfing into something elemental" (5). And as befits a text that so obviously recalls by the name alone of its titular character biblically ordained meteorological events of cataclysmic proportions, *The Death of Noah Glass* foregrounds the weather, in particular watery immersions that Martin Glass seems to will into being: "Martin looked skywards and hoped that the cloudburst would catch them … rain began to fall in emphatic drops. Dark coins appeared on the shoulders and bodice of Evie's dress. Martin had always adored these sudden transformations."[5] Later in the narrative, when

---

2   Gail Jones, *Sorry* (North Sydney: Vintage, 2007), 19. All subsequent references are to this edition and appear in parentheses in the text.
3   Gail Jones, *Five Bells* (London: Harvill Secker, 2011), 58, 47. All subsequent references are to this edition and appear in parentheses in the text.
4   Gail Jones, *Dreams of Speaking* (Milsons Point, NSW: Vintage, 2006), 46. All subsequent references are to this edition and appear in parentheses in the text.
5   Gail Jones, *The Death of Noah Glass* (Melbourne: Text, 2018), 23–4. All subsequent references are to this edition and appear in parentheses in the text. Martin's former wife is of an altogether different mind. Her attitude towards the rain is diametrically, and tellingly, opposed to his own: "'Another day ruined,' she laments, rearranging her hair following an unexpected shower (61). Martin's sister, Evie, recalls that this phrase was frequently used by her former sister-in-law when "she and Martin were together, always expressed emphatically" (61). To evoke the vernacular, the implication is that their relationship was stormy.

everyone is wearily sardonic on account of "this splendid [rainy] weather", Martin jokes, "I would prefer more rain" (182). More rain is what he gets.

This chapter proposes to trace the weather in instances of Jones' writing to suggest that it provides more than unremarked scenery or determines if a character should grab an umbrella on their way out the door, which the characters in *The Death of Noah Glass* are well advised to do if they wish to avoid a soaking. In *Five Bells*, umbrellas are put to their original purpose, to create a shady shield against the sun, while their commercial value in modern Sydney is foregrounded: "Umbrellas bearing coffee-logos fluttered in the breeze" (5). Rain is so ubiquitous in *The Death of Noah Glass* that Martin Glass pauses in recognition of a moment in which "it was not raining" (117), and determines that rain is "how he measured time now: *it is raining, it is not raining*" (184). The one day it is sunny – "No rain, Martin thought, ah, no rain" (250) – he is brutally beaten without warning or obvious reason by unknown assailants, and left for dead. The violence committed is thus a double-shock. The emergence of literary sunshine should, by convention, usher in warmth and clear vision, and a kind of happiness that Catherine in *Five Bells* experiences when, at Circular Quay, she "rejoiced in the sunshine" (122). Instead, Martin is damaged, hospitalised, the hand with which he once effortlessly drew now "a weighty lump" (287). The elements are meaningful in Jones' textual worlds, even if their significances are oftentimes implied rather than obvious. Evie Glass' joy at the presence of her young niece in *The Death of Noah Glass* is made gently evident by the air – "Evie's affections flew in a swift gust to the child's sweet face" (59) – suggesting that her adoration is something fundamental, and not easily arrested by language.

Snow, winds, heat, storms and rain are therefore the subjects in Jones' writing in ways they might not be for meteorological instruments – phenomena to be predicted, gauged and graphed. Cass may well end up with soggy socks thanks to the slush that accumulates on the streets of Berlin. But she also reads the below-freezing temperature illuminated on an *Apotheke* sign she passes not as a public record of meteorological fact but rather one of many "untimely signs" that surround her and which "were registers of a fake or redundant knowledge" (37). In *Dreams of Speaking*, Alice Black, as a child and with her sister Norah, liked to watch the television weather report but not because she wanted to know the next day's temperature forecast or the monthly rainfall measure. (The televised weather brings the elements indoors, a largely uncommented-upon feature of everyday modern life.) Alice and Norah are attracted by its reliable regularity, and their quiet, nightly ceremony recasts the ordinary as something special. They are fascinated by the stop-motion televisual representation of the weather:

> Each evening, before the list of tidal figures and temperatures and barometric predictions, one of the stations showed a wide-angled prospect of the city … Eight hours were filmed and condensed to one or two minutes … Light arose and receded, clouds streamed in from the ocean, gathered and dispersed, rain filtered down in drifting, diaphanous waves, swept the screen with shadow, then disappeared in an

instant … The film of the weather was transfixing because it was so unnatural, yet it provided the illusionist gratification, at once terrifying and beautiful, that one might speed up time, that one might push nature faster, that there was a perspective, somewhere, somewhere up very high, of panoramic relativity. (81)

If this modern vision of the weather is also a vision of time travel, the entrance of Anna Griffin into the narrative of *Black Mirror* is notably marked by the weather and folds in time. The would-be biographer is said to remember herself later as "feeling her legs swept by water from passing cars".[6] Yet, in the present she figures herself aesthetically – "a modernist composition … caught in the possibilities of the elements and their visual trickery" – and linguistically saturated by her wet environment, saying her name reassuringly to herself in a "watery whisper. *Anna. Anna*" (1, 2). In *Dreams of Speaking*, Alice casts rain as resolutely unmodern, "so messy, importunate" (131), and also as magnifying of modernity. Travelling on a train with her former lover to Charles de Gaulle Airport, Alice glances out the window and notices the "[d]ark rain splattered the glass, sliding horizontally across the window. Mysterious signatures of neon flashed and departed" (53). The rain effect not only exaggerates the lit colours but also occasions Alice's technological reverie:

> It was as if, outside the train, the world had converted to a system of electrical communication, wrought by arrangements of light answering light … Alice imagined people with transmitters affixed to their heads … beaming statements, questions, existential cries, their faces lacquered with bright responses. (53)

The rain prompts Alice to imagine a future wherein light, rather than words, is the means of communication. The melting ice crystals that numb Cass' feet in *A Guide to Berlin* are similarly figuratively abundant, and tell difficult stories that Cass cannot speak.

The focus of this chapter is on how such atmospheric phenomena are imaginatively represented and materially evident, and why they are metaphorically suggestive in Jones' writing. The weather can be obvious – the clap of thunder; the hot sting of the sun's rays – but it is also frequently unexpected, inexplicable and shape-shifting, lending itself to concerns both material and metaphysical that preoccupy Jones' narratives.

One of the issues that arises when the weather is singled out for discussion, however, is that it is seemingly an unpromising subject. Cass herself acknowledges at one point in *A Guide to Berlin* that the topic is entirely "unoriginal" (138): she introduces the weather into her discussion with Marco Gianelli at an uncomfortable moment so that the two new lovers might find "neutral

---

6   Gail Jones, *Black Mirror* (Sydney: Picador, 2002), 1. All subsequent references are to this edition and appear in parentheses in the text.

territory" (138). A little later, in bed, they revisit their earlier weather conversation, with Marco recommending "the third chapter of Pliny the Elder's *Natural History*, which he said was full of oddball speculations and historical musings on things like lightning, sunshine, tornadoes and shadows" (142). In so doing, Cass rehearses a well-established assumption, which the novel itself declines to endorse, namely that the weather is the stuff of small talk. It is an idea also explicitly entertained in *The Death of Noah Glass*. Characters make "small talk in lowered voices. They commented on the predictable or unpredictable weather" (155) and elsewhere in the narrative they comment on the "[c]hangeable weather" (208) and apologetically recognise "the inevitable small talk about the rain" (113). It is evident too in *Dreams of Speaking*, wherein a reunion after many years between Mr Sakamoto and his former girlfriend, Clare MacDougall, commences with "[s]mall talk … talk about the efficiency of the Métro, the volatile weather, the physical changes evident in Paris" (149). The weather is seemingly something insignificant, a prelude to the forming of conversational intimacies.

In the context of early twenty-first century debates over climate change, serious scientific conversations about the weather have been cast as anything but trivial, scaled up to utterly essential global talk. It is a discussion in which literature has also participated, with the advent of the genre known as cli-fi.[7] And yet, even as the weather has reinserted itself into contemporary consciousness as something that demands worldwide attention and action, the idea lingers that Cass rehearses and *The Death of Noah Glass* echoes, namely that talking about it in everyday conversation is banal. Speaking about the weather is something resorted to when there is nothing else to say.

If the weather is an ordinary subject, then in some literary circles and thanks to Edward Bulwer-Lytton (or an abiding prejudice against melodrama) it has also been accused of being simply too overwrought. Bulwer-Lytton had hoped that his wildly popular 1830 crime novel *Paul Clifford* would bring about penal reform; its now much-lampooned first words – "It was a dark and stormy night" – came to be held up as everything that is wrong with the weather in English literature.[8] It did not help, perhaps, that the sequence coming directly after this otherwise inoffensive clause was the advent of rain falling in torrents, checked at intervals by gusting winds that agitated feeble light sources and rattled London roofs. Bulwer-Lytton's weather was artlessly over-the-top. That its readers then, and now, were, and are, well trained to leap upon such literary weather signs is in no small thanks to the religious undertones the weather has never really sloughed – unexpected weather events are still referred to as acts of God, in line with Old Testament punishments meted out as ruinous weather – and the Romantics. These poets took weather

---

7 See Adam Trexler, *Anthropocene Fictions: The Novel in a Time of Climate Change* (Charlottesville: University of Virginia Press, 2015).
8 Edward Bulwer-Lytton, *Paul Clifford* (London: G. Routledge, 1848), 13.

seriously as an uncontrollable, revolutionary variable, which Enlightenment laboratories tried hard to keep out of their regulated indoor atmospheres.[9]

This example from *Paul Clifford* points to the overt literary presence that weather can have. As it happens, it is a cyclonic storm, terrifying and sublime, that is the scene of Cass' shameful childhood trauma in *A Guide to Berlin*, so the weather can, and does, have a dramatic role in Jones' writing. But the interest of this chapter additionally lies with how the weather in Jones' work is also elusive. Following her first sexual encounter with Benjamin, for example, Evie Glass in *The Death of Noah Glass* steps from the house, looks skyward and sees reflected there her affective tumult and sexual stirrings: "Thunderheads were sweeping from the east, across the ocean. The sky was flaring with antique heraldic colours, gules and purpure, a touch of azure, increasing the impression of emotional drama" (247). If the sky's palette paints the airstreams of Evie's inner life, the weather also makes its presence known by the barely perceptible effects it has on characters and things.

It is this feature that the young child, Nina Glass, intuits in *The Death of Noah Glass* as she rests her hands on a window surface that "shudders in a gust" (307). Her seemingly incidental experience of wind on glass is expressive of her difficult coming to hearing from deafness: "The whole world is shuddery now, as she fights the thunder of surround sound and the raucous jumble of spoken words" (307). In *Dreams of Speaking* and as an adult, Alice Black inhabits both intellectually and physically a world abuzz with the inventions of modernity that – among other capacities and as Nina is now learning – afford sound and information to be transported seemingly effortlessly through the medium of air.

Alice's experiences remind her, though, that air is not submissive to the human claims made on it; the wind makes its own demands on Alice. In her determination to learn to windsurf as a teenager, Alice has to undertake "daily push-ups and back-strengthening exercises" so that she might steady the board and have the strength to manoeuvre the sails (123). Only then was Alice "finally able to catch the wind, to move across the river like a skimming bird … Sky seemed to be everywhere … It was the body almost naked, lashed by spray and tutored by wind" (123). In *Five Bells*, Pei Xing is not so much instructed by the weather than she embodies it. As a seven-year-old girl living in Shanghai with her family, she carries the charming child-conceit, encouraged by her mother, that she is responsible for the snowfall that reshapes the world. It is the purchase of her new scarlet coat that calls forth the snow outside, she thinks, and which makes its literary appearance indoors as her father translates Boris Pasternak's *Doctor Zhivago* (1957), a novel in which nearly every surface is covered with snow. As a much older woman living in Sydney, where snow on hat brims and window ledges is unheard of, Pei Xing retains this connection to the weather. When she listens to music in her apartment, she hears memories of her childhood that are recalled as the weather: "the descent of the snow … there was

---

9   See Arden Reed, *Romantic Weather: The climates of Coleridge and Baudelaire* (Hanover, NH: University Press of New England, 1983).

the floating of single flakes and their moist feathery touch" (189). Out of doors, Pei Xing momentarily *is* the weather, performing a Tai Chi movement spontaneously in the sun and fresh wind, "her arms upraised: the soft sway of a movement known as 'cloud hands'" (113). In another time, place and form, certain Romantic poets might have fantasised about becoming a cloud to escape corporeality, but Pei Xing is not Percy Bysshe Shelley. Instead, her physical strength and grace are emphasised: "She felt the shape of her body and the fine balances it could achieve, muscles taut, or relaxed, or forming a woven pattern of crimson chords tucked deep inside her" (113). As a cloud, Pei Xing both moves "into eternity for a few precious seconds", and is resolutely specific and bodily present (113).

If Cass is at all right about the weather being an unoriginal topic of conversation, then she also inadvertently points to something crucial about its discursive potential. In as much as the weather might be understood as a safe topic of conversation, or what could be termed a phatic expression, talking about the weather is also to be not speaking about the weather at all. The weather has undeniable narrative dimensions that extend beyond itself. Mr and Mrs Ramsay's dispute over the weather forecast in the first pages of Virginia Woolf's *To the Lighthouse* (1927), for example, which Jones perhaps subtly references in *Sixty Lights* with the idea that "[e]very person was a lighthouse, a signal of presence",[10] is the barometer of the emotional pressure in their household. It is this quality of the weather that is also apparent in Jones' narratives, in particular in the two novels singled out for discussion in this chapter – *Sorry* and *A Guide to Berlin* – on the basis of their shared snowy imaginings.

This pairing is likely unexpected given that snow appears briefly in *Sorry* in dreams only, while in *A Guide to Berlin* snow is inescapably everywhere. But both novels treat snow as though the scenes on which it falls are located within a snow globe, and their narratives are subject to the kind of revolutionary shake-up along the lines that philosopher Walter Benjamin, whose writing is expressly discussed by characters in *A Guide to Berlin*, attributed to those objects.[11] As his friend and

---

10 Gail Jones, *Sixty Lights* (London: Harvill Press, 2004), 171. All subsequent references are to this edition and appear in parentheses in the text.

11 Marco's passing reference to Benjamin's writing is aimed at "correcting" Cass' interpretation of Nabokov's "A Guide to Berlin", the short story that lends its name to the book in which this discussion is taking place. Marco implicitly evokes Benjamin's figure of the angel of history to make his case for how to read "A Guide to Berlin" properly: "'It's the whole point of the story,' Marco insisted, 'Not an angel looking backwards, seeing ruins and history blown away, but an old man, gentle and kind, looking at ordinary things, and seeing mystically into the future memory of a small child'" (143). This is considerable post-coital conversation, and open to debate, which Cass is not keen to pursue. The old man is arguably less mystical than presumptuous to cast himself as a fixed image and future memory in the mind of another, insisting on the narrative control Benjamin's angel is denied. Further, Marco's casual reference to Benjamin's ninth thesis on the philosophy of history evokes the weather. In Benjamin's scenario, the indifferent, turbulent wind is rendered a sign of the empty, homogenous and sequential time of progress itself – "a storm is blowing from Paradise". The wind pins open the impotent angel's wings and renders him a witness to the rubble of the past that piles up before his widened eyes.

fellow philosopher Theodor Adorno related it, among the things that Benjamin liked to collect were snow globes, approaching them as philosophical toys for play and contemplation.[12] The dialectical image they offered of natural history (the snow) and history (the small world scene) had Benjamin expectant that, with their stilled focus on an isolated, frozen scene, snow globes might make visible historical relations and enact a seismic shock at being shaken back into life. He accorded big responsibilities to such a little object, and these are at play in the two novels discussed in this chapter.

Benjamin's broader meteorological musings resonate in Jones' texts beyond *Sorry* and *A Guide to Berlin*, however. Benjamin, who wrote from exile of his childhood in the city that serves as the setting of *A Guide to Berlin*, is not an explicit presence in that novel in the way that Vladimir Nabokov, another Berlin resident, is. His thought is referenced in it, however, just as it is in another of Jones' novels, *Sixty Lights*. Benjamin's much-quoted aphorism – "Knowledge comes only in flashes" – plainly prefaces part two of *Sixty Lights*, and given that text's sustained interest in mid-nineteenth century photography, the metaphor of sudden, fleeting yet startling disclosure – the flash – seems entirely apt (79).[13] And yet, the flash to which Benjamin is referring in that aphorism is akin to the blinding light of a burnt magnesium ribbon camera flash only because it serves as its natural model. For Benjamin, the flash that knowledge resembles is lightning, the sudden electrostatic discharge produced by stormy circumstances. This celebrated insight is directly, if subtly, credited to Ellen, the four-month-old daughter of *Sixty Light*'s photographer-protagonist, Lucy Strange: "still startled by the dazzling novelty of the world. She looked at faces as if they appeared in a flash of lightning before her" (169). And Benjamin's thinking continues along such weather lines. If knowledge as revelation appears like lightning – it is a paradoxical moment of blinding seeing – then the narration that tells of this insight is the elongated rumble that temporally lags behind: "Text is the thunder rolling along afterwards," Benjamin suggests.[14] As a text, *Sixty Lights* should, by Benjamin's meteorological designs, roll along, but with the logic of the flash as its formal principle, its sixty brief chapters approximate the revelatory glimpse that the lightning flash promises.

This was not the only time Benjamin looked skywards. With his gaze directed towards outer space, Benjamin insisted on cosmic thinking, suggesting that just as constellations link the stars, ideas enable the perception of relations between

---

Walter Benjamin, "Theses on the Philosophy of History", *Illuminations*, trans. Harry Zorn, ed. Hannah Arendt (1968; London: Pimlico, 1999), 249.

12 In his portrait-essay of his friend, Adorno writes that among Benjamin's favourite objects were "small glass balls containing a landscape upon which snow fell when shook". Theodor Adorno, *Prisms*, trans. Samuel and Shierry Weber (Boston, MA: MIT Press, 1967), 233.

13 For a recent account of the history of flash photography, see Kate Flint, *Flash!: Photography, Writing and Surprising Illumination* (Oxford: Oxford University Press, 2017).

14 Walter Benjamin, *The Arcades Project*, trans. Howard Eiland and Kevin McLaughlin, ed. Rolf Tiedemann (Cambridge, MA: Harvard University Press, 1999), 456.

objects.[15] And closer to the earth, with the troposphere in sight, talking about the weather was anything but banal for Benjamin. It is essential and nothing less than a fundamental sign of individual integrity and intellectual enquiry:

> The mere narcotizing effect which cosmic forces have on shallow and brittle personality is attested in the relation of such a person to one of the highest and most genial manifestations of these forces: the weather. Nothing is more characteristic than that precisely this intimate and mysterious affair, the working of the weather on humans, should have become the theme of their emptiest chatter. Nothing bores the ordinary man more than the cosmos.[16]

Whereas in earlier times the cosmos might have provoked an experience of heavenly revelation or the sublime, in modern secular life it induces a kind of world, and word, weariness which Benjamin identifies by means of the conversational petrification of the weather. Against this habit, Evie Glass entertains another sort of meteorological thinking in *The Death of Noah Glass*. She recognises that "the rain, which was unceasing" signified "some larger sense of the world beyond human control" (178). Her father is similarly imagined as looking upwards at the night-time sky and feeling "a helpless awe, like an ancient man deciphering the drama of weather" (299). In a comparable spirit, Mr Sakamoto in *Dreams of Speaking* reminds Alice Black that the sky resists historical determinations: "There is nothing modern about the sky" (21, 65), he says. This observation is not to suggest that there is no temporal aspect to the sky but rather that its timescale extends beyond human ones. Alice's father seems to share this insight. Having survived a mine cave-in, he works installing electricity in houses, and "[s]ometimes he stood on a roof just to feel the sun on his face, the intensity of daylight and the immeasurable arc of the sky" (48). And the mournful, snowy thinking of Catherine in *Five Bells* oscillates between human scale and that of the cosmos: "Upon all the living and the dead. This was how Brendan haunted her, visiting at unexpected moments, falling over her, as if from the sky, smoothing her own definition" (58). Her intimation of literary snow while in sunny Sydney is unforeseen, but it is rendered both intimate and universal, and yoked with her welcomed memory of her brother. Likewise, Benjamin persisted with the idea that the weather is one of the cosmos' "highest and most genial manifestations". And he turned to snowflakes to pursue the point.

Benjamin wrote of snowflakes explicitly in his 1930s memoir *Berlin Childhood Around 1900*. Writing in exile of Berlin, the city of his childhood now on the cusp of modernity, and aware that he would most likely never see this place again, Benjamin looked out at the snowy weather through a window and wondered

---

15 Walter Benjamin, *The Origin of German Tragic Drama*, trans. John Osborne (London: Verso, 2003).
16 Benjamin, *The Arcades Project*, 101–2.

how to write of an impending obsolescence in the past. "Images and allegories," he insisted, "preside over my thinking."[17] And among the governing images are snowflakes remembered from childhood:

> But sometimes in winter, when I stood by the window in the warm little room, the snowstorm outside told me stories … What it told, to be sure, I could never quite grasp, for always something new and unremittingly dense was breaking through the familiar. Hardly had I allied myself, as intimately as possible, to one band of snowflakes, than I realised they had been obligated to yield me up to another, which had suddenly entered their midst. But now the moment had come to follow, in the flurry of letters, the stories that had eluded me at the window.[18]

The flurries Benjamin compares to the play of words on the page, his apprehension of snowflakes and stories, is his very own project of mimesis and a meditation on the making of allegory itself. And at the same time, there is the somewhat mystical suggestion that words and things are connected materially, and that these connections unfold at varying velocities – this sequence surges and tumbles – and invite a surrendering of the self, an imagined letting in of the snow. *A Guide to Berlin* and *Sorry* share these gestures, with the snow-filled dreams Stella Keene has in *Sorry* serving as a starting point for an exploration of them:

> And that night, for no reason, Stella dreamed that there was snow falling softly in the desert. As if beneath a plastic dome, or confined in the more expensive glass ornaments, she saw the slow descent of flakes, a little too large, and petal-like. In her dream she opened the front door and walked across its threshold, but did not feel the chill of snowflakes settling on her skin; they seemed to evaporate before they touched her. The place looked the same – barren, Australia, the light was glaring orange and the sky extensive – but held suspended this dissolving, impossible drift. In her new country Stella would dream this dream many times. It was always the same. There was always the stepping through a doorway, a sense of keen disconnection, of indefinable loss, and then of the air filled with delicate, illogical presences. She loved to tell it; her snow dream. She told it to anybody who would listen. She must have told me her snow dream ten or twenty times. (19–20)

Stella has been recently uprooted from Cambridge, England.[19] She has relocated to a cattle station "in the scrubland of spinifex and rocky outcrops" in the north of the state of Western Australia when she first has this dream (15). The year is 1930, and the

---

17 Walter Benjamin, *Berlin Childhood Around 1900*, trans. Howard Eiland (Cambridge, MA: The Belknap Press, 2006), 39.
18 Benjamin, *Berlin*, 59.
19 This travel trajectory is reversed in *The Death of Noah Glass*. Noah travels from Western Australia to Cambridge to write his art history thesis on Piero della Francesca (and to meet his future wife, Katherine White).

reason for her arrival at this place of spikes and protrusions is her husband, Nicholas Keene. Keene is an aspiring anthropologist with grandiose ambitions to "crack open the code of primitive humanity, return to Cambridge triumphant, drink sherry with the dons, wear a long cardinal gown with an ermine trim, receive a silver badge on his chest, rosette-shaped, from the King, and an accolade detailing his discovery, in full, in the *Sunday Times*" (30). He has attitudes in common with Herbert Morrell, the rich white mine-owner in *Black Mirror*, who "had opinions on every race and nation on earth and had systematically ranked them" (158). While Keene wishes to exercise knowledge over the Indigenous people he considers primitive, Morrell's grand capitalist design is genocidal in intent: "Australia would advance, he believed, only when the extirpation of the Aborigine was complete" (159).

Things do not quite turn out the way Nicholas Keene plans. Nicholas' ostensible objects of study are unexpectedly (at least to the ethnographic assumptions Nicholas carries) "intelligent and quick-witted" (23), as his unwanted daughter, Perdita, well knows. These people befriend and nurture Perdita in ways that her own parents are incapable of doing. On learning of Stella's pregnancy, Nicholas' reaction is to order "a medicine to make it go away" (22); at the moment of her birth, Perdita is described by her mother as "a bloody mess and utterly unlovely" (24). In contrast to this parental disinterest, Perdita casts her own arrival into the world as resonantly coincident with the dramatic workings of the weather:

> Rain was beating on the iron roof so that there was a density and amplification to the world of substances; plashing, drip-drip, the cascade of waterfalls and spouts, frog-life, scampering things, clay earth subsiding into overflowing sluices and channels. Thunder boomed in the sky. The humid heat was unbearable. (24)

Whereas her mother sees nothing but ugliness in the birth of her unwanted child, Perdita imagines her arrival in the world as a watery creation and baptism, noisily announced by the sympathetic elements.

Nicholas' failed future does not come as a surprise. His death, signalled by the glimpse of a blue dress "spattered with the purple of my father's blood", is told and concealed by a whisper on the novel's first page: "*don't tell them*" (3). The narrative returns to this scene at intervals, with each of its arabesques slowly accumulating detail so that the whispering voice, the dress, and Perdita as child-witness, recalled by her older self, are gradually brought into focus.[20] Further, very early on in the

---

20 Roseanne Kennedy describes the narrative in terms familiar to theories and experiences of trauma, "*Sorry* does not immediately reveal Perdita's complicity in her father's death and Mary's incarceration. Rather, the narrative mimics the structure of trauma as a belated memory that is not directly accessible to consciousness." Roseanne Kennedy, " Australian Trials of Trauma: the Stolen Generations in human rights, law and literature", *Comparative Literature Studies* 48 no. 3 (2011): 349. Diana Brydon suggests that *Sorry* is a novel searching "for a form adequate to the difficult forms of knowing with which Australians need to engage, once the state has officially apologized for colonialism and recognized some of its injuries". Diana Brydon, "'Difficult Forms

narrative, Stella intuits her husband's inflated foolishness and feels acutely and keenly, as her name would suggest, her physical isolation and emotional distress. (The weather on their wedding day had foretold of their unhappiness; it had been "a gloomy day, with the threat of rain" (9). The rainy Saturday wedding that takes place later in the book is not a sign of anything, but rather is signed by finger patterns and bodily gestures as a minor part of the mute groom's visual address to his guests.) The dreams the two characters have on their first night on the station also seem to tell of the true situation in which they find themselves. The first dream told is unusual for a narrative that otherwise gives scant attention to Nicholas' inner life. It is of the anthropologist initially sharing a meal with an Indigenous family, only to soil himself when unable to digest the prepared meat and leading to his mockery by an Aboriginal elder. This is a dream of humiliation, and it clearly settles where narrative approval lies. The second dream, told immediately after Nicholas' and so positioned for comparative contemplation, is Stella's snow dream.

Given where Stella is and what she is quickly coming to realise, the dream could be read as a nostalgic remembrance of the wintry England she has recently left behind. That the dream occurs as if in a snow globe, an ornament linked inextricably with kitsch, which in turn is popularly interpreted in scholarly circles as a commentary on inconsolable loss, would seem to push in that interpretive direction.[21] The narrative, though, warns gently against any such easy conclusions. Whereas Nicholas' dream serves the unambiguous purpose of again laying bare his wretched absurdity, Stella's dream is had "for no reason" (19). And as dreams are wont to do (or, at least this is a feature they are often attributed with), this one makes the familiar strange. Not only is it impossibly snowing in the desert, but the falling flakes themselves are also of ever-so-slightly unusual proportions and shapes. Their suspended dissolution is an unlikely affirmation.

Rather than any meaning or location they might reference, it is instead the flakes' aesthetic qualities that are emphasised, and Stella herself declines to interpret her snow dream. The dream prompts a narrative retelling of it which becomes her daughter's inheritance, and this bequest is suggested formally by the novel's almost imperceptible shift from an omniscient perspective to Perdita's first-person point of view. This play between narrative levels, which the novel insists on throughout, identifies Perdita as the specific recipient-listener of her mother's snowy story but also prompts questions about re-presentation. What is the true version of events? Whose truth is offered? The rest of the narrative turns around these questions as it works its way towards the abstruse verity of the whispered denial that announces Nicholas Keene's death on the novel's first page.

---

of Knowing: enquiry, injury and translocated relations of postcolonial responsibility", *Postcolonial Translocations: cultural representation and critical spatial thinking* eds. Marga Munkelt, Markus Schmitz, Mark Stein and Silke Stroh (New York: Rodopi, 2013), 15.

21 See Esther Leslie, "Snow shaker", in *The Object Reader*, eds. Fiona Candlin and Raiford Guins (New York: Routledge, 2009), 516–18.

As such, it is significant that the narrative ends with Perdita recalling in first-person present tense her much younger self and willing into mind her mother's snow dream. Perdita is now an adult. She no longer suffers from the dysfluency that she developed suddenly following her father's death, and which gave her mother further reason to be impatiently disdainful of her prodigious daughter.[22] What allows Perdita to recover her fluent speech is not entirely attributable to reason – "There is a margin of mystery … that every doctor allows," her kindly therapist willingly concedes – subtly aligning Perdita's story with the winter tales of improbability to be wondered at, rather than believed, that her Shakespearean namesake inhabited (200). But this recuperation is assisted by both her being well versed in iambic pentameter – Stella Keene recites the Bard's verse as a talisman and solace, and her daughter calls on the "bizarre resource of maternal impersonation" to recover her tongue (191) – and a near-relative of the dreamed-of snow globe: a beautiful glass paperweight.[23] Contained within its smooth vault is "a multi-petalled flower of startling turquoise, the like of which could not possibly exist in nature" (159). As Perdita holds the cool object in her hand, Dr Oblov encourages his young patient to imagine it as containing her voice "coming, like magic, out of the centre of the blue flower" (160). The glass paperweight, like the snow dream, seems to evoke affective sophistications that might otherwise belong properly to the unconscious, with its associations, displacements and condensations.

It is while Perdita is holding the paperweight and reciting a passage from *Macbeth* that she is suddenly flung back in memory to the time of her father's death, and a belated recognition of her own culpability. Mary, a young Walmajarri woman whom Stella thinks of as a sister, had been falsely imprisoned for the killing of Keene when she confesses to the crime. But she was herself the victim of Keene's sexual violence, which Perdita witnesses and ends when she "simply took up the carving knife lying on the table and walked steadily towards him" (193). She is also subject to his ideas about Aboriginal people that are by no means his alone. The condescending attitude Keene exhibits towards his chosen anthropological subjects is shared by the government in whose service he works, with damaging consequences. That Mary is within Keene's reach is because government policy, informed by race theories and anxieties about miscegenation that supported and discomforted colonial projects respectively, has decreed that her light skin means she should be forcibly removed from her mother, placed in a mission and sent to a city convent to "learn to be

---

22 Perdita's dysfluency has attracted critics' attention. Christopher Eagle reads Perdita's stutter as one demonstration of the "many ways in which individuals can be deprived of voice and forced to adapt through other means in order to achieve some level of self-expression". Christopher Eagle, "'Angry Because She Stutters': stuttering, violence and the politics of voice in *American Pastoral* and *Sorry*", *Philip Roth Studies* 8 no. 1 (2012): 26. Julie McGonegal suggests that "Perdita's stuttering is a kind of text, as it were: it contains meanings hidden beyond or beneath the surface and thus demands to be decoded and interpreted." Julie McGonegal, "The Great Canadian (and Australian) Secret: the limits of non-Indigenous knowledge and representation", *ESC* 35 no. 1 (2009): 77.
23 Paperweights are also collected by Benjamin in *The Death of Noah Glass*.

a whitefella" (55–6).²⁴ From there, Mary is recruited as domestic help when Stella Keene is institutionalised for a time with a psychiatric disorder.

The final snow dream comes after what – if this story were to be told in another genre or register – might be called this revelation towards which the narrative is moving, even as the dream first occurs well before that knowledge is made possible and even earlier than it is subsequently remembered. Perdita is part-suspicious of her memory's reliability and fixations, likening her recall to "the opening shot of a second-rate movie" (212). And yet to represent visually that the last snow dream forms part of the older Perdita's present memory of the night she returned with her mother to the house in which she murdered her father and began to forget would take some seriously creative on-screen fashioning. Whereas Perdita quietly insists that she "did not will it" (213) – that is, her forgetting – she does emphasise that she made herself "think instead of Stella's snow dream" (214), having been repeatedly rejected by her mother and finding herself nested outside with her sleeping pet dog. It is a resolve that sits in contrast with her still earlier effort to conjure the same dream, also in the face of maternal absence.

When her mother is admitted to hospital for psychiatric care,²⁵ Perdita thinks of the snow dream and imagines that one day she will see snow for herself somewhere distant: "She would go to distant Russia and see the snow" (45–6).²⁶ In that hypnogogic moment, with the war the USSR was entering reaching the Keenes only belatedly by means of news reports that paper their living room, Stella's dream becomes Perdita's "own private treasure; she fell asleep imagining a soft drift, an endless vertical sadness, a delicate slow sinking, a whiteness, a whiteness" (46). The dream of snow that inhabits the inner lives of both Perdita and her mother is a wishful singular intimacy, the words on the page gently accumulating like the dreamy soft drift, inducing sleep.

The effect of the last snow dream is decidedly different. Perdita tells of remembering her younger self thinking about

> Stella's snow dream: a field of flakes descending, the slow transformation of the shapes of the world, the slow, inconclusive, obliteration. I saw a distant place,

---

24 This circumstance is also that of Lily-white in *Black Mirror*, "a mission girl, compliant, well-trained for housework and general slavery" (178). Naomi Orb offers a reading of *Black Mirror* that acknowledges this context and presents "a close examination of the relationship between Indigenous and non- Indigenous Australians within the text". Naomi Orb, "Mirroring, Depth and Inversion: Holding Gail Jones' *Black Mirror* Against Contemporary Australia", *Sydney Studies in English* 35 (2009): 112.

25 This is often the fate of Jones' mothers. In *Five Bells*, James' apprehension of his mother's reduced mental life, necessitating institutionalisation, is couched in meteorological terms, "the blizzard in her mind that she liked to call her 'snow'" (69); Anna Griffin's mother in *Black Mirror* suffers after the birth of her daughter and needs "time away, in a hospital" (123).

26 It is from Russia, and with Anton Chekhov, that snow comes metaphorically to colonial Ceylon in Jones' short story "Snow". It carries imperial impulses that are sexually enacted. Gail Jones, "Snow", *Fetish Lives* (Fremantle: Fremantle Arts Centre Press, 1997), 9–21.

all forgetful white, reversing its presences. I saw Mary, and Billy, covered by snowflakes. I saw my mother's bare feet beneath the hem of her nightgown. Everything was losing definition and outline. Everything was disappearing under the gradual snow. Calmed, I look at the sky and saw only a blank. Soft curtains coming down, a whiteness, a peace. (214)

What Perdita remembers is a process of forgetting, and the moment she recalls resembles her mother's dream only because of the presence of snow. Otherwise, and contrary to how the remembering Perdita might have them, the two dreams are quite unalike. Whereas the snow in Stella's dream is suitably dreamy – indistinct, illogical – snow in this waking instance (Perdita is not asleep, but thinking) takes on a metaphoric charge, part transforming, part cancelling out those whose lives have been radically altered by Perdita's response to her father's violence against Mary. The snow here "obliterates" and causes everything to "disappear", albeit gently. Forgetting, as a snowy whiteness, settles on the word "peace" as the narrative's conclusive word, and the calm that Perdita remembers feeling seems to draw the story to an end.[27]

But the book does not end there, exactly. The narrative stops in the recalled past, but what follows directly is "A Note on Sorry". This is a paratextual address to the novel's (international) audience. And it gives explanation of both the various Indigenous meanings of the term "sorry" and the unmet non-Indigenous responsibilities towards Aboriginal people. In the context of Australia's ongoing colonial legacies and the refusal by the Federal Government of the time to acknowledge past and present wrongs committed against Aboriginal people and cultures, "sorry" is recognised in this postscript as a highly charged word and concept. "Sorry" is the simple yet also freighted word Perdita does not say to Mary, who continues to be imprisoned for Keene's murder even after Perdita determines to "claim her guilt" (201). As the *Macbeth*-reciting witness to Perdita's killing of her husband, however, Stella Keene puzzlingly refuses to support her daughter's admission; she is not motivated by any obvious maternal concern. So Perdita is not judged credible.

Mary articulates what she sees as the limits, anyway, of seeking recognition or restitution by means of the law: "'No one will believe the word of a bush blackfella. Unless,' she added, 'they're confessing a crime'" (203). To seek something approaching justice from the social institutions that determined Mary should be wrenched from her mother because of her race, and which continue colonial habits

---

27 The snowy curtains coming down on the narrative also suggest the theatrical direction *exeunt*, and provide a reminder that a section of Antigonus' speech from Shakespeare's play *The Winter's Tale* prefaces part one of *Sorry*'s four parts. The sequence that starts with a dream and ends with a storm – a rough lullaby for the abandoned baby Perdita, which the thunderous birth of Perdita Keene in *Sorry* echoes. Antigonus himself is then most infamously pursued off stage by a bear. Perdita, fully aware of the literary inheritance her name carries, declares that she "hated this bizarrely particular detail" (27).

of conflating indigeneity with criminality, is of little use. Even the expansive elements are incapable of countering their damaging power, with Mary knowing that once she was taken away as a young girl, "her mother spoke to her in the wind, and that she was crying too, full of whispery breath, overflowing and spreading out, coming like wind-spirit across the land to find and to claim her. But it was no good, they never saw each other again" (55). Mary's incarceration is expressly imagined as a state cut off not only from the weather but also from her mother and the land, and from memory: "to be closed against the rustle of leaves and the feel of wind and of rain, to be taken from her place, her own place, where her mother had died, to be sealed in the forgetfulness of someone else's crime" (204). The tying of the wind to Mary's mother, and Mary's loss of her mother, only underscores the cruelty of the young woman's unjust imprisonment and the act of forgetting. That Perdita and her childhood friend Billie step out into a downpour following their first meeting with the imprisoned Mary emphasises the differences between the two women and allows the weather its signifying function:

> Perdita and Billie left disheartened. As they stepped outside the building it began to rain and soon they were both drenched. They made their way back to the bus stop, up the rain-blue suburban streets, in a dripping sad silence. Skeins of white rain chilled and enveloped them. Cars skidded past, sending up sheets of water. Everything was darkening, wintering, becoming night, conveying in the very elements their inexpressible woe. (172)

If Mary is resigned to her weatherless incarceration – "I teach reading and writing. I have my friends, my place" (203) – then she is also knowing of the circumstances that have brought her to this point in a way that Perdita is not. Perdita is tellingly described as "apprehensive" when she visits Mary soon after her memory of the murder is returned. She is both fearful of what Mary might say or how she might react, and coming to difficult knowledge: "she was beginning to understand the true dimensions to things" (202). And yet in the face of Mary's disbelief that an appeal to the law can make her wronged situation somehow right, Perdita still insists on pursuing this course of action, telling Mary, "I can write letters, visit lawyers. I can tell them the truth" (204). The truth Perdita sidesteps with her legalistic quest for justice, as it is proposed in the novel, is that something almost unsayable (as suggested by the narrative's opening hushed whisper), yet unable to be changed or fixed, has occurred between Perdita and Mary.

The act of apologising – of saying sorry – is offered as the alternative by which Perdita might acknowledge that wrong and accept responsibility for it, without defence, and therefore be placed in a vulnerable state, knowing that Mary might refuse her apology. By saying sorry, Perdita would also be admitting there is truly nothing she can offer that will be sufficient for what Mary has experienced and suffered. This is a ritual, a social exchange founded on a speech act, that seeks to recognise and reshape the moral order that has been breached, and it is one that Perdita declines to initiate. Only later, when Perdita is older and she learns of Mary's early death, does she come to realise and understand what she did not say: "*I should have said sorry to my sister, Mary. Sorry, my sister, oh my sister, sorry*" (211). That the belated apology-never-made is italicised is not merely a typographical convention signalling internal thoughts; it links visually that which is not said to the repeated emphasis made of Mary's decisive directive to Perdita in the immediate aftermath of the murder: "*don't tell them*" (3). Whereas Mary's concern for silence, with withholding an account of what has just occurred, is later interpreted by her as the way to protect Perdita (but might also be bound up with the shock and misplaced shame of her own violation), Perdita's silence is full of belated regret at her own incapacity to apologise, and her unawareness of why saying sorry might matter.

In that context – but also apprehended by a future that Perdita cannot know and which is the present of the text's writing (and reading), alive to the significances of (not) saying sorry – the final snow dream that is remembered directly after the sorry-not-said offers more than the quiet, conclusive peace it seems to promise. The field of flakes, reshaping Perdita's proximate memories, might well have provided necessary comfort to Perdita as a traumatised child returning to the house where her father had lately died by her hand. But told by the adult Perdita at the story's end, the recollection of snowy forgetting is unsettling. Perdita's comely imagining of snow as "forgetful white" – placed in the narrative after Mary's death and her explicit critique of neo-colonial discrimination against "blackfellas", and just prior to the paratextual explanations of "sorry" that emphasise the book's contemporary political context – seems both poetic and pointed. Everything "losing definition and outline" looks less like a wish than a warning. Dreams of snow in the desert might momentarily delight Stella, and in turn become her daughter's melancholic inheritance in which momentary comfort might be taken. But the blanketing snow as forgetting in *Sorry* also raises questions about the acts of covering over that it facilitates, and which the novel itself works hard against as it insists on, both formally and thematically, the necessity of complicated remembering.

It is not incidental, perhaps, that this snowy landscape is said to be had in dreams "as if in a plastic dome". What this link between the unconscious mind and the snow globe encourages most immediately is an attention to the otherwise repressed scenes each might be said to entertain. Stella's dream extends the access usually afforded an external, distanced viewer of the snow globe by having Stella fantastically inhabit the object from the inside. In turn, the snow of the dome is transferred to the microclimate of the dream. Dreams, like snow globes, are mythopoetic spaces where what is impossible in waking life can be imagined. Yet, they are so very unalike in many respects. Snow globes exist to be physically held; dreams are a lot less graspable. The plastic domes encase a miniaturised scene stopped for extended viewing; dreams move visually and dissolve on waking, more often than not. Domes are produced *en masse* and distributed widely; dreams feel intensely private.

But regardless of their differences, and beyond their shared speculative landscapes, the analogy made in *Sorry* between dreams, the unconscious mind and the snow dome, also holds the promise of turning upside down the current state of things. As frozen as they might appear, the whole point of snow domes is surely the momentary disruption of their fixity, with the movement of the artificial snow in their watery environment the very sign of such disturbance. Whereas a hand action sets the snow globe in motion, it is the effort to remember in *Sorry* that unsettles the "peace" the accumulated flakes at rest suggest. While Perdita might recall her younger self seeking precious solace in the snow dream, her action of remembering this desire is undertaken in the persistent knowledge that what "remains is broken as my speech once was" (212). Perdita's recollection of her efforts as a child to conjure her mother's snow globe-like dream catches the snow's process of obliteration in mid-shake; the transformative tremors afforded memory are realised in the falling snow.

The very brief and unlikely appearance of snow in *Sorry* speaks to a concern attendant to Perdita's remembering of the repressed scene that comprises the novel's beginning, namely for "the shape that affections make, the patterns that love upholds in the face of any shattering. It is not sentimentality that drives me to claim this, but the need – more explicitly self-serving, perhaps – to imagine something venerable and illustrious beneath such waste" (212). If the snow of the dome-dreams is marked in *Sorry* by the shattering of remembering, it is also afforded the possibility of reshaping and transformation as it settles again on a suspended scene that comes to look different because of its new snowy arrangements. It also points to an abiding interest in Jones' work in the potential of metaphorical language, of aesthetic form, to discern patterns in contingency, coincidence and "waste", however transitorily. The minor, fleeting presence of gently accumulating snow, dreamt of in *Sorry* as if beneath a plastic dome, gestures towards such a desire.

The abundant snow in *A Guide to Berlin* might also be approached as if within a glass dome. In other words, the snowy weather that comes to absorb Cass in this novel is not some icy backdrop to the narrative's action. Rather, the snow-dome qualities of suspension and shattering are also redolent for thinking about this novel and its ethics.

If the claim for approaching *A Guide to Berlin* as a snow globe holds at all, it is prompted in part by its protagonist's own fleeting but exuberant recollection of patterns caught in a smooth, clear sphere when she first notes snowflakes netted by the wind. At that moment, Cass "was reminded of the coiled colours lodged magically in her brothers' glass marbles. She felt an instantaneous, novel delight" (103). Up to this point in the novel, the wind has been something to combat, and not only because of its physical force. The wind blows away human individuality: "Everyone wore black padded jackets in a kind of mournful uniformity, and battled the same bladed wind that swept across the open spaces, their fists jammed into pockets, their heads resolutely down" (39). "Everyone"

– and there is no sense of solidarity imputed – is frozen and compressed, and hardly recognisable as themselves, with their faces "eroded by the cold" (44). It is little help to the overall feeling of despondency this wintry environment evokes that it also takes on the palette of the city's history, a "fascist grey" (103). With the coming of the first snow, however, Cass is imaginatively enlivened. With no concern whatsoever for the mundane fact that she has just stepped out of the shower with wet hair, Cass opens the doors to her small balcony and ecstatically welcomes the weather: "She remembered reading somewhere that if one watches falling snow long enough, it would seem as if one's building is floating upwards. This was true. Verifiable. Already she was ascending, already her elation was a levitation" (102). From then on, each time "she found herself in snow she felt again the charm of the first moment she had rushed to her window. Each time she faced the fierce arctic air, she was relieved when it sprang alive with a bulge and billow of soft flakes" (111). And when it is not falling, "she wanted snow. Cass wanted that powdery light, that world-filling softness. She wanted total immersion" (135).

This desire for encircling absorption is suggested by both the marble memory that arises when Cass witnesses the play of snow on the wind and the walk she takes in the snowfall immediately after this recollection. The description of this everyday act has Cass inhabit a similarly imagined globed swirl: "It was her first experience of enwrapment in the soft surround of snow" (103). The sibilant embrace Cass receives has the wintry season out of kilter with its habitual poetic associations with absence, monotony and arrest, and she is at a loss to understand why everyone around her seems to want to "defer the 'real' Berlin until spring" (139). In the snow-globe world of the novel, how each character reacts and thinks about the weather says much about them. Cass' response to the weather is presented as contrarian. Her enthusiasm for snow is understood by Gino Scattini, Marco's friend, who confides, "I also love the snow" (149). He is vying for Cass' sexual attention, however, so his meteorological appreciation is a little calculated. And he does end up admitting that the story about the weather he adores the most is one concentrated on suns. It involves Descartes' early seventeenth-century observations while in Rome of parhelia, and sees Gino admiring Descartes' suitably rational response to the seeming appearance in the sky of three suns: "He did not panic, he did not lose his religion, he did not resort to lunatic theories or apocalyptic speculations. Instead he stood looking up at the sky … and knew how good it was to be a man, with his senses fully alive, his brain figuring out all the equations of angles and reflections" (153–4). By contrast, when Cass looks skywards, she sees a "white ceiling" (155) and her response to snow is spontaneous and sincere, and not entirely rational (if Descartes' thinking about suns is taken as a measure of manly reason, as Gino suggests). But it fits with her image of herself as precocious, serious and internally fissured.

Cass travels to Berlin in the knowledge of the city's traumatic and shameful past, and carrying a small hope that in Berlin she "might recover her own presence" (34), a hint at hidden personal catastrophe that later emerges in the narrative. Her ardour for the writing of Vladimir Nabokov sees her drawn, almost despite herself, to a group – by her own admission she's not a "joiner" (15) – whose five other members share her literary fervour and promise connection. They volley between themselves phrases from Nabokov's stories to share, to impress, to seduce. Replacing with a hyphen the comma punctuating the imperative title of Nabokov's autobiography, *Speak, Memory* (1951), the group convenes to participate in speak-memory disclosures at vacated dwellings. The characters form a cosmopolitan collective; they identify as Jewish-American, Italian, Jewish-Italian, Australian and Japanese. And they take democratic turns across a number of weeks and gatherings to tell aspects of their life stories, which are bound up with wider national and religious histories and traumas. This willingness to speak about what might otherwise prove to be too painful to articulate gives shape to connections across difference, rather than inviting comparisons, as each speak-memory is interlaced with Nabokov's narratives and vocabulary, and reveals an innermost vulnerability.

With the commencement of these meetings, Cass finds intellectual companionship within the group, whose staging is announced by the theatricality of the soliloquies each character speaks. It is also pronounced by the costumes they wear. Victor, a Jewish-American academic, self-reflexively plays the part of the tourist by sporting a shapka "of artificial fur … the dangling earflaps looked childish and comical" (76) and Cass notes repeatedly the complementary clothing worn by the young Japanese couple, Mitsuko and Yukio. As signs, she reads onto them the couple's class position. (They are rich, Cass determines). But the costumes also perhaps model the lovers as the twinned wings of the butterfly. With snowflakes, the butterfly is the novel's sovereign airborne image, recalling Nabokov's pursuit of lepidopterology.[28] The stories told in these sequestered spaces accelerate intimate

---

28   Part of *Speak, Memory* was published as an essay titled "Butterflies" in 1948, and Nabokov saw in butterflies what he sought in art: "The mysteries of mimicry had a special attraction for me. Its phenomena showed an artistic perfection usually associated with man-wrought things. Consider the imitation of oozing poison by bubblelike macules on a wing (complete with pseudo-refraction) or by glossy yellow knobs on a chrysalis ('Don't eat me – I have already been squashed, sampled, and rejected') … When a certain moth resembles a certain wasp in shape and color, it also walks and moves its antennae in a waspish, unmothlike manner. When a butterfly has to look like a leaf, not only are all the details of a leaf beautifully rendered but markings mimicking grub-bored holes were generously thrown in. 'Natural selection,' in the Darwinian sense, could not explain the miraculous coincidence of imitative aspect and imitative behavior, nor could one appeal to the theory of 'the struggle for life' when a protective device was carried to a point of mimetic subtlety, exuberance, and luxury far in excess of a predator's power of appreciation. I discovered in nature the nonutilitarian delights that I sought in art. Both were a form of magic, both were a game of intricate enchantment and deception." Vladimir Nabokov, *Speak, Memory: An Autobiography Revisited* (1951; London: Penguin, 2012), 90–1. For Jones' thoughts on butterflies and Nabokov, listen to the podcast of her speaking at the Sydney Writers' Festival, "Spiral Time, Biscuit Tins, Butterflies: how Nabokov enlivens us", 22 May 2016. It is an intuitive association to recall that Benjamin shared Nabokov's fascination with butterflies, keeping in his bourgeois childhood bedroom a cabinet of "[c]abbage butterflies with ruffled edging, brimstone butterflies with superbright wings". Benjamin, *Berlin*, 50. Virginia Woolf, another of Jones' literary guides, was also an enthusiastic butterfly collector.

friendships between characters while the snow outside slowly builds, suggesting simultaneous temporal registers within the world of the novel.

Snow comes to be everywhere in *A Guide to Berlin*. More than telling of Cass' snowy desires, like the flurries they describe, the words themselves have about them a sense of mellifluous descent, repetition with quiet variation and gentle accumulation. The winter's falling snowflakes further suggest corresponding dynamics of language and story-telling that are resonant with another instance of Jones' writing – the short story "Speaks Shadow" in *Fetish Lives*. Like *A Guide to Berlin*, this story turns on images of snowflakes. As the narrator relates: "It was my Jewish lover who told me that every snowflake is an image of the Star of David … In the image, said my lover, lies its shade, its shadow."[29] The narrator's Jewish lover, David Heller, thinks of snow allegorically and experiences an "excess of imagining" (160), as do Victor and Marco in *A Guide to Berlin*.[30] Victor, the oldest among the group and a man for whom Cass develops great affection, suffers from both not knowing his parents' Auschwitz experiences and the guilt of being youthfully incurious. He admits that "every torment is possibly theirs, and nothing wholly is; I insert them into any memoir, anxiously imagining, then have to remove them again" (22). Marco tells in his speak-memory of consoling his Jewish mother with the promise that he will "one day" write her story hinted at by isolated words: "Disappearances. Adoptions. Conversions. Secrets" (121). Here particularly, and in a novel that repeatedly stages displacement in a city attempting to face its brutal past, the phrase "one day" suggests deferral rather than a definite future date.

Further, "Speaks Shadow" gestures towards an ethical position that *A Guide to Berlin* seeks to imagine, and is suggested by Dominick LaCapra's notion of "empathic unsettlement".[31] This ethical, affective response to the suffering of others calls for listening and understanding that resist full identification with, and appropriation of, specific traumatic experiences of others. It also speaks directly

---

Virginia Woolf, *Moments of Being: Autobiographical Writings*, ed. Jeanne Schulkind (London: Pimlico, 2002), 113. Butterflies are everywhere apparent in her work as literary images and metaphors. As Bernard in *The Waves* insists, "When I grow up I shall carry a notebook … I shall enter my phrases. Under B shall come 'Butterfly powder.' If, in my novel, I describe the sun on the window-sill, I shall look under B and find butterfly powder. That will be useful." Virginia Woolf, *The Waves* (1931; London: Penguin, 1992), 26. It is hard to disagree.

29 Gail Jones, "Speaks Shadow", *Fetish Lives* (Fremantle: Fremantle Arts Centre Press, 1997), 151. All subsequent references are to this edition and appear in parentheses in the text.

30 Their experiences recall what literary theorist Marianne Hirsch terms "postmemory". For Hirsh, "postmemory" approximates the transgenerational diffusion of trauma that is so profound it comes to overwhelm and constitute the memory of the second generation. In this scenario, histories in the form of certain images, stories, objects, behaviours and affects are passed down family lines, rather than by means of direct memory. Marianne Hirsch, *The Generation of Postmemory: Writing and Visual Culture After the Holocaust* (New York: Columba University Press, 2012), 29–54.

31 Dominick LaCapra, *Writing History, Writing Trauma* (Baltimore: Johns Hopkins University Press, 2001), 41–7. LaCapra's ideas were first articulated in his article "Trauma, Absence, Loss", *Critical Inquiry* 25 no. 4 (1999): 696–727.

to Paul Celan's ethical project of *Schatten Sprach*, his language of shadows, which moves towards silence at the same time that it encompasses the obligation to speak and bear witness.[32] Following the break-up with her lover, the first-person narrator of "Speaks Shadow" questions whether their intimate relationship had been a means for her "to claim the suffering of the Hellers as my own special suffering" (162). In its way, *A Guide to Berlin* writes back to this earlier short story, with the soliloquies that constitute it offered as a response to this call for perspicuity and responsive listening, which the unnamed narrator of "Speaks Shadow" fears she has occluded. It is the snow dome-like suspension of the novel that seems to make this ethics possible.

The apartments in which the group cloisters itself in *A Guide to Berlin* encourage the feeling of englobed separation. Little is known of the histories of the former owners and occupants of these spaces; the only traces left are the shadows on the walls of removed objects that bring to mind the past traumatic evictions of Berlin's Jews. Yet, it would be wrong to suggest that the group of six is simply removed from circulation and isolated from history, as objects placed in a glass dome might seem to be. Yukio is on Twitter and "Facebook with many, many friends" (192). Marco moves freely through the city in which refugees have taken temporary shelter and with whom Gino has formed something resembling friendship. And the Japanese lovers of Cass' own age enthusiastically head out "to hear a famous Japanese DJ play remixes of David Bowie. Super-cool!" (66). The Berlin in which the speak-memories take place is an image of contemporary globalisation.

It is Cass' experiences, however, which the narrative focalises, that suggest this snow-globe circumstance, with its stilled time. The contrast presented between Cass and Yukio and Mitsuko is instructive. Not only are the lovers imagined and retained in Cass' thinking as a couple, while Cass sees herself as solitary; Mitsuko and Yukio participate in Berlin's nightlife while Cass determines to listen to "Mischa Maisky on cello" on her laptop, alone (136). Just to underscore her separateness, she anticipates and welcomes her future as "an old woman one day, alone in a dark room, with only Bach's cello to keep her company" (136). With all that desire for physical and mental absorption, and at the same time all that drift of distance (and indeed all that snow), it really is hard to avoid the idea that the world Cass inhabits resembles a snow globe.

And if, as the cultural critic Celeste Olalquiaga tells it, early Victorian snow globes most commonly encased small figures holding umbrellas,[33] then the pervasive presence of umbrellas throughout *A Guide to Berlin*, from the epigraph

---

32 Beth Hawkins, "The Washing of the Word, the Washing of the World: Paul Celan and the Language of Sanctification", *Shofar: An Interdisciplinary Journal of Jewish Studies* 20 no. 4 (2002): 36.
33 Celeste Olalquiaga, *The Artificial Kingdom: A Treasury of Kitsch Experience* (New York: Pantheon, 1998), 63.

onwards, can be remarked on in terms that both exemplify the symbolic convergences at which the book's characters marvel and underscore the suggestiveness of thinking of Cass' world as a snow dome. As part of his speak-memory, Victor tells of his father working as an umbrella maker, and he later exclaims "Umbrellas" (130) on seeing the contractile bodies of the jellyfish at the Berlin Aquarium, another glass-enclosed space, when he and Cass set off to find the tortoise Nabokov saw when writing his tale that gives the novel its title. It is a response Cass determines as a sign of his "personal aesthetics, derived from childhood enchantment and the authority of ideal forms" (130), although equally the reference could derive from the language of biology (exumbrella; subumbrella). On dropping her umbrella in a Berlin street, Cass notices properly for the first time the *Stolpersteine*, the commemorative brass plaques marking victims of Nazism. But even as Cass is unexpectedly confronted with the past in this manner, as she makes her way through wintry Berlin her experiences are nevertheless presented as dreamlike and at some remove: "She felt somehow tenuous and unbelonging; her riding [on the S-Bahn and U-Bahn] was the symptom of absent centre and inexplicit purpose" (159).

If Cass is geographically displaced, her inner life is suspended by the shame she feels at her childhood response to her brother's death. It is only when she relates her memory of it to Marco that a future is possible: "Alexander could rest in peace and she could fall in love with Marco. It felt as if she had scooped at a pond of icy water, dashed her face clean, felt a shock intake of breath, and then come suddenly alive" (190). Cass' re-entrance into the flow of historical time is provisionally admitted with this private speak-memory. Away from the group gatherings, Cass relates to Marco the circumstances of her brother's accident:

> I was twelve, he was thirteen … There was a cyclone, a fierce one, which swung in from the ocean … We were inside with my parents, crouching under the kitchen table, which was bordered with mattresses. We could hear our dog, Nip, barking frantically outside … Alexander lunged from our shelter and rushed out into the storm to retrieve him … A falling tree struck him on the side of the head. My father struggled through dangerous winds to locate him, then returned within minutes carrying his wet, bloody body. Together we pulled him beneath the table. We sheltered against the roar of the wind and the shaking of the house. (181–2)

The death of Cass' brother is cast as a random, terrible accident of wild weather, cinematic in its recall and literarily resonant with a scene in *Sixty Lights* which sees another young boy, Jacob Webb, and another dog, Red, also caught up in fierce weather – "an astonishing hailstorm" (203) – and requiring paternal rescue.[34]

---

34 In *Dreams of Speaking*, Alice Black's father also heads out into storms to fix damaged electricity poles. It is a role for which Alice "heroicised him extravagantly" (120), and suggests that in Jones' novels, stormy weather is often cast in childhood imaginings as the stage for admirable

Jacob sees in the weather "the direct violence of the hand of God" (205), evidence of which is his (loosely interpreted) biblically inscribed body, *"Ring-streaked and spotted"* (204). Whereas Jacob survives the heavenly blows of ice to witness shortly thereafter the death of his father – he had interpreted the cataclysmic weather as an augury of some coming calamity – Alexander's death in *A Guide to Berlin* becomes "the family secret" (183), not to be spoken of and not to be grieved. Like Perdita in *Sorry*, but in very different circumstances, Cass is also "confronted by the question of what is at stake in staying silent or in speaking" (183), a question that takes on further charge as the narrative of *A Guide to Berlin* progresses. Cass carries her witnessing of her brother's death quietly and internally; it is a remembrance also marked by a particular shame.

Cass' heightened defiance, which is made apparent throughout the novel by her enthusiastic apprehension of snow, is notable in her spontaneous childhood response to her brother's accident remembered as an adult. Rather than the grief her family quickly prohibits, Cass recalls "an indecent sense of adventure" (184) and an aesthetic illumination: "It had been a vision, an anomalously charming vision. Cass knew that this too was part of her shame, that she had found the wreckage alluring" (182). If Cass wonders at what might emerge from ruin, her instinctive inclination towards aesthetics troubles her intellectually and emotionally as an adult. To help her think through the enormity of her brother's death, she turns almost involuntarily to the weather: "Death had its own weather. Death was uncontrollable as cyclones" (206). The repetition of "death" here suggests Cass' uncertain testing out of her analogies, or an incantation. Cass is brought up short, however, by the image her invocation elicits: a vision of her father shrouding his damaged son in a curtain which "bore a decoration of autumn leaves of a kind she had never actually seen – European leaves of an unbelievable orange, regularly shed in unbelievable seasons" (207). At this moment, looking to the weather for signs, for ways of understanding, is presented as preposterous. The gaudy weather scene is out of place – a European autumn suspended on fabric in an Antipodean interior – and a "decorative cliché" that encloses her brother's body and which "meant nothing; the expedient offence of it, the simplification" (207). The weather, which has been so meaningful to Cass, is reduced to a domestic print without significance that cannot remove from sight her loss.

If the weather has come to signal such nothingness, then it is due in part to the circumstances in which Cass finds herself. She has these unbidden thoughts about death, her brother and the weather as she is gathering coats and scarves

---

fatherly fearlessness. In *Sorry*, it is not Nicholas Keene who cares for Perdita Keene and her mother during a cyclone, but rather Kurnti, an Aboriginal man who had "been in chains … as he laboured outside the Continental Hotel" (84). Kurnti is best able to interpret the wild weather, "Kurnti said simply: 'Wait; comin' back' … 'Bloody good one, eh?' He rose, looked around. 'Safe now. C'mon" (85, 86). In *The Death of Noah Glass*, Martin Glass as a young boy is hauled indoors from a hailstorm by his father, with the event an occasion for an art lesson in pointillism that leaves in memory for Martin "the word pied" (87).

for those who are assembled beneath her balcony in the snow, where the stilled body of Victor lies. Intimate revelation and reciprocity had once constituted this speak-memory group, but the community is broken asunder by a peripeteia, physical assault and the tangled roles each character has as witnesses to it. Drug-affected, Gino has cast Victor from the landing on which Cass had first rapturously encountered snowflakes. In a grotesque mirroring of the snowflakes' gentle vertical descent, "Gino lifted Victor, rested him, and then let him fall" (202). His death, or rather an unspecified death, has been anticipated by the book's prelude, which commences with Marco speaking of the impossibility of speaking, or writing, about death to a confused, grief-stricken group. "The death of any human was incomparable. It was not a writerly event. It was not contained within sentences" (1), Marco intones. What is entirely shocking and unexpected for Cass is not so for a reader who comes to the scene with different narrative knowledge. Cass' recall of her brother's shrouded body at this moment encourages a memory of that earlier, anticipated scene because the gathered group is similarly said to be "enshrouded", in this instance in snowfall as a "feeble wind spun the flakes" (1). Just as the autumn leaves on the curtain are rendered a cliché, the poetic resonances that the snowflakes accrue narratively after, and temporally before, this scene are called into question.

From that terrible moment, "an irrevocable plot had taken over"; the characters are "slipped into a genre" (209), and for Cass snow itself marks this narrative turn, or shake-up: "no geometry of flakes but a chaos of elements, no poetic impulse, but disgust and ruination. The tense shimmer, the snowy sky, was an unbearable thing" (217). Marco is propelled into shocked but purposeful motion to protect his friend, with Cass, Yukio and Mitsuko thrown into stunned complicity with Marco's resolve to bury Victor's body in the icy Havel river.[35] Flurry-words are emptied of their poeticism and put into the service of explanations designed (perhaps unconsciously, as displacement would have it) to protect, conceal and solicit consent to the reality they construct. "It was a terrible accident," Cass feebly says (250). Victor's death prompts reconsideration of all that has come before, with the credulity of the speak-memories that laced the characters together rendered radically uncertain: "The most earnest and open story still meant nothing assured" (254). Bearing witness not only to Gino's act and Victor's resultant death but also to each other as "cowardly and passive" results in the group's rapid dissolution (209). Characters that had previously spoken at length fall mute, their intentions to speak out registered – "And I need to tell Rachael [Victor's daughter], Cass thought" – but never realised (231).

A Guide to Berlin calls on the metaphoric resonances of snow it has established to represent Victor's death as splitting open time. Snow also presents itself to Cass as a "consolation" because of its imagined capacity for silencing, a "lush erasure

---

35 *The Death of Noah Glass* commences with a story of resurrection from ice.

of signs" (255). Whereas once snow promised euphoric alterations, it is its literal capacity to cover up that Cass turns to in her anguish at Victor's death and as a reluctant criminal accomplice: "The obliterations of winter had use-value, after all" (196). As in Perdita's remembered snow-globe dream in *Sorry*, snow for Cass becomes a sign for forgetting: "there might be a white-washing now, and a more complete covering over" (255). Further, snow is also asked to carry the (misplaced) promise of new beginnings; Cass imagines later that she and Marco might resume their relationship with the fall of the new snow (255). This anticipated pace of their future romance is brought to an abrupt halt, however, with the iced-up qualities of snow transferred to both time and Cass' sense of self. Jilted by Marco – he fails to meet her at an agreed-upon hour – "[t]here was only her waiting and her freeze-frame emptiness" (259). Stalled like a scene in a snow dome, Cass is returned at the novel's end to the S-Bahn, where she was first seen looking out to an unfamiliar Berlin through the train's window, anticipating the 411 whose transformative tremors come to be uneasily resettled in conclusion.

Jones' characters might think (at first) that mentioning the weather is no way to start larger, deeper conversations about the world and their place in it. The novels themselves suggest, though, that the weather is far from being the stuff of small talk, attributing to it significances that are befitting of its omnipresence and which allow for the otherwise unsayable traumas to be registered and represented.

2
Time

The Death of Noah Glass begins in coral light – as though submarine – with Martin Glass hypnopompically remembering a story on the morning of his father's funeral:

> Two brothers in their late seventies attended the funeral of their father, aged forty-two. The father had disappeared as a young man skiing across country, and in an unseasonable thaw, years later, his frozen body had been exposed. The bright sun shone upon him, ice melted and slid away, and he became a gruesome, implausible and shiny surprise. The body might have been a slow-motion swimmer lifting through the surface of the water … They would have been silent, observed by strangers, formally bereft, looking down at their dead, impossible father. Both must have felt the collapse of time. One brother, the younger, died three weeks after the funeral. The older followed a few months later.[1]

The first paragraphs of *The Death of Noah Glass* alert a reader to the novel's complicated interests in time. The story Martin summons is an untimely story, a story about time's untimeliness, a story about narrative and time, and a tale about the frozen time of grief. At its heart is the idea that a man, long-disappeared, might be surprisingly released from the ice into time, and his elderly sons are more recondite than bereaved at the temporal distortion revealed by this astonishing return from the dead of their now younger father.[2] It is the father – who died too early – who seems to have survived the human transitoriness to which both sons soon necessarily succumb; his reappearance is both a denial of time and a palpable

---

1 Gail Jones, *The Death of Noah Glass* (Melbourne: Text, 2018), 3–4. All subsequent references are to this edition and appear in parentheses in the text.
2 "And so they are ever returning to us, the dead," acknowledges the narrator of W.G. Sebald's novel *The Emigrants*, which also tells of a frozen man released by a glacier some seventy years after his initial disappearance. W.G. Sebald, *The Emigrants*, trans. Michael Hulse (London: Vintage, 2002), 23. Sebald's text is one of many written and visual narratives that includes a story of restoration from frozen time.

reminder of its elusive passing. That the ice melts into water and the man long dead is cast out as a swimmer suggests that time might be conceived of as something shape-shifting, not only moved through but also exerting its own forces in which narrative structure is implicated.

In interviews, Gail Jones has acknowledged the influence of cinematic philosophies of time on her thinking and writing. These theories, she suggests, "attend to the symbolic and artificial dimensions of time through crafting points of amplitude and contraction, fast editing and slow-motion".[3] Andrei Tarkovsky and his conception of cinema as a form of "sculpting in time" is particularly suggestive in this regard. Known for his long-takes, Tarkovsky argues that "[t]he dominant, all-powerful factor of the film image is *rhythm*, expressing the course of time within the frame".[4] Gilles Deleuze's work on the time-image is also intellectually provocative and turns to Tarkovsky's cinema (as well as the time philosophy of Henri Bergson) to assist in the setting up of the concept's contours. For Deleuze, "Tarkovsky challenges the distinction between montage and shot when he defines cinema by the 'pressure of time' in the shot. What is specific to the image, as soon as it is creative, is to make perceptible, to make visible, relationships of time which cannot be seen in the represented object and do not allow themselves to be reduced to the present."[5] Certain cinema, Deleuze suggests, holds the potential for us to see time's operations. For all their formal differences from cinema, Jones' narratives share this interest in making time rhythmically present.

According to both the tenets of narrative theory, as expounded by critics such as Gérard Genette, and ideas about narrative time, philosophically entertained by Aristotle and more recently by Paul Ricoeur,[6] narrative has the capacity, if not duty, to interrupt and rearrange "raw" events that otherwise take place causally and chronologically. It does so to offer other representations of temporality and prove literature's own temporal autonomy.[7] In the instance of Jones' scenario in *The Death of Noah Glass*, however, the story remembered relies on the chronological sequence of events – the skier disappears years before; his sons grow old in the meantime; the petrified man returns comparatively youthful; the sons die – for its account of time's incongruities and complexities. This narrative feature is underlined by the one isolated word that immediately follows Martin's recollection – "Wednesday" (4).

---

3   Gail Jones, "The Interview", interviewed by Michele McCrea, *Wet Ink* 3 (2006): 28; Gail Jones, "The January Interview", interviewed by Summer Block, *January Magazine*, 2008, https://www.januarymagazine.com/profiles/gailjones.html.
4   Andrew Tarkovsky, *Sculpting in Time: Reflections on the Cinema*, trans. Kitty Hunter-Blair (London: Bodley Head, 1986), 113.
5   Gilles Deleuze, *Cinema 2: The Time-Image*, trans. Hugh Tomlinson and Robert Galeta (Minneapolis: University of Minnesota Press, 1989), xii.
6   Paul Ricoeur, "Narrative Time", *Critical Inquiry* 7 no. 1 Autumn (1980), 169–90. Ricoeur is interested in both the aporia that arises when thinking about time in time and the capacity of narrative to interleave lived and cosmic time.
7   Gérard Genette, "Boundaries of Narrative", trans. Ann Levonas, *New Literary History* 8 no. 1 (1976): 1–13.

As a conventional marker of calendrical time, this word pulls Martin back into adult responsibilities and the standard time the story recalled promises to unsettle: "Today he must retrieve the suit he was married in and prepare himself. He must be cautious of his own precarious feelings, he must be manly, and upright, and not lose control, or weep" (4). Coming as it does on the first two pages of Jones' latest novel to date, this story about time both anticipates an abiding preoccupation of the narrative that follows, and can be read as a reminder of a concern that also finds representation in much of Jones' work.

It is a risk, of course, to suggest so casually that time finds expression in Jones' writing. Such generalisations can fall flat, appear lazy, and be proven incorrect. But exceptions to this claim are hard come by. In some instances, time is of overt interest. In the earlier short story "Touch (The Births of Walt Whitman)" in *Fetish Lives*, for example, time is bifurcated – it is both public and private – and imagined as poetically abundant: "Outside it was springtime, May 1819; but inside time was transfigured and elastic. Time was an accordion unsqueezing and a book blown open."[8] For Alice and Norah Black in *Dreams of Speaking*, watching the nightly weather report on television is a form of shared time travel: "The sisters watched it together, sucking at ice cubes, lying on their bellies with their four legs waving in the air. Time-travelling in their lounge room with the aid of the camera's shrewd lie."[9] In *Black Mirror*, Anna Griffin is sent on a search for an hourglass, although in a novel that interlaces memory, dreams and the present, the device is not required as a timekeeper but rather is a symbol of a lost mother and an object of beauty from another time: "It was a splendid thing, an eighteenth-century specimen ... The ampoules were bulbous and firm, and of a glass which had within it traces of bubbles and imperfections ... Inside was not sand, but finely ground egg-shells, sieved so that each grain was exactly the same size."[10] In *Sixty Lights*, time is stopped, or at least the pings of mechanical devices that signal the passing of time, and its increasing standardisation in the mid-nineteenth century, are silenced. The father-in-law of Lucy Strange's brother is a watchmaker, "and all around the parlour stood clocks of many eras, shapes and kinds, some half-disembowelled, their brass innards gleaming".[11] All of the clocks are quietened because his wife cannot endure "the false liveliness of clocks" (176). Rather than standardising and telling the time (and regulating labour), these disassembled objects are reminders of other

---

8   Gail Jones, "Touch (The Births of Walt Whitman)", *Fetish Lives* (Fremantle: Fremantle Arts Centre Press, 1997), 127.
9   Gail Jones, *Dreams of Speaking* (Milsons Point, NSW: Vintage, 2006), 82. All subsequent references are to this edition and appear in parentheses in the text.
10 Gail Jones, *Black Mirror* (Sydney: Picador, 2002), 138–9. All subsequent references are to this edition and appear in parentheses in the text. For another reading of *Black Mirror* that considers the novel's interests in space (rather than time), see Fiona Roughley, "Spatialising Experience: Gail Jones' *Black Mirror* and the Contending of Postmodern Apace", *Australian Literary Studies* 23 no. 2 (2007): 58–73.
11 Gail Jones, *Sixty Lights* (London: Harvill Press, 2004), 176. All subsequent references are to this edition and appear in parentheses in the text.

times. As ruins of sorts, they endure the so-called ravages of time, surviving and superseding the temporal ephemerality and rationalisation their chimes would otherwise sound.

If the mechanisms of physical clocks are halted in that novel (as they are in Charles Dickens' novel *Great Expectations* (1861), from which the characters of *Sixty Lights* quote in confirmation of their affectionate connections), it is photography that affords other ways of thinking about time and liveliness in *Sixty Lights*. Lucy practises her own form of time travel through this visual form. On looking at the prints she made of the wedding of her brother and Violet, Lucy marvels:

> She had by magic and illusion travelled them through time, made them ever-alive, endowed their faces with the nacre of wet seashells and the promise of persisting youthfully, on their marriage day, for generations to come. "Behold me," each face called from the past to the future. (177)

In *A Guide to Berlin*, Yukio recalls as part of his speak-memory one of the conversations he and Mitsuko first had: "She told me her strange ideas about time: we all live in different times, and only sometimes these match. This is called friendship, or love, this matching time. We talked about forever, what that might be."[12] In other moments, time makes itself felt narratively such as when Lucy's remembrance of her witnessing of a man's death in *Sixty Lights* is told proleptically in the introductory pages, in anticipation of its later occurrence in the narrative. A similar interruption in chronology occurs in *A Guide to Berlin*, when Marco Gianelli addresses in the first pages a huddled gathering, shocked and numbed; later it is told that one member of this group has killed another, and the first vision afforded by the novel is what comes after this event. And the prologue of *Black Mirror* sees Anna Griffin caught not only in the rain but also in a jumble of time: "She pops open her umbrella, holds it close above her ... And later, when Victoria is dead, she will remember how on this day of their very first meeting she was so distracted she became soaked" (1). In the same moment, Victoria Morrell imagines herself cinematic and outside of time: "Victoria can also see herself as though filmed ... She is a profile in winterlight, a woman not entirely visible, and obscurity releases her face from time" (3). Time is truly everywhere in Jones' writing.

---

12 Gail Jones, *A Guide to Berlin* (North Sydney: Vintage, 2015), 62. As Jones herself acknowledges, the literary hero of Yukio and Mitsuko, Vladimir Nabokov, was "so afraid of the passing of time that he knew how many heartbeats he had in an hour". Gail Jones, "Interview", interviewed by Susan Wyndham, *The Age*, 8 August 2015, 24. The first paragraph of *Speak, Memory* has Nabokov introduce himself expressly as a "young chronophobiac". Vladimir Nabokov, *Speak, Memory: An Autobiography Revisited* (1951; London: Penguin, 2000), 5.

2 Time

But are not all narratives about time?[13] Surely it is impossible to think about literature without also thinking about time. In a very obvious sense, all stories see events unfold in time. (The metaphor here suggests that the purpose of narrative is to smooth what might otherwise lie about, crinkled and corrugated, something Jones' writing declines to do.) While time might be apparent in Jones' stories, it is arguably one of the trickier concepts to get a handle on. Time is not an object that can be seen or touched, but neither is it entirely abstract, nor a general notion or idea. It is arguably not a wholly natural phenomenon, but the natural and physical sciences, together with literature, have offered significant attempts to understand it. To ask "what is the time?" poses few challenges for those for whom world standard time, first proposed at the 1884 International Prime Meridian Conference in part to prop up imperial trade, is a basic measure of quotidian life. To ask "what is time?" is to enter fields of philosophical headaches and debates, including linguistic ones. As J. Hillis Miller has pointed out, "Expressions of the inscrutability of time have punctuated the history of thinking about temporality in the West," and the word "time" itself is a catachresis in that it does not ensure knowledge of the entity it names.[14] Further along these lines, Hillis Miller suggests that "The word 'time' is posited, without authority or possibility of verification, as a figurative expression for something unknowable."[15] That might be so, but scientists, philosophers and writers, and anyone waiting for the arrival of what feels to be an excruciatingly slow bus, nevertheless continue to think about, and through, time. Or, perhaps it is because of this enigmatic inscrutability that time continues to intrigue and make itself felt in various ways.

Indeed, the concomitant idea about narrative time, which goes beyond but is also exemplified by specific instances of Jones' work, is that narration itself gives shape to (other) orders of time and can explore and represent varying temporal schema. A story can occur *in medias res*, can be discontinuous, and can abide by a form of now standard chronology. Within the world of a text, the pace of time can be sped up; years can pass in a sentence, even though the characters themselves might not be aware of this, as with Stella Keene in *Sorry* who returns home from hospital treatment but is "at first unaware of the elapse of time".[16] Or, time can be slowed down, possibly to imagine psychological or private time. The opening section of *Dreams of Speaking*, for example, yokes space walking and mourning, with Alice admitting that "Anything in slow motion … was intrinsically sorrowful" (3).[17] And in the short story "The House of Breathing" in the volume of the same name, the capacity of narrative to transport to another time is suggested by the

---

13 For the theorist of the novel, Georg Lukács, time is a constitutive principle of the form. See Georg Lukács, *Theory of the Novel: a historico-philosophical essay on the forms of great epic literature*, trans. Anna Bostock (Cambridge, MA: MIT Press, 1971).
14 J. Hillis Miller, "Time in Literature", *Daedalus* 132 no. 2 (Spring 2003): 88.
15 Hillis Miller, "Time", 89.
16 Gail Jones, *Sorry* (North Sydney: Vintage, 2007), 75. All subsequent references are to this edition and appear in parentheses in the text.

narrator remembering as a child her grandmother's tale of being aboard the ill-fated *Titanic* voyage and her "room floodlit with the power of her descriptions".[18] Bridget, the grandmother, keeps other times. She obsessively recounts her story and at night, in dreams, she roams the decks of the long-sunk ship.

Narratives themselves move through time, too. That Perdita Keene in *Sorry* recites Shakespearean verse in mid-twentieth century Australia to a surprised but receptive Dr Oblov is testament to this claim. And it is one that is complicated in *Sixty Lights*, with Lucy Strange attributing a foretelling capacity to narrative, musing to her brother, "Strange … how fiction predicts" (102). This facility is given over to Lucy, too. From her ostensible historical standpoint in the mid-nineteenth century, she foresees narratives to come. For example, Lucy anticipates the future writing (from her temporal moment) of Virginia Woolf and determines that "One day someone will write this" (218).[19] Lucy can be understood as expecting some future only because it constitutes the past for the novel's readers (if they have knowledge of such things).[20] And in so doing Lucy suggests, perhaps counterintuitively, that the movement of narratives through time is not unidirectional, and indeed that time might be something other than a passive or indifferent medium facilitating the passage of stories and memory.

This model of absolute time that Lucy disavows is evoked in *Sixty Lights* by means of the name of Lucy's benefactor and friend, Isaac Newton. "Names were foolishly entailing" (196), the novel readily concedes, inviting readers to make such speculations and connections. The seventeenth-century scientist, the other Isaac Newton, not only devised theories of colour and white light that inform Lucy's practice of modern photography, and which her lover-to-be, Jacob Webb, instantly recognises when first learning of her "married" name: "Mrs Isaac Newton … Ah, prisms! … Whiteness shattered! The spectrum revealed!" (196). Newton also proposed theories of time of which his contemporaries were not altogether convinced. But, they neatly came together with universal ideas of time that were being increasingly entertained as part of the project of European modernity, and

---

17   In an essay on mourning, photography and the moon, Jones notes how the footprints left by astronauts are an implicit violation "of the aesthetic and symbolic autonomy of the moon". Gail Jones, "Five Meditations on a Moonlit Night", *Le Simplegadi* 14 no. 16 (2016): 16. Jones also writes about memory, mourning and the moon as a metaphor for the face in the short story "The Man in the Moon", and acknowledges that: "The moon has drawn poetic impulses, just as it draws the heavy sad tides. It invites metaphorics. It recruits metaphysics. It is a round-shaped screen, obligingly receptive, for any number of loony projections." Gail Jones, "The Man in the Moon", *Fetish Lives* (Fremantle: Fremantle Arts Centre Press, 1997), 140–1.
18   Gail Jones, "The House of Breathing", *The House of Breathing* (Fremantle: Fremantle Arts Centre Press, 1992), 149.
19   The essay Lucy anticipates is, appropriately enough, Virginia Woolf's "Modern Fiction", *The Common Reader*, vol. 1, ed. Andrew McNeillie (1921; London: Vintage, 2003), 146–54.
20   In *Dreams of Speaking*, Woolf's much-quoted provocation in the essay "Mr Bennett and Mrs Brown" – that everything changed around December 1910 – is rehearsed to denote the newness of modernity (21). Virginia Woolf, "Mr Bennett and Mrs Brown", *A Woman's Essays*, ed. Rachel Bowlby (1924; London: Penguin, 1992), 70.

enjoyed some degree of cultural and scientific prominence until the beginning of the twentieth century. It was with the emergence of quantum physics and Albert Einstein's general theory of relativity, which proposed an understanding of the universe that rested on an infinite number of different times, that Newton's universal time was radically challenged. Newton had imagined times with distinct ontologies. Universal time, Newton posited, was "[a]bsolute, true, and mathematical time", as "equally without relation to anything external",[21] and markedly distinct from the far more mundane idea of time as simply a measure of a period of motion, "relative, apparent and common time".[22] In the mechanistic universe of Newton, time was universal and unchanging, and the medium through which everything moved.

Time is very far from being understood in *Sixty Lights* as pure, objective and consistent. The novel entertains the thematic and formal possibility that "time might distort … might loop lacily and suddenly fold over" (29). Together with *Five Bells* and *The Death of Noah Glass*, *Sixty Lights* can be read as foregrounding narrative as an art of time. Whereas scientists and philosophers might strive towards some universal definition of it (which does not imagine time itself as universal in the now debunked Newtonian sense) by means of logical methods, incremental processes and advancing explanations, literary texts can work under different conditions, which Jones' work foregrounds. They reflect on, and respond and give shape to, the complex and varied histories, imaginings and experiences of shared as well as personal temporalities.

The three texts chosen for discussion in this chapter offer meditations on time's aesthetics and rhythms as well as its political and social dynamics, and pose challenges to the ways in which standard time might work to unify and organise social life in the service of particular knowledges. Admittedly, this concern is not unique to these novels.[23] Nicholas Keene's anthropological project in *Sorry* is an important reminder that time can be an exercise in social power. Among other dubious principles, his enterprise is founded on the denial of the contemporaneity of the Aboriginal people he proposes to study: "like all primitive peoples, [they] had

---

21 Isaac Newton quoted in Stephen Kern, *The Culture of Time and Space* (Cambridge, MA: Harvard University Press, 2003), 11.
22 Isaac Newton, *The Principia: Mathematical Principles of Natural Philosophy*, trans. I. Bernard Cohen and Anne Whitman (1687; Berkeley: University of California Press, 1999), 408. Quantum physicists working at the subatomic level and with the Heisenberg Principle now hypothesise that state vectors are procedures independent of time. Mendel Sachs, "Changes in concepts of time from Aristotle to Einstein", *Astrophysics and Space Science* 244 no. 1–2 (1996): 269–81.
23 Jones' short story "Modernity" pointedly understands the clock located in the intimate space of the babushka's bedroom as part of wide-scale political programming: "The clock that used to stand in her grandmother's bedroom ticked in totalitarian and purposive circles. Its hands were definitive, its face as indisputable and blandly commanding as a uniformed apparatchik … And history itself – by government decree – will later submit to subsections of Five Year Plans." Gail Jones, "Modernity", *The House of Breathing* (Fremantle: Fremantle Arts Centre Press, 1992), 12–13.

a tendency to expire on contact with a superior race. It was the sad duty of Civilised Man to raise or erase the lesser humans, to enable the March of Progress and the Completion of God's Plan" (12).[24] Keene's investment in progress as a metric of value, which rests on the idea of time as a steady, sequential continuum dovetailing with a form of social evolution, is displaced by the novel's preferred model of time: "Time looped back and replayed" (93). A conception of time as something other than relentlessly forward-moving is offered in *Sorry* and makes possible, the novel proposes, the telling of forgotten or suppressed stories and experiences.

A moment in *Five Bells* that might otherwise pass unremarked also shares the concern of *Sorry* with how time is harnessed to produce and perpetuate social relations of power. In very precise temporal terms, Pei Xing remembers Mao Zedong going for a long and energetic swim:

> Less than a year before her parents were taken, Mao had famously swum in the Yangtze River. It was 1966, he was seventy-three years old, and there he was, plunged into the brown water near the Wuhan Bridge. Posters appeared everywhere: Mao chubby-cheeked and tubby-shaped, beaming robust health and totalitarian command. He was reputed to have swum thirty Li, fifteen miles, in only sixty-five minutes. Pei Xing remembers the figures exactly, because her father had scoffed, doing a quick calculation.
>
> "Our leader is superhuman," her father announced with a wry smile.[25]

Mao seems to have not simply swum with great gusto, but also to have achieved the impossible: he has defeated time itself. While measures of distance are presented as culturally variable, if equivalent (Mao is reported to have swum thirty Li, or fifteen miles), markers of standard time – the calendar year, Mao's age, his herculean swimming feat recorded by objective clock time – announce publicly the leader's achievements and are expressly linked with his (desire for) absolute authority. Pei Xing's father sounds a note of caution about this political manipulation and abuse of time that seeks to create a universal temporal connection everywhere. This desire is announced by the propaganda posters in the name of a timeless and immortal leader. That his own disappearance, adjunct in his daughter's memory to Mao's vanquishment of time, is recalled in terms that are less temporally precise – "[l]ess than a year before" – suggests the novel's interests in challenging claims that might be made on behalf of, or by, standard time.

Jones' narratives do not simply disavow standard time. There are a number of instances where time is marked in a familiar, clock or calendar-standard way (which is not to overlook that lives beyond these texts are certainly lived and

---

24 Johannes Fabian makes this point about time's role in shoring up colonial practices and ideologies in *Time and the Other: How Anthropology Makes its Object* (New York: Columbia University Press, 1983).
25 Gail Jones, *Five Bells* (London: Harvill Secker, 2011), 187. All subsequent references are to this edition and appear in parentheses in the text.

measured by timekeepers other than the Gregorian calendar). That *Five Bells* takes place over the course of a day suggests an obvious preoccupation with the social structuring of time. Yet, it is also committed to other temporalities, including the "*here-now*" of the sunny Saturday the characters are living in and remembered past moments (1). As Ellie marvels while waiting for a bus: "A bus-stop wait could cover all of this, all this complicated history … death, time, recollected acts of love-making – all together, simultaneous, ringing in her head" (141). As this thought suggests, Jones' texts are preoccupied with how relationships in time can be made meaningful, and meaningfully, rather than, say, in the service of suspect jingoism, the profit-making mantra of capitalism, or avaricious colonialism. In these narratives, metaphorical and formal patterns represent human relationships and connectivity temporally, and in ways that might be understood as less instrumental than those commanded in certain contexts by standard time.

One way to start examining this proposition is to recognise that Jones' work resonates with ideas about time that are a revelation to Ellie and James as school children in *Five Bells*. Unlike their classmates, who were largely "bored and perplexed", these two "intelligent twelve-year-olds" are deeply affected by the ideas of time related to them by their teacher, who asks her charges "to consider how human time was measured" (96). The very fact that this lesson is of significance to them marks the two children out as special, or at least unusually attuned to questions about time that the novel also shares. Miss Morrison goes on, "Is it really kept inside your watch? … Does time really tick? Or work by numbers? Or pass in neat measured segments? Might there be a time that flows, or indeed does not flow?" (96). The teacher's counter-example to the wristwatch is an instrument brought into disuse by the widespread use of clocks: the clepsydra.

Clepsydrae are described in the novel as "vessels that dripped or leaked, flowed or seeped, making use of floating pointers or measures, sometimes of gears. It was a process, she said, of emptying and filling, of fluent time-passing, not one chopped into pieces" (96). Miss Morrison's focus on fluid mechanics means she only acknowledges in brief the historical uses of these time-marking devices. Approvingly, she notes that the Chinese "devised particularly ornate and complex clepsydra", but presumably aware of her charges' short attention spans, she declines to acknowledge that the instrument was designed to complement the telling of time by the stars and the sun (96). The clepsydra had advantages over both as it was able to function indoors and in cloudy weather, and was independent of the earth's motion. It regulated daily life in small villages and towns; medieval doctors used them to time the human pulse; as late as the sixteenth century, mercury clepsydrae were integral to Galileo's experimentations with falling bodies and the celebrated astronomer Tycho Brahe measured the motion of stars with them. Clepsydrae were also relied on to control the hours that slaves worked in Ancient Rome, and were implemented to limit the speech of loquacious orators, who were known to bribe those who set the clepsydrae in motion. By adding a little sand to the contraption, the flow of water could be slowed and the time for speechifying could be expanded.[26]

Five Bells is especially interested in the philosophical suggestiveness of Miss Morrison's accounts of the dripping clepsydra. What Miss Morrison teaches her students (and therefore the readers of *Five Bells*) is that the idea of time the clepsydra models is one that is shifting and relative, rather than conforming to a uniform flow. It is also susceptible to pressures and variables both atmospheric and political. Thanks to Miss Morrison's instruction, the clepsydra serves as a helpful metaphor for thinking about how the narrative of *Five Bells* works and imagines time. The narrative moves across and between four narrative strands that are told by means of third-person focalisation and are linked respectively to the four main characters, Pei Xing, Catherine, James and Ellie. It is their thoughts, memories and desires that constitute the text. And the narrative shifts not only between these different points of view but also between the present of the text and "the curve of lost time and unbidden recurrences" (18) to approximate "leaky" time in a way Miss Morrison credits to the clepsydra.

For Ellie and James as fourteen-year-old lovers, their shared memory of the clepsydra lesson is erotically charged. The day they remember the lesson about time is also the same day they first have sex in secret, and the narrative makes this association, and the entwining and layering of memories, explicit in a way that formally approximates Miss Morrison's tutorial on the time of the clepsydra.

Ellie first recalls having sex with James while walking to the restaurant where she is to meet him for lunch following years of silent distance between them. Earlier in the novel, as he slowly makes his way through the streets of inner-city Sydney to their agreed-upon meeting place at Circular Quay, James also recalls their encounter on the blanketed floor of a disused iron foundry. That the two considered the location for their liaison "their *hideout*" suggests their youthful playfulness and hints at the idea that, in the eyes of others (and in particular the law), their experience at such an age would be felonious, "as if they were sexual criminals" (35). For Ellie and James, however, the experience is remembered as mutually consensual and pleasurable, if somewhat clumsy and brief.

Ellie's recollection of this sexual experience is then replayed in the last pages of the novel. Ellie is unknowing that James will suicide that night, slipping quietly and unnoticed into Sydney Harbour weighted with whisky, his guilt and grief at not having prevented the accidental drowning of one of his young students, profound existential despair, and the ghost of his poetic antecedent, Joe Lynch, elegised in Kenneth Slessor's poem "Five Bells".[27] In terms of the narrative sequencing of

---

26 Edward Graham Richards, *Mapping Time: The Calendar and its History* (Oxford: Oxford University Press, 1999), 51–5.
27 Kenneth Slessor, *Five Bells: XX Poems* (Sydney: Frank Johnson, 1939). Jones' novel explicitly references Slessor's poem in its title and by one of its epigraphs, making explicit the two texts' shared interests in time and grief. Joe Lynch met his death in the same waters as James. Whereas

events, though, James' suicide precedes Ellie's second recall of their younger selves, rendering poignant her glimpses of their possible future together: "And now he was returned, her James, the body remembered above others, and in the saturated time of his return Ellie felt something open before her, another scale, a refashioned future, the glimmering of something half-concealed up ahead" (211). Adjacent and asynchronous, the patterned placement of their respective narrative strands details that Ellie and James have differing capacities to think about themselves in time, which constitute and reflect their sense of self. Whereas James is first introduced in unambiguous terms as "obstinately unjoyful" (4), he concedes elsewhere that Ellie is "still the optimist; she believed in redemptive futures" (111). Ellie is said to wake "each day to the world, not expecting catastrophe" (20), although she is certainly not unaware of its horrors. Unlike James, who has difficulty seeing himself in some coming time, Ellie's sense of time and self is shaped by the expectation of futurity. Further, the fashioning of James' reappearance to Ellie is in terms of "saturated time", subtly recalling Miss Morrison's lessons on the clepsydra's wet time and resonating with Ellie's memory that as young lovers the word clepsydra had become "a kind of code between them, an erotic trigger and a flag of assignation" (210). Even if James is reluctant or unable to admit a time-to-come, he instantly recognises this amatory temporal code.

At lunch, the two characters politely exchange their compressed autobiographies: "Ellie had moved to Sydney to take up a postgraduate scholarship ... and worked part-time in a hole-in-the-wall coffee shop on King Street; he was a med-school dropout but committed schoolteacher" (106). When Ellie unexpectedly introduces the memory of Miss Morrison – she has been thinking all morning with affection about her former teacher and the clepsydra lesson – James' thoughts turn immediately to the clepsydra and the sexual experiences he has shared with Ellie in the past: "Across the table this young woman was recalling their first time: he knew it" (107). Fittingly, the force of desire this "code" releases rearranges and collapses standard time in the measure of a clock-second, so that the past and desire surge into the present moment:

> In a confused second between mouthfuls he wanted nothing more than to slip his hand beneath her skirt and remove her panties, to find himself back in the foundry, to enjoy *adolescent* lust. Their lovemaking had been simple, blundering, making up in lewd vigour what it lacked in sure knowledge. (107)

Earlier in the narrative, Ellie thinks of the re-emergence of James into her life in expressly temporal terms, too, as "counter-time ... that splashed light in its own theatre" and which brought new ways of seeing, and of seeing time: "She'd not noticed it before, how for a brief time each day the shadows at a certain angle

---

it is the speaker in Slessor's poem who feels the "wet push its black thumb-balls in" the night his friend suicides, it is James who is the recipient of this liquid force in Jones' *Five Bells*.

might project a light-shadow effect" (28). Wracked with longing and the welcome confusion of time, all James can do in the act of having a casual lunch is sorrowfully self-medicate by pouring himself yet another glass of wine, and agree to talk with Ellie "tomorrow", a future he will not live to see (111).

This more familiar sense of time, which has one day follow another, is made apparent in the novel because of the quiet rhythms of life and labour that accompany the sun's steady movement through the day and the narrative. These quotidian endeavours are represented by the minor character of Aristos, an ice-cream vendor who serves the Saturday crowd thronging to Circular Quay and whom Pei Xing, a fellow migrant to Australia, has known "a long time" (9). Pei Xing encounters Aristos during the day, and while she intuits his "intractable dying" (10), she also imagines him simply returning home when she notices a shift in the colour of the sky, with a "fine salmon streak to the west" anticipating sunset and signalling the end of his shift (188). And these temporal rhythms are also made apparent by Pei Xing's homeless friend, Mary, who keeps different times. She seeks a safe sleep "nestled in the home she had made beneath her hoarded plastic bags" (188) while the rest of the city's population goes about its early-evening business.

The three main female characters – Catherine, Ellie and Pei Xing – all look to the sky during the course of the day and take passing notice of the light, the warmth and the sun, which come after a night of rain: "It was a kind of tropical summer, cool in the dawning, steaming up as the sun rose, raining in late afternoon or at night" (19). James does not. He sleeps badly. He is awake at 3 am, with this clock-time recorded precisely by the narrative, and he wakes at 9 am, thinking of René Magritte, his favourite painter – both grieve their lost mothers – and to whom his mournful thoughts return repeatedly during the day. He also reminds himself of Salvador Dalí's painting about the unfixity of time and inevitable decay, *The Persistence of Memory* (1931). He does so when contemplating how a Surrealist might have gone about painting the Opera House, the architectural landmark that each character encounters and apprehends differently throughout the day. James' first impression of it is as simulacra: "It appeared on T-shirts, on towels, even trapped in plastic domes of snow; it could never exist other than as a replication, claiming the prestige of an icon" (5).

James contemplates rejecting this time that has explicitly marked his insomnia and awakening into consciousness by staying in bed and in the sunless gloom of his hotel room, "refusing the real-time of the city for a dead-beat retreat" (30). By contrast, Ellie, on her day off from work, is seemingly released from this mode of time-keeping that might otherwise regulate her daily routine. She experiences the 3 am rain as puddles pooling in the morning and is grateful for the "seamless sunshine" (28). The weather provides the conditions, and metaphors, for Miss Morrison's clepsydra lesson, which imagines time other than segmented in the way that clock-time would figure it. James, though, has little interest in the sun and the notions of time it might be understood to mark, keeping instead to "the blue shadows of the café" (7). Since the death of his student, "the blazing sky" for

James has proven too immense, "too huge to look at"; neither aesthetic nor full of portent but rather "piss-coloured behind his sunglasses" (149). In the afternoon sun he sleeps, waking at 6 o'clock and glancing "at his watch a second time, for confirmation. It was as if someone had scissored out a slice of the day, destroying time" (202). The time his watch tells is confirmed by the altered light, a change in the weather and a slight thinning of the crowds, and dusk is announced by the light transforming to purple as "yellow was draining to the west" (204). Counterintuitively perhaps, it is the dark of night, not the sun, that comes to James "in a lustrous rush" (205), and it is into "black wet … the mothering darkness" that James is washed as he slides over the edge of the ferry (208).

The female characters' observance of the sun and the sky also involves the valuing of a particular conception of time. When Ellie attends an open-air market in the late afternoon, for instance, before James' suicide at night but also after it in the sense that her excursion is related directly following the account of her childhood lover's drowning, the sun is not only a sign of the day's approaching end. It also serves to tie the idea of time that the movement of the sun is asked to carry in the text with a particular way of thinking about human connectivity:

> The market was a joy … It was near closing time, so stallholders were looking rather hot and bored, but pleased too to see browsers still wandering about and relaxed into friendly chit-chat and casual light banter … The sunlight was now orange and the day was drifting away; it gave the shoppers a healthy non-commercial glow. They were defeating all market predictions by their delight in trash and treasure; they held up crumpled cast-offs and cracked old teacups; they leafed through children's books from the 1930s, they paused over someone's collection of rusty tools, most superceded these days by something electrically loud. Ellie bought an old hammer so that she could hang a small print on her wall. The man who sold it was pleased, he said, that his hammer was going to a good home. (208–9)

The trash and treasure market trades in testaments to enduring past times. And its advancing closing time is expressly linked with the waning of the sun, whose light casts the browsers as members of a meaningful, if transient, community rather than as individualised producers and consumers in a capitalist economy wherein time is not their own, or at least is sold and exploited for wages. Profit is not the sole motivation for bringing together these people in this way. Ellie purchases a hammer in the service of her aesthetic interests – the print she wishes to hang is "another item she rescued from obscurity at a market stall" (213) – and the man from whom she buys it considers his tool to be moving between "homes" rather than circulating in an abstract and impersonal marketplace. Buyers and sellers exchange not only money and pleasantries but also values. They talk and salvage remnants of the past from the relentless rehearsal of the new. This characterisation of modernity is overseen by an idea of "chopped up" public time, the real-time of the city that James would prefer to avoid but which is strapped to his wrist, and is countered by the movement of the sun.

If the trash and treasure market is one special space in the text where the value of time and human community is cast in terms other than those of capitalism – here time is certainly not money – then the characters' shared interest in music is another way that temporal connections between them are imagined, and ideas about the time of memory are suggested.[28] The book opens by foregrounding sound, the very substance of music, and it resonates through the text: the first line is repeated some ninety or so pages later, as though an echo or a coda. This line reads "*Circular Quay*: she loved even the sound of it", with the sound that the word "quay" makes when spoken carried over into the next sentence and transformed into the "key to a new world" (1). The interplay between the written word and sound is playfully but meaningfully emphasised in this gesture, and there is a hint, perhaps, that Circular Quay and the sound it rings out might be read as fundamental to the text's narrative organisation – a key, as it were – much as the concept of key is central to the tonal system that has formed the basis of Western music art since the eighteenth century.[29]

This kind of associative thinking is encouraged by the text, which is organised not by action-driven plot but rather connections that are forged sonically, metaphorically and mnemonically, as suggested when Catherine, far from home, is pictured pausing before a not entirely beautiful fountain at Circular Quay. She is an instinctive student of Miss Morrison's clepsydra lessons, with her observation of the fountain's descending wet beads – the movement of which is echoed in the clauses of the sentence in which it is related – evoking an unbidden memory of her dead brother and his love of James Joyce's short story "The Dead": "There was something in the falling of fine water drops that reminded Catherine obliquely of snow; and snow reminded her of the story Brendan loved above all others" (58). Catherine then wonders at the workings of memory – James elsewhere conceives of memory temporally, as a form of "time-lapse" (141) – and of the kinds of time remembrances involve:

> [She] might be rising from coffee in a good mood and remember his funeral, so that she might be walking in the sunshine in another country entirely, so that she might be heading for the Opera House or wishing she had written to her mother, and think suddenly, irresistibly, of the intimate presence of snow. (58)

---

28 For an interesting, if more generalised, discussion on music and time, see Georgina Born, "Making Time: temporality, history, and the cultural object", *New Literary History* 46 no. 3 (2015): 361–86.

29 Ella Mudie discusses sound, trauma and representations of the city in *Five Bells* in her essay "The Synchronous City: aural geographies in Gail Jones' *Five Bells*", *New Scholar: an international journal of the humanities, creative arts and social sciences* 3 no. 2 (2014): 11–22. In part she takes her cue from Robert Dixon's essay "Invitation to the Voyage: Reading Gail Jones' *Five Bells*", *JASAL: Journal of the Association for the Study of Australian Literature* 12 no. 3 (2012): 1–17.

To be thinking about death and snow on a summery Sydney day after a pleasant morning coffee is testament to the jumbled time of the *"here-now"*, which the characters' passing encounters with the Sydney Opera House denote in a different way. At various points during the narrative, each of the four characters comes across this well-known architectural feature, and each offers an individual response to it, while also projecting onto it private desires and anxieties. As Ellie is well aware, "Monuments addressed us this way: pause here, consider. What hunger is driving you? What loss? What ambition? How does this place figure in your dreams?" (94) Initially, James views the building as carnivorous and insatiable, "Its maws opened to the sky in a perpetual devouring" (5), although he finds himself surprised to reconsider this first assessment, conceding that "it was an art-object after all, it contained multitudes, suggested metaphors" (102). On a ferry ride, Pei Xing observes the building from across the water and sees shapes "like porcelain bowls, stacked one upon the other, fragile, tipped, in an unexpected harmony" (12). On her return journey, she looks anew at the form she never tires of and determines that it resembled "folded paper, like one of those shapes children produce under instruction from a teacher" (186). On viewing the structure for the first time, Catherine likens it to a *"bowl of blown roses"*, prompted in part, perhaps, by a line of imagist poetry that had arisen to mind some moments before (15). And for Ellie, the edifice is a Futurist's dream, "[a]n unfolding thing, shutters, a sequence of sorts … an assemblage of planes and curves" and also a receptacle for music, "poised in a kind of alertness to acoustical meanings, concentrating on sound waves, opened to circuit and flow" (3).

Their viewing of the Opera House has the characters respond immediately and creatively; their thinking is given over to the present moment, when so often their thoughts are looping back to earlier reflections and experiences that the text suggests are otherwise inseparable from the now of the day in which the novel takes place. Time is paused with the characters' attention turned to the Opera House; or, more accurately, the current moment is made present. This impression of a temporary stillness is given in a narrative, which only works as words on the page are read in linear sequence, because the characters conceive of the Opera House as aesthetically poised, composed of folds and planes and petals and balancing bowls. That Ellie takes a photograph of the building – with such a gesture understood in this instance as removing from time a slice of itself – only underlines this idea: it is their different but shared aesthetic responses to, and apprehensions of, the Opera House that synchronise them, far more so than the coordinated time of clocks.

If the Opera House returns the characters to the *"here-now"* and suggests that their connections might be fashioned through aesthetics and the patterning of narrative, rather than some standardised measurement of time, then music is the other "key" to the novel's interest in time and human connection.[30] James makes this

---

30 Leigh Dale also notes the importance of music in *Five Bells*. Leigh Dale, "No more boomerang? 'Nigger's Leap' and 'Five Bells'", *Journal of Australian Studies* 37 no. 1 (2013): 48–61. In *Dreams of*

point implicitly early in the text. While killing time (as it were) in anticipation of his lunchtime rendezvous with Ellie, he takes refuge in a café, where everyday urban sounds are uncomfortably intensified: "Chatter rose with the clack of cutlery and the chink of teacups, the infernal din of the coffee machine and the roar of steaming milk" (7). What is additionally displeasing to James is the sonic presence of "[t]he summer of Vivaldi's *Four Seasons* playing in a jangled slur" (7). Far from calming his nerves and already annoyed that his own mind seems hostage to "the curse of his generation, to have a soundtrack enlisted for everything" – Coldplay's song "Clocks" had just "swam into his head" – James is clearly frustrated at this musical intrusion (7). It appears to him as a crude and seemingly inescapable example – a jangled jingle – of the reach of commodity capitalism: "How he hated this: music treated as a background accessory" (7). This version of Vivaldi is but one scrap of the disposable commercial detritus he sees littering his immediate surrounds: "torn sugar sachets, food scraps, the bits and pieces of commercial junk people left everywhere" (8). Later, a t-shirt worn by a fellow train-passenger has James thrown back in time to his nineteen-year-old self watching an unsettling Nirvana video-clip, which he now determines to be "cut-price Surrealism" (75). Along similar lines, although without the harsh judgement that James metes out, Pei Xing – she is not sure if she imagines it – hears an aria from Mozart's *The Marriage of Figaro* used as a mobile phone ring tone (13). Earlier in the narrative, Ellie perceives in passing a "tinny ring-tone" version of a Rolling Stones song (4). Pei Xing also notes the "pleasant chime" of G major announcing the start-up of a laptop (12). What the characters hear is the music of vernacular modernity.

If music might be thought of as an art of time – not time conceived of as a historical period that might go by the name of "modernity" but rather one that makes use of time as a formal element; the temporal ordering of tones, together with the "kinetic interplay of tonal phenomenon (rhythm)",[31] is exploited for musical perception – then James' objection to the playing of Vivaldi's four violin concerti also partly lies with how their status as "background noise" obscures duration as a subject of attention. After all, James explicitly, if involuntarily, recalls Coldplay's "Clocks", and not another of the band's many singles, so for him at least (but it can also be said about the novel itself) music and ideas about time are closely aligned. And when Pei Xing listens in the evening to a CD of Liu Fang's pipa solo, she hears not only the descent of snow but also "the sense of stilled time and

---

Speaking, Mr Sakamoto similarly calls on a particular piece of music to suggest how time might be an expression of human relations; he nominates "Yesterday" as his favourite Beatles song because it "combines the simplest of rhymes ... with the simplest anguish ... and constructs it all as a spectre of lost time ... The idea, think of it, that yesterday might come *suddenly*. Time itself, split open by abandonment" (33). For Alice Black, with whom he shares this idea, "yesterday" is the mode of the photographic image, "It is always time-bound but out-of-time, always anachronistic. In its fidelity to moments, to split-second slices, it carries the gravity of testimony and the lightness of chance. This paradox endears us: this is its clever intercession" (36).

31 Philip Alperson, "'Musical Time' and Music as an 'Art of Time'", *Journal of Aesthetics and Art Criticism* 38 (1980): 410.

Buddhic possibilities" (189). When music is attended to intently, time makes itself felt. Pei Xing furthers this connection between time and music when she proceeds to reflect on the pieces she hears and acknowledges that they have endured time as some are centuries old: "this was sound ever-flowing, ripple-effecting, beyond clockface time" (190). The metaphors Pei Xing conjures to imagine her timeless music recall the watery time of the clepsydra, and this figurative gesture has its own ripple effect: it serves narratively to connect characters who are otherwise unknown to each other. While Ellie and James might once have been lovers, a distance of some years is now between them, and neither of them can be said to "know" Pei Xing, who has the briefest of encounters with Catherine when both women cross paths during the day as potential witnesses to the disappearance of a young girl. It is not standard time that brings these characters into accord but rather their thinking about time in this musical and aqueous way.

Further, the assigning to music a secondary status as the café environment seems to do deprives it of the potential that Ellie, and the novel, insist on. Music for Ellie – and Ellie's notion of music is inclusive of all kinds of sounds – might generate connections and social collectives that are neither regulated nor brought into being by standard time. Unlike James who, in his consuming grief, is largely disdainful of crowds, seeing them as "indistinct", "blithely autonomous" and "unconnected" to him (7), Ellie is characteristically more optimistic about what such groupings might mean. When first alighting at Circular Quay, she sees herself as part of "the democratic throng, in the pandemonium of the crowd" (2), which is looped by "the sound of a busking didgeridoo with an electronic backbeat, *boum-boum, boum-boum; boum-boum, boum-boum*. The didgeridoo dissolved in the air, thick and newly ancient" (2). The crowd itself intones a "melody of voices" and Ellie happily thinks of herself "at the intersection of so many currents of information" (4). An Aboriginal man plays the instrument and insists on his singular communion with the music he plays: "Like the best buskers, he paid no attention to the crowd but entered his music as though it were a room he might rest in" (122). Catherine gathers herself into the group of listeners the didgeridoo music attracts, acknowledging that even as she is conjoined with others through her listening, she knows little about the meanings the sound might carry for the man playing it, and worries that her understanding might be a form of romanticism.[32]

Standing at Circular Quay, Catherine is surprised at the range of the didgeridoo sound, "at times like a human voice … at others like wind, or blown rain, or the amplified sighing and heartbeat one hears during illness or love-making" (123). And it is this music that James also hears just prior to falling asleep in the afternoon

---

32 Catherine is not known in her family for being musical in an intellectual sense. As a child, she was refused instrumental tuition and was given to play instead the triangle whose "shiny tingle-ring" could nevertheless be heard through "all the other sounds" (170). But as a young woman she "cultivated with an exclusive, almost irrational, devotion" an interest in "journalism and rock music" (91), and during the day unbidden fragments of song emerge from memory and transport her back to Ireland, her younger self, and her brother for whom she grieves.

on a grassy slope. He detects "a didgeridoo playing, a muffled soothing sound, and the distant busy din of traffic and people; he could hear the whole world jangly and abuzz on a Saturday afternoon" (202). He sets himself apart from this sonorous community, however, by slipping into sleep. That he is distant from the connections the music forges is telling of his present alienation. After he and Ellie first have sex as teenagers, his impulses are musical and his speech is a coda: "'I feel like singing,' he said. 'I feel like singing'" (98). He also thinks of his name and childhood self in similarly melodious ways: "*Gennaro DeMello* … The sing-song of someone he used to be" (201). Ellie remembers with fondness that as children they also chanted "in a sing-song fashion" the names of birds and times-tables, and the "listing and repetition became a kind of music" (213). As a new teacher, James' contentment is signalled by music; he listens agreeably to "Bob Dylan and the Triffids" (146), and his peaceful welcoming of a future time is imagined as "easy as music, a long melody of story" (146).

Following the death of a student in his care, however, James' depression is marked by a radical change in his response to music. Music he once found companionable crashes in his "jangled head … The song repeated its screeching message and its frenzied violins" (149). When he does think of music it is with a sense of violence: "Nirvana's 'Tourette' was an instrument of torture at Gitmo" (150). And the future time music had once favourably signalled collapses around his grief. The only music he allows in on the summer's day in Sydney is a mental recitation of Ellie's name, "a kind of inward music" (38). In the present moment, though, James cannot bring himself to identify outwardly with a community briefly laced together by music. Neither can he conceptualise himself in time with a future. He considers silence a relief, only to slip into the watery depths, emptying himself of past time that had been "leaking in" (38). As concerned as the novel is with imagining times other than those that regulate and dehumanise, there is the attendant unease, focused on James in particular, that the propensity of grief to stop time, to imagine the self as flooded by the past, carries its own despairing and damaging effects.

In contrast, and while (still) waiting at the bus stop, Ellie is attuned to the sounds of the crowds and is pictured "listening to the community of life around her and the mechanical and human sounds that together, a rough orchestra, filtered through the streets of the city" (141). She is pulled back into the standard clock-time time by which public transport (ideally) runs when the bus eventually arrives, but it too contributes its own percussive elements to Ellie's musical imaginings. It expels "a low pneumatic sigh" that breezes across the narrative as the focus shifts from Ellie's thoughts to James' recall of his failed medical studies and the sad irony in learning about breath from the stilled, sawn-open chest of a corpse (141). Whereas the chest is the cavity on which the lesson in breath is focused, for Ellie the entire city is a musical chamber. It is a note on which the novel concludes as she listens at night to "the musical sound of rain on her roof" and inwardly incants the four-bell intonation "*must ring James, must ring James, must ring, ring …*" (216). Ellie looks to, indeed inwardly sings, a future time that the ellipses gesture towards and which James cannot imagine and will not inhabit. And her shifting thoughts that bring the narrative to its close not only lift lines from Joyce's "The Dead" (1914), thus linking her thinking with the mind of Catherine, but also approximate the wet workings – the fluent and musical time passing – of the clepsydra:

> Ellie is thinking of rainfall over the Opera House, thinking of the Harbour swept shining and mystical by rain light, thinking of the time-lapse of all that she has known and read, and of James, and with James, ever and ever and abiding … seabirds rising up and rain coming down and the falling, falling, upon the living and the dead, ever and ever and abiding. (216)

This is how the wet time of the clepsydra moves and sounds in narrative form, the novel suggests.

Like *Five Bells*, *The Death of Noah Glass* is also preoccupied with how experiences of mourning and expressions of love might be realised in temporal terms not readily captured or measured by clock-time. Certainly, in the novel time ticks along, and weeks pass. The framing story takes place across some weeks following Noah's funeral: at one point, Evie tells her new employer that her father "had died five weeks ago" (124). And the narrative tells in temporally precise terms that "Noah Glass was born in Perth, Western Australia, in 1946. He died in Sydney sixty-seven years later, fully clothed, face downwards, in the pristine turquoise swimming pool attached to his apartment block" where he was found by a neighbour "at about seven a.m." (38). But these conventional understandings of time are given little weight. They are conceptions of time familiar to pro forma police reports; it is surely no coincidence that Evie and Martin first meet Detective Malone, whose motives the siblings are deeply sceptical of, in an office adorned only with a handsome clock.[33]

These standard temporal measures seem to say little of the lives that inhabit these times, and which are of interest to the novel. Having given this fact-like, temporally bound account of Noah's life and death, the narrative immediately slips to "this time and this place [that] had shaped him more than any other, but he rarely spoke of, or wished to recall" (39). Noah had lived as a child in a leprosarium in northern Western Australia with his religious and hard-working but emotionally distant doctor father and the institution's exclusively Aboriginal patients. The seemingly small matter of forgetting as an adult the name of his childhood friend's uncle (Jeremiah – the narrative voice remembers it) privately distresses him, as does

---

33 That the policeman is depicted as somewhat hapless is suggestive of the Glass' shared social status. In *Sorry*, a Nyoongar man named Joey tells Perdita Keene who is in search of Mary's whereabouts, "Lotsa blackfellas … in trouble with the law. And them whitefella p'licemen just love to stick us all in gaol" (148). The experience Evie and Martin have with the law is not expressed racially as it is for Joey.

his boastful teenage casting of himself, in the manner of *Ben-Hur* (1959), as the saviour of that same boyhood friend, Francis. Such experiences are of no interest to Detective Malone, but they constitute the story of *The Death of Noah Glass* and require other ways of conceiving of time, and indeed of narrative.

Noah's death itself marks out time both for his children and the narrative in terms of before and after. The time that comes after, the present time that Evie and Martin inhabit, is interposed with the time before – the desires, thoughts and experiences of their deceased father that commences with his boyhood and concludes with Noah's death. Narratively speaking, this event has already occurred, but as a consequence of the narrative alternation between these times, they are presented in parallel as well as conjoined, but also (at the same time) distinct. The novel then concludes with a chapter written in the present tense that gives the impression of linking in narrative time Noah's surviving granddaughter and lover (two characters that have not to this point been afforded an extended focalised narrative point of view), and his adult children. If the novel insists on Noah's ongoing presence in the lives and memories of his grieving children, whose points of view the narrative moves between, it also puts limits on their knowledge about him. In a staging of dramatic irony, the adult children know next to nothing about their father's experiences as a young child, and indeed as an older man with a new lover. They are steadfast in their disbelief that their academic father might have been an art thief; that he turns out to have participated in the crime is not a point of revelation or resolution that the text lingers on, or determinedly works towards. Rather, *The Death of Noah Glass* thematically and structurally turns on Noah's death. Like the long-dead skier Martin recalls on the morning of his father's funeral, astonishingly released from ice into time, Noah Glass, dead at the novel's beginning, is recovered in narrative. Yet the narrative time his readmittance announces and is afforded by is not so much that which might be associated with slow thawing (and narrative cause and effect) as with perforation.

Noah himself uses the term "punctured" (224) to describe a particularly dizzying experience of time that jet lag is imagined to induce and which the narrative more broadly might be said to entertain. It centres on a woman serving sake in an airport departure lounge. Exhausted, guilty (in his luggage is the stolen Ragusa bust he has agreed to carry for his lover, Dora Caselli), and a little drunk, Noah momentarily imagines the woman as the wife of the artist whose work he is smuggling out of Italy: "Eleanor Ragusa – Kiyohara Tama – had returned and was serving sake at Narita airport. She had punctured time, risen from the dead, and come to offer him a drink" (224) – not unlike Noah himself. He is then momentarily returned to the present, aware of "familiar accents circulating around him", only to "be revisited by an old regret" (224, 225) of giving his young son palliative alcohol. Noah is then reminded of the present by calculating the time differences between Tokyo and Rome (from where he has recently departed), only to recall, prompted by the shape of the sake-serving woman's kimono, how his wife, pregnant with Evie, had brought to mind at the time Piero della Francesca's image of *Madonna del Parto* (1460). As Noah asks of himself, "What state was he in, visited by such resemblances, stretched to breaking with desire for Dora Caselli?" (227). It is a state centred on the intangible experience of everyday moments, wherein things from the past are not contained to that time, and can come unbidden to mind by a fold of fabric. And at the level of form, the event-driven narrative tending towards closure, the story in which Detective Malone is cast as he (unsuccessfully) seeks out the art thief, is displaced by the meditative idea that one thing might not lead to an end but rather unexpectedly connect with another. In this sense, Noah's tucking of an encoded note in the cardboard backing of his favourite St. Jerome icon is less a "clue" to the location of the stolen Ragusa sculpture than a letter of love from beyond the grave to his daughter as "Only Evie would understand the code" (299).

While Noah is in turn troubled by, surprised at and grateful for these projections and memories, which are propelled by desire and marked by perforated time, his adult children also experience time in a particular way. Their grief at Noah's unexpected death both figures them as out of time, and prompts their heightened awareness of it. As Martin walks through Sydney streets towards the harbour, he considers his present action as "[p]ushing into time" and thinks, as an artist might, about avant-garde visual representations of time and movement, of "Marey, of Muybridge, of the fascist Futurists. No one since them had seen it better" (55).[34] And while she is walking through the same streets the morning following her father's funeral, Evie has a profound awareness of being removed from the daily temporal rhythms of working life, a state she attributes to her mourning: "There was vivacity everywhere, people starting the new day, streaming to work in cars and trains … Perhaps this too was grief, she thought, this omnipresent liveliness, marking one's own exclusion" (21).[35] Her grief also sees her conceptualise her father's apartment in Sydney, where she is staying, in temporal terms. It is a place where time has stilled, a time capsule filled "with his relics and his various leavings intact", and iced over: "it

---

34   Étienne-Jules Marey's chronophotography most famously informed Marcel Duchamp's *Nude Descending a Staircase* (1912) and lay the groundwork for modern cinema.
35   This time of grieving is interspersed for Evie (unlike James in *Five Bells*) with future possibilities. In *Black Mirror*, the characters similarly contemplate "hazarding loss as a premise for the possibility of redemption" (131) and the idea, and hope, that "*Out of desolation, promise*" (138). Jones has also commented in an interview, "I do think grief is one of the most tenacious emotions. It does not go away easily and it does wreak damage, and I've thought a lot about what it is that gets people through, what does it mean to move from grief into affirmation." Gail Jones, "Artistic Light into the Future: interview with Gail Jones", interview by Bron Sibree, *The West Australian Weekend Extra*, 28 August 2004, 7. It is a future time when the willing of such relief might not be so pressing, although Evie is also cautious about grief ending tidily, or being temporally bound and experienced as a discrete period: "This ease cannot last," she tells herself (245). In *Dreams of Speaking*, Mr Sakamoto expresses a similar conviction when he tells Anna of a recent night-vision of his wife, having not dreamt of her since her death many years previously: "It was a perplexing thing. Like being hauled backwards. This is one thing I should have learned by now: that grief never finishes …" (131). The time of grief, Mr Sakamoto suggests, is eternal, confounding and non-sequential.

looked like an apartment frozen in time" (243). And as she sleeps there, Evie herself is said to have "relinquished time" (244).

Both Evie and Martin are experiencing what the novel proposes from its first pages as the temporality of grief. The morning after Noah's funeral Evie wakes at precisely "[s]ix a.m." only then to reflect on her sleep and the time that mourning keeps: "To be nothing for thirteen hours: what sweet relief it had been" (15). To be released from her consciousness of time and the knowledge of her father's death is a momentary reprieve for Evie, and it is a condition that Evie expressly discusses with Martin so that its importance for the book is highlighted.

Talking about time is something that the siblings have grown up doing as a consequence of their father's efforts to instruct them in art history and composition, and with a mix of gratitude and resentment. The currency of this discussion between them is such that when her brother has been beaten and lies half-conscious in a hospital bed in Palermo, Evie talks to him about time: "He heard 'multiplicity, not unity'; he heard 'co-presence of the finite and infinite'; he heard her say something about serial time giving way to curves and bending motions. He could understand nothing. Was it the medication?" (292). If Martin, damaged and drugged, cannot apprehend his sister's inherited lessons on time and art at this moment, he was earlier impatient with his father's theories. "For fuck's sake," he tells Noah as a teenager, as his father attempts to explain his artistic theories of time at the beach (158).

So, speaking about time is not out of the ordinary for the Glass siblings. And it is worth noting that the conversations Evie and Martin have about time often occur on Skype, with each sibling in a different country and in a different time zone. Moreover, the technology they use to facilitate their discussion is itself fancifully imagined by Evie to be transcendent of their chosen subject; Skype affords a "timelessness" where brother and sister can meet virtually and meaningfully (235), and come to new understandings. For Evie at least, talking about time gives pause to reassess their sibling relationship: "she must learn to take him more seriously," she decides (237). It is only following the Skype call, when Martin mentally conjures images of his sister in Sydney, that he, however, feels time most forcefully and his affection for his sister is enlarged: "Dilation, that was it; Martin felt the dilation of time. Evie would be settling down for the night in Sydney: across the planet he pictured her in their father's apartment, rising from a chair, moving towards the bedroom on bare feet with an air of self-possession" (240). Skype might synchronise Martin and Evie and their talk about time, but their private thoughts are more temporally complicated and divergent.

The prompt for their Skype conversations about time is a plaque Martin saw in Palermo. It officially commemorates the place "where Garibaldi slept … for two hours in May in the year of 1860" but is additionally perceived by Martin as a "verification of weariness … and time out of time" (231). His understanding of the sign contrasts with that of Frank Malone, the Sydney-based detective who has unexpectedly turned up in Palermo, pursuing leads relating to the art heist and with little time for this kind of reflection. "So what's the big deal?" he asks Martin (231). As far as the novel is concerned, the big deal about time is its connection with human vulnerability and consciousness, with sleep imagined as the condition that pulls together, and apart, these two states.

Prompted by her brother's query about whether sleep is "in or out of time" (237), Evie, as a former professional philosopher, tells Martin: "My first response would be that there is no time without consciousness" (237). It is an answer her brother had already intuited as a teenage artist, and raises the question as to how narratives, the sequencing of their words wedded with linear time, might faithfully represent the proposed non-time of sleep. The response is familiar to comic-book depictions of dozing. Martin draws above the head of his sleeping sister "a scalloped dream cloud, and in the dream cloud Martin rendered her sleeping alphabetical: *zzzzz*" (298), a state into which Evie, as an adult, is said to slide away "darkly uncertain, on the inner surf of her zzzs" (37). (On the evening after their father's funeral, Martin watches his sister sleep with an artist's eye and remembers his recollected story: "Her eyelids were cyan blue, her blotched skin was pasty … her face was creased against the cushion. The two French brothers must have looked at their father in this way" (12).) For Evie, who internally recites compulsively but comforting word lists that run in an orderly fashion from A to Z, this depiction of sleep – slurring past the end time of the alphabet – supports graphically her philosophical position that she later confirms when listening to her lover, Benjamin, sleep at her side. She determines that sleep "is a sound without alphabet … that arrives only with images" (311). As her teenage brother had understood, Evie too believes that the image, which can achieve the stationary, is more suitable for representing the non-time of sleep than time-conscious narrative.

This interest in the novel with the time of the image is also represented earlier in the narrative. Before, in this same apartment where Evie speaks by Skype to her brother, Noah himself is depicted as sleepless on his return to Sydney with the Ragusa sculpture. Unable to rest, he recovers from beneath his bed the image Martin drew of Evie sleeping as a teenager. For Noah, the image from the past of Evie's release from time and consciousness is both "like a living thing" and ghostlike, his daughter's face "a spectre, disappearing" (298), not unlike the man released from ice that Martin recalls. Martin's drawing has moved through the time Evie's sleeping denies, and is received by the adult children's father with "powerful feelings" (298) because the image evokes convergent ideas he carries as both a father and an academic with a special interest in pictorial representations of time. The image provokes an indistinct moment of recollection – "Evie blue-coloured and almost drowned" (304) – but loops back to an earlier episode in the narrative in which Noah's fears for himself and his children are laid bare. Depressed, the children's mother is said to have left Martin and Evie "to fend for themselves" (74); it is nearly forty years later that Noah remembers the detail of removing the infant Evie from a cold bath and wrapping both her and her brother "in the towel, making them one beloved package … *saved, now they are saved*" (304). For now, the siblings are saved from the end of time, the knowledge of which is perhaps present and portent in the ghostly image of Evie as a sleeping girl that sets the older Noah's hand trembling.

These folds in time that the recovered image prompts accord with the radical reordering of time that Noah experiences with the birth of his children. As new parents, Noah and Katherine are said to have felt time anew: "It raced and it stalled; there were wearisome nights and accelerated days" (73). And as an older man, with his children grown, Noah's love for them opens up time so that as children they are as present in his mind as they are as adults in his here-and-now. Sitting on a beach in Palermo, his thoughts turn to Evie and Martin:

> He was thinking again of his children. He was unable to say how being a father moved and engaged him, how Martin and Evie, even at times of estrangement, were his centred world. No hypothetical eternities, but their actual now. And the memory of them when little, dressing, undressing, pulling garments on and off their vulnerable bodies, the incandescent light falling like seawater over their small bent backs. (160–1)

This image of luminous, preciously specific love is tied for Noah with his academic study of the Renaissance paintings of Piero della Francesca, in particular *The Baptism of Christ* (after 1437). His memory of the children, their baptism in light, is overlaid with his interest in this picture's bending figure pulling a diaphanous shirt over his shoulders: "something in his contemplation of images had led him here, to see his own children in the figure of the man wriggling in or out of the shirt" (157). That something is cosmic time.

Whereas Noah believes that scholars to date have talked endlessly about mathematics and geometry in Piero della Francesca's work, Noah draws on his faith, which his children do not share, to propose that this painting is a meditation on "the mystery of time"; that the image of the man, whose face is shielded, might well be an image of time – a flash-back, or flash-forward, of Christ himself – "so the audacity of the painting would exist in imagining a man exceeding time" (156). Beyond this one painting, Noah suggests that all of Piero della Francesca's everyday settings – something that distinguished his art thematically from the medieval vision he inherited and which Noah and Dora view through binoculars at the Monreale Cathedral in Palermo – insist that the scenes of miraculous events they depict did not just happen long ago. They are also happening forever in eternity, occurring all the time. (It is a lesson Evie has learnt well from her father as she relates to her beaten, hospitalised brother "the fresco sequence [by Piero della Francesca] called *The Legend of the True Cross* … A piece of wood appearing and disappearing throughout history, and its afterlife in millions of icons around the world, substance remade as image, continuing in time" (292).) But even as Noah captures his children within an image of cosmic time, he also insists on their modern, temporal existence – "the actual now" – which Noah feels intensely. For

Noah, it is the affective pull of his children – his adoration of them holds them together as a triptych – that contemporises secular and cosmic time.

Martin is still part-baffled as an adult by his father's thinking about time. When contemplating a new artwork on the morning of Noah's funeral, Martin's mind turns to the geometry, rather than the temporality, of Piero della Francesca's early works. Evie, though, shares her father's intellectual, if not religious, temporal and visual interests (some of which also preoccupy Lucy Strange in *Sixty Lights*). Like Noah, Evie has trained her intellect on the image. She tells her new employer, Benjamin (who is to become her lover), that when working as an academic philosopher, she once wrote a paper on "miraculous images, things made without hands, just appearing" (125). (The narrative is correspondingly mischievous: Benjamin's hands immediately claim Evie: "She liked his hands, veined and purple" (125).)[36] Rather than the still images that are the subject of her father's devotion and study, Evie has begun speaking moving images for this man who is blind. Her new employment has Evie enter a new time, "rolling along in movie-time" (125). It is a description that suggests film, as a smooth serialisation of still images, might create or carry its own distinct set of temporal interests and speeds; that Evie's first assignment is to watch a Hitchcock film in preparation for her later viewing of it with Benjamin also suggests the repeatability of this film-time – thanks to modern technology rather than religious mystery.

If the narrative of *The Death of Noah Glass* allows for these complexities of multiple times, then *Sixty Lights* shares its preoccupation with time and visual images, in particular the nascent technology of photography, which constitutes its presiding formal and thematic interest. Even without a camera in hand, from a young age the novel's protagonist, Lucy Strange, is said to have a special propensity for photographic seeing. It is a proclivity that prompts her to keep a book in which she records special things she has, and has not, seen and it also leads her to contemplate the ideas about time that photography affords. These meditations on time are central to how Lucy conceives of herself and her relationships with others, and they take on a heightened charge in the knowledge of Lucy's impending death from consumption. While ethereal women might waste away in the art and literature of the nineteenth century, in which Lucy is well versed, Lucy's own impending passing draws her into thinking intently about the time of photography.

Even before Lucy is diagnosed with her illness, her interest in this new technology marks her as having a particular relationship with time. In short, Lucy herself is new. The novel is careful to attend to how race and class have roles to play in the creation of Lucy's distinctiveness in Bombay (where she is viewed as a foreigner despite wishing "herself Indian" (136)) and in London (where, as an orphan, it is deemed proper that she work in an albumen factory, but with

---

36   Jones' skiagrapher would understand this interest given that she contemplates the idea that "women might unconsciously choose lovers on the basis of their hands". Gail Jones, "Skiascopy (or, The Science of Romance)", *Fetish Lives* (Fremantle: Fremantle Arts Centre Press, 1997), 60.

women who are suspicious of her bookish learning). And the novel establishes too her differences from the women Lucy loves most. Her sister-in-law, Violet, and her childhood carer and adult companion, Mrs Minchin, are clearly presented as good-hearted but not entirely understanding of her photographic ardour, and Lucy is depicted as yearning for professional and philosophical female companionship: "If I could locate another woman interested in photography, I feel sure I could speak honestly and openly of these matters and defend more confidently my maculate aesthetic" (199).[37] Within the world of the text, this desire for collegiate sympathy is unrealised, and Lucy's originality, singularity and separateness are underscored.

But more than a novelty, Lucy is also presented as out-of-time. Her newly found passion for photography has her wondering about the timelessness of that enthusiasm. She comes surprised to a possibility she has already intuited, that "somehow – was it possible? – she had always been a photographer" (141). And this concern to imagine Lucy and photography in terms of time is reinforced when the narrative casts her as a figure of prolepsis: "Chemicals, glass, mechanical reproduction – these combined to make Lucy feel entirely modern, a woman of the future" (141). Lucy is anachronistic, existing as adjunct to historical time.

It is in this proleptic capacity that she imagines herself in terms akin to a Romantic poet. She is a seer – "She saw lucent intimations of worlds to come" (233) – and anticipates the modern invention of the x-ray, cinema and other mechanical forms of vision of which photography forms the basis. These technologies are presumably known, and known as historical, to a reader at the time of the book's publication. But as far as Lucy's contemporaries are concerned, they are not yet thought of. The reception of her prognostications by her lover, Jacob Webb, is telling in this regard. In addition to relaying to him these future ways of seeing, she also "quotes", with variation, Virginia Woolf's elegant lines in the 1921 essay "Modern Fiction": "'In the future,' pronounced Lucy, 'people will understand that life is not a series of gig lamps or gas lamps symmetrically arranged; it is more encompassing, more immersing, more like an ulterior halo'" (218). Jacob Webb's response is one of bewilderment, yet his determination that "[s]he spoke like someone who was watching history unfold, like someone who knew beforehand of her own death, and was speaking posthumously" (218) is fully sympathetic to Lucy's ideas about time. Lucy's confident predictions of its future telling render her anachronistic in his eyes.

That Lucy might foretell the future, including the invention of technologies of seeing, is because she understands photography to afford a kind of time travel. Lucy

---

[37] Lucy's dedication to the maculate aesthetic puts her in sympathy with a real-life near contemporary, Julia Margaret Cameron. Cameron, Jones imagines, "loved the shadows where each soul would come artistically to rest. She loved differentiation, the un-echoing quality of each self. And though her hands were always blackened with the effects of her processing chemicals, and her skirts perpetually (and scandalously) collodian-stained, what she engaged in was less physical than it was metaphysical – the mysterious aspects of the capture of light." Cameron is the kind of woman-photographer Lucy wishes to encounter. Gail Jones, "Five Gifts Told by Echo", *Fetish Lives* (Fremantle: Fremantle Arts Centre Press, 1997), 173.

comprehends photography in terms of time that are instructively different from the man to whom she is apprenticed in Bombay, thanks to the financial support of her friend and benefactor, Isaac Newton. For Victor Browne, photography is unambiguously "science .... not prettified seeing. It is pure calculation" (141). In contrast, photography for Lucy is not a matter of aesthetics or science – she sees the two as inseparable – but rather a relationship with time.[38] It is this attribution of time to photography that has Lucy determine with distaste that her teacher "sedated and mortified all that he saw" (141). Browne unthinkingly stops time and his example is upheld as the antithesis of Lucy's photographic aesthetics, ambitions and understandings. Lucy imagines the as yet unrealised potentialities of photography for physical and temporal travel. In addition to conceiving of "a mobile apparatus, one that travelled everywhere", she also determines that images might examine the structure of appearances and discern "the capability of all things ... to be seen singly and remarkably" (141) across the time they render complex.

Lucy has ended up at Browne's photographic establishment as a result of Isaac's suggestion that "he and Lucy should have a portrait photograph taken, before – as he so indelicately put it – her shape betrayed her, an image, he said, that would help later on and might even serve as consolation to the future child" (139).[39] Lucy's shipboard sexual encounter with the "utterly caddish" William Crowley during her passage to India has put paid to any hope her uncle might have had in uniting his niece and his friend (128); Isaac's unrequited affections for Neville also mean that the projected marriage was never likely to eventuate.

Isaac nonetheless has grown fond of Lucy and he proposes the photograph in the knowledge that the story it might tell of the pictured couple can reach beyond the time of its taking. That the story is a complete fabrication, something Isaac is counting on, is underscored by "the little world of props and false objects" Lucy immediately encounters on entering the studio (139), and is realised in the image that Browne's lens creates of "Isaac Newton and Lucy Strange as a legitimately married couple in an English park" (140). If the photograph transports Isaac and Lucy out of the studio in India and into a nondescript landscape at the centre of empire, it also propels them into individual forms of time travel as "The power of the flash had removed some of Isaac's years; he looked both younger and more solid than he appeared in real life; Lucy, on the other hand, appeared older and less substantial" (140). Further, the narrative itself shifts forward in time so that immediately following this description of the photograph Lucy is imagined in a future time "[l]ater" looking at this past representation of herself and finding "no

---

38 In her study of nineteenth-century photography, Jennifer Green-Lewis discusses the connection her subject has with a crisis of memory (rather than time), partly attributable to an unmatched expansion in knowledge. Jennifer Green-Lewis, *Framing the Victorians: photography and the culture of realism* (Ithaca: Cornell University Press, 1996).

39 That Crowley introduces Lucy to the word and concept of bioluminescence is possibly his one redeeming quality, although it must be said that Lucy never expected more than sexual satisfaction from their fleeting intimacy, anyway.

pool of portrait beauty over which to linger and transform" (140). She is then represented as thinking proleptically to a time in the further future when she is dead and the image will endure and be viewed by others *as* her, rather than as the contrived construction she knows it to be. Lucy is alert to photography's mnemonic function, and its complicated imaginings of time.

The image Lucy settles on as the one she wants to be remembered by has her appear in a collective portrait as already ghostlike because "Lucy, having moved during exposure from her initial position, appeared in print as blurred and residual" (236). Despite requests from her lover and fellow artist to have the photograph taken once more, "[s]he would not pose again" (236). For Lucy, this photograph is marked by the maculate – "error and chance" (243) – which differentiates her style and preference, and indeed politics, from "*the men of the Society of Photographers*" who decree that: "*The photograph should appear ... as if God had breathed it onto the glass*" (199), as she writes in a letter to Isaac. Thanks to her experience in Victor Browne's studio, Lucy is all too aware of what lies behind the production of such a veneer. Her viewing in London of magic lantern images that cast Indians as "snarling barbarians" (185) in the story they tell of the First War of Independence (the 1857 Indian Mutiny) suggests the interests such seemingly God-given images might serve. This suspicion about images passing themselves off as "natural" is also rehearsed through Lucy's doubts about the "luminous image" conjured by the medium, Madame d'Esperance, who Lucy's uncle earnestly consults for news of his deceased sister, Lucy's mother (94). While she witnesses and acknowledges her uncle's impassioned response to the revenant, Lucy herself "imagined trickery and hidden contraptions" (94). And although she does not state it outright, Lucy's preference for this other sort of ghostly image, beholding her after her death in anticipation of that event, lies with the prospect that it is a photograph less of Lucy than of pleats in time.

More precisely, the possibilities photography holds for Lucy lie not so much with documenting (however partial) a time as signalling "a shift in time itself, and a celebration of the lit-up gaze" (142), although she worries that this "wish to beautify" might be ethically suspect: "How, she wondered silently, to attest it all?" (147). The shift in time that Lucy imagines photography to mark involves more than the presupposition to capture a moment in time in the knowledge of its future contemplation, a conceit that carries its own temporal complications that the novel acknowledges: "Looking at photographs cracked open time" (233). That is, the presence of the photograph disrupts any assumption that time might move smoothly and inexorably from the discarded past to the novel future. This shift also allows for the dislodgement of the official, historical time Lucy sees screened at the magic lantern show to grant "moments arcane, seductive, trivial, breathtaking, that waited for the sidelong glance, the split-second of notice, the opening up of an irrefutable and auratic presence" (142). And it further permits Lucy's half-formed notion that photography might conceptualise time in unexpected ways. As Lucy muses to Isaac about the photograph Victor Browne took of them, she again relates her aesthetic preference for the "blossom-looking shadows"; that which is "[m]arked and shadowed, and flecked with time" (146). In determining to eradicate the maculate from his image, the professional photographer conjures temporal terms to declare the presence of those shadows as "Bad timing" (140). Browne declines to recognise that the interplay of light and shadow that affords photography might also comprise time.

Like the photographs she produces, as well as those she does not take, and also the sixty non-sequential short chapters in which she appears, Lucy is a time traveller who troubles the linear sensibility of time that such a term might carry. She cherishes the possibility of meetings across times that she intuited when conjuring a photograph-not-taken of her mother. In this imagined image, her mother

> as a child of seven or eight … looked directly ahead, but squinted slightly, as though she were peering into the future to meet her adult daughter's gaze, as though, in fact, the child knew it was possible that time might distort like this … It was a canny image: the child seemed to know something of the future. (29)

Lucy's discernment of a future-directed gaze that she meets when looking to the past in this image-not-taken forges a connection, and connective pattern, between mother and daughter that the time told by the clocks, now-stilled on Max and Matilda Weller's mantelpiece, cannot comprehend, measure or gauge.

Sixty Lights, *The Death of Noah Glass* and *Five Bells* imagine time in terms other than those proposed by chronological and linear conceptions of it. It is what escapes these common conceptions of time that preoccupies Jones' writing as it seeks in representational form to glimpse, and give serious consideration to, private moments, unbidden memories, thoughts and dreams, and everyday experiences which are understood to have their own temporal patterning and rhythms. Alert to how time might be harnessed to regulate and discipline social relations and conceptions of the self, these three novels exemplify how narrative might afford other ways of imagining meaningful and ethical relationships in, and with, time.

3
Reading and Writing

When Cass Turner takes leave of the falling snow in *A Guide to Berlin* and enters one of the apartments where she and five others are to share their speak-memories, she coolly surveys her unfamiliar surroundings and discovers almost immediately the absence of books:

> Kępiński's sitting room was lavishly appointed. There were thick brocaded curtains, of emerald-green damask, frilly standing lamps, not entirely perpendicular, and commodious settees and armchairs, all corpulence and plush. There were touches of gold around mirrors and on the frames of mediocre paintings, and in the light over all. At the centre of the room hung a giant chandelier, which on closer inspection was missing more than a few of its crystals. And at the periphery was an old oak desk, clearly never intended for use, upon which stood a tulip-shaped reading lamp, fashioned in a tone of pink not unlike that of the blooms in Cass' studio. No bookcases anywhere, no books were visible.[1]

Who Kępiński is, is unclear; Jewish Victor jokes that "Kępiński is probably a long-lost cousin" (114). The apartment is one of the up-market properties for which Marco Gianelli is seeking an occupant and which has at its doorstep tessellate *Stolpersteine*, commemorative brass plates inscribed with the names of the Levi family who had lived at the residence, before being subjected to Nazi terror. Inside, and under Cass' steady gaze, the apartment's surface veneer of wealth is found wanting. It is not that Cass minds the damaged chandelier or the unexceptional

---

1   Gail Jones, *A Guide to Berlin* (North Sydney: Vintage, 2015), 113–14. All subsequent references are to this edition and appear in parentheses in the text.

paintings edged with gold. Rather, what catches Cass' eye and deeply troubles her, as the repetition of the negative suggests, is the conspicuous lack of books.

For Cass, the want of books is possibly highlighted because of her specific circumstance. She is in Berlin, in a comparatively bare apartment, with plans to write her own book: "Her block, number 50, faced a cemetery. It looked plain and forlorn. At least it would be quiet, she thought. At least she might work here. Write here. Find a foreign sense of purpose" (33). But more than this personal endeavour, books – and reading books and talking about writing – are markers of what matters in the world of *A Guide to Berlin*. The notable absence of books in the unoccupied apartment takes on a particular historical and political charge with Marco's election of Micha Ullman's memorial – bookcases buried in the Bebelplatz – as his most meaningful site in Berlin. He tells the rest of the group's members, "They commemorate the book burning there by the Nazis in 1933 … you peer into a lit square, as down a deep well, and you see only empty shelves. I like the simplicity of his installation, and the accuracy of the idea" (195). Together with the other group members who gather in this "stately old apartment in Wilmersdorf", Cass esteems books and reading (111). These characters have come together because of their shared love of Vladimir Nabokov's writing, and Cass expressly couches her acceptance of participating in the speak-memory gatherings as admitting "the possibility of a literary fellowship" (16). This promise of solidarity is something that Marco also acknowledges in his address to the group: "There is an isolation to reading, just as there is a community. There is a philosophical learning, impossible to unlearn, and we have all, each of us here, discovered this form of enchantment" (122). Later, as the first speak-memory held in the apartment draws to an uncomfortable close – its members bristle at the implication made by one of their party that their meetings are a form of therapy – Cass admits to herself that the disclosures had been a kind of delirium whose transporting effects are intensified because they have occurred in "this over-decorated room, reeking of tasteless excess and bookless ignorance" (124). For this community of readers, books are markers of understanding. But on her entry into the apartment in which these sentiments are articulated, Cass is struck by the staging of a very different notion of value, one that is bound up with the practicalities of attracting a rent-paying tenant in the market economy, which she clearly rejects.

Contrary to the furnishings of Kępiński's apartment but in line with Cass' own thinking, this chapter turns on the observation that Gail Jones' texts are very much concerned with books and reading. Jones has herself commented on how

> The artefacts of human life are super-numerous and I suppose we are each called upon to establish our own orders of value, to decide whether it is a car or a novel that furnish meaning, whether the new carpet or a bowl of slowly inclining, flame-coloured tulips offers aesthetic satisfaction and ineluctable delight.[2]

---

2   Gail Jones, "On Small Things", *The Weekend Australian Review*, 8–9 January 2005, 2.

In *A Guide to Berlin*, the artefacts of life Cass chooses to value are evident. Not only does she purchase a "paper sheath of tulips" (18) that the reading lamp on Kępiński's desk also brings to mind; together with Jones' *oeuvre* more broadly, she and the other speak-memory members agree that books are central to ethics.

Many of Jones' protagonists are authors, or would-be authors, and the presence and vocation of these characters in Jones' texts give pause to the processes and purposes of writing within both their story-worlds and the narrative that tells of them. In addition to Cass, there is Lucy in *Sixty Lights* who keeps a book of "*Special Things Seen*" in which she records the images the world offers up to her.[3] Alice Black in *Dreams of Speaking* is writing a book on modernity, and *Black Mirror* tells the story of Anna Griffin who has been commissioned to write Victoria Morrell's biography. Evie Glass in *The Death of Noah Glass* once wrote academic essays on *acheiropoieta*; Catherine Healy in *Five Bells* is a journalist. Further, Jones' two short-story collections, *The House of Breathing* and *Fetish Lives*, both relate lives and deaths official history declines to record as well as imagine private experiences of recognised authors.

Related reflections on reading – what it might involve, how it might feel, what it might afford – are also apparent throughout Jones' work, which also deliberately entwines itself with the writings of others. It is easy enough to suggest that this preoccupation is self-reflexive; that the interest Jones' writing displays about reading and writing cleverly draws attention its own construction and reminds a reader of their participation in the meaning-making process. But the commitment Jones' work has to reflecting on books is more an ethics that is also often tested in the imaginative worlds Jones offers.

Attending to the notice Jones' texts give to books, and writing and reading, suggests that this emphasis is dedicated to thinking through their limits and possibilities, particularly when it comes to testifying to historical injustices and the complexities of individual lives and deaths.[4] In Jones' writing, the central characters often single out books because they conceive of them as enacting ethical understandings that might create sympathetic and meaningful relationships. The narratives that tell of this hope are more circumspect, however, allowing for the ethical import the characters credit reading and writing, but also admitting their limitations.

Because books, and references to reading and writing, appear so often in Jones' work, this chapter moves across a number of texts – *A Guide to Berlin*, *Five Bells*, *Sixty Lights* and *Dreams of Speaking*, as well as a selection of short stories. It also considers at some length the novel *Black Mirror*. Of all the authors in Jones' work, it

---

3   Gail Jones, *Sixty Lights* (London: The Harvill Press, 2004), 86. All subsequent references are to this edition and appear in parentheses in the text.
4   Gail Jones has approvingly noted in others' works this abiding concern with the importance of reading and writing. In her review of Brenda Walker's book *Reading by Moonlight* (2010), Jones notes: "Reading and writing are taken seriously as that which might sustain and rescue." Gail Jones, "In the darkness, words to the rescue", *The Australian Literary Review*, 5 May 2010, 16.

is Anna Griffin in *Black Mirror* who is pictured grappling with the ethics the writing of her dying subject's biography involves.

Perhaps the most obvious place to start contemplating the importance of books and reading to Jones' narratives is to acknowledge the presence in them of fragments from other stories, poems, plays, films and philosophies, as well as allusions to various genres, styles and authors. Such inclusions promote the notion that the text being read is a constituent of a literary community, and that the conversations this meeting of narratives prompts are a means for thinking through literary ethics. This creative re-visioning of canonical as well as popular forms insists that texts and the meanings they carry are not isolated or restrained by their origin. Jones' narratives seek to connect with what has come before in order to acknowledge the extensive entanglements of responsibility and influence between past, present and future moments of writing and reading. These temporal markers are made permeable in this ongoing process, and the opportunity for critical reflection on, reinterpretation of, and intervention in the value of reading and writing, as well as the ideas circulating in and across texts, is apparent.

These possibilities notably preoccupy *A Guide to Berlin* and its characters, who are enthralled by the writings of Vladimir Nabokov. This literary devotion is exemplified by their adaptation of the title of Nabokov's autobiography, *Speak, Memory* (1951), to denote their own experiment in literary friendship and disclosure. Nabokov's memoir, with its spiralling narrative and ornate prose, is replete with acute distress and a longing for a home to which the author could not return because of the Bolshevik Revolution. *Speak, Memory* is also a story of how the redemptive possibilities of memory might surmount loss. As Nabokov writes:

> The act of vividly recalling a patch of the past is something that I seem to have been performing with the utmost zeal all my life ... A sense of security, of well-being, of summer warmth pervades my memory. That robust reality makes a ghost of the present ... Everything is as it should be, nothing will ever change, nobody will ever die.[5]

What is found in *A Guide to Berlin* is quite different, however. Making memory speak does not necessarily "alleviate ... deep misery" (108); it might even worsen traumatic states, leading to tragic ends. The novel offers circumspection and sagacity, rather than deference, in its dialogue with the writings of an author routinely recognised as one of the twentieth century's greatest.[6]

---

5   Vladimir Nabokov, *Speak, Memory: An Autobiography Revisited* (1951; London: Penguin, 2000), 50, 52.
6   In *Five Bells*, another intimate relationship is initiated by a discussion of *Speak, Memory*, although Luc, Catherine's lover, is more distrustful of Nabokov's image repertoire: "Every shape, said Luc, was already filled up with death ... Poor Mr Nabokov." Luc prefers instead "Pushkin and Dostoevsky. I loved Gogol and Tolstoy", and he particularly adores the epic novel associated in the novel with Pei Xing, "'And *Doctor Zhivago*,' he added. 'I really loved *Doctor Zhivago*.'" Gail

Sixty Lights also engages with two texts that are held up today as literary greats: Charlotte Brontë's *Jane Eyre* (1847) and Charles Dickens' *Great Expectations* (1861). It does so in part to suggest that the past does not obediently stay put in historical time. The novel's temporal setting might be loosely nominated the mid-nineteenth century, but the narrative is less concerned with representing or recreating that time than acknowledging the role literature has in mediating the past.[7] Like the Strange children who feel that *Great Expectations* "made London seem altogether more actual" (84), the novel's engagement with these (now) canonical texts is bound up with its interests in imagining time as well as affective relationships. For example, one specific line from Dickens' serialised *Great Expectations* – "'Partickler when he see the ghost!'" (85), an exclamation that itself refers to Joe Gargery's spontaneous response to his first attendance at a performance of *Hamlet* – is repeatedly quoted by Lucy Strange, her brother Thomas and their uncle Neville to underscore their love and connections. It was their "private three-way joke" (85). Unlike Joe Gargery, these characters know their literary references, and they get the witticism.

Just as this line from Dickens acts as a coda of sorts in *Sixty Lights*, *Jane Eyre* is also directly summoned in the same novel. This book, with selected passages carefully underlined, is found by Lucy as a child in a box of private things belonging to her mother, Honoria, who has recently died from childbirth complications. As a young woman, Honoria identified strongly with Brontë's romantic protagonist, Jane Eyre: "*I am Jane Eyre,* she secretly told herself. *I am honourable but unnoticed. I am passionate and strong. I need a lover who will carry my future in the palm of his hand*" (12). While it is true that Honoria is partly aware that *Jane Eyre*'s romance script is "preposterous", she simultaneously determines it to be "wonderful" (47), an enthusiasm in which the novel knowingly indulges. As the heroine of an early episode in the novel, Honoria soon finds herself admiring the shape of Arthur Strange's "large hand", in which her future is presumably destined to be carried (13).

If two texts Anglophone criticism considers to be nineteenth-century literary classics echo throughout *Sixty Lights*, it is various writings by Shakespeare – the author celebrated today (not without considerable debate) as the pre-eminent English language writer and dramatist – that are recited repeatedly and at length in *Sorry* by Stella Keene and her daughter Perdita. The novel makes numerous allusions to at least eight Shakespearean dramas, which Stella has memorised and quotes from regularly. Because of this habit, she cuts a strange figure in a place marked "by the call of butcher birds in a nearby tamarind tree, and by a clanking

---

Jones, *Five Bells* (London: Harvill Secker, 2011), 127, 130. All subsequent references are to this edition and appear in parentheses in the text. In contrast, the characters in *A Guide to Berlin* identify strongly with Nabokov's writing: Yukio thinks of himself as the "little Russian boy" in the story " First Love", for example (64).

7   For a different perspective on the novel and its historical imaginings, see Kate Mitchell, "'The alluring patina of loss': Photography, Memory, and Memory Texts in *Sixty Lights* and *Afterimage*", *History and Cultural Memory in Neo-Victorian Fiction: Victorian Afterimages* (London: Palgrave, 2010), 143–76.

metallic sound that turned out to be a group of Aboriginal men in iron chains, linked painfully by their ankles".[8] While Stella's turn to Shakespeare is a searching for solace, Perdita quietly but meaningfully questions her mother's unwavering conviction that "Shakespeare has identified ... *all* the 'big' questions" (38). Perdita wonders instead if the knowledge her Mandjabari friends live by and relate in song might pose "*small* questions ... Or perhaps – the idea subversively filled her head – there were *different* big questions" (38). It is a prospect the novel is committed to as it seeks to relate what the "big questions" sidestep. If Perdita queries the cultural and epistemological status her mother affords Shakespeare and his writing, it is nevertheless the books her father ordered from Sydney that she understands retrospectively, and rapturously, as forms of protection, imaginative escape and intellectual revelation:

> By the time I was ten, when I began seriously to read ... half the front room was crowded by books. ... In the darkness the pillars of books seemed to tilt and arch over me, yet I fancied not collapse, but a kind of shelter, the roof-shaped protection of open volumes. After my father died ... we read. There is no refuge so private, no asylum more sane. There is no facility of voices captured elsewhere so entire and so marvellous. My tongue was lumpish and fixed, but in reading, silent reading, there was a release, a flight, a wheeling off into the blue spaces of exclamatory experience, diffuse and improbable, gloriously homeless. All that was solid melted into air, all that was air was reshaped, and gained plausibility. (31)

Perdita attributes to books and to reading a revolutionary potential to remake what is known and understood. For Cass in *A Guide to Berlin*, books and reading are nothing less than markers of an individual's integrity and worth. The novel gives expression to this notion by means of Cass' changing attitude towards a man who is first introduced in the narrative as the caretaker of the building in which Cass' decidedly non-bourgeois apartment is located. The newly arrived Australian initially thinks of Karl as kindly, although she misinterprets his concern as transactional only, offering him money he rejects for his service of carrying her suitcase upstairs. This first impression shifts slightly when he appears – a *deus ex machina* – at the Pergamon Museum to assist Marco through his epileptic convulsions while Cass looks on helplessly. Cass' thoughts about Karl change once again when he shows up at her apartment unannounced. Initially, his presence

---

[8] Gail Jones, *Sorry* (North Sydney: Vintage, 2007), 46. All subsequent references are to this edition and appear in parentheses in the text. This unusual faculty is rehearsed by another of Jones' characters in an earlier short story, "The Word 'Ruby'". In this story in *The House of Breathing*, Jones' barrister protagonist recalls the case of a man who, while unable to remember his role in his mother's murder, can recite from memory, and by heart, all of Shakespeare's sonnets. He is committed to an asylum rather prison.

provokes displeasure as Cass is hosting two members of the speak-memory group, Mitsuko and Yukio. But her annoyance quickly gives way to solidarity when he produces an old book filled with etchings of snowflakes, the very meteorological phenomenon she is preoccupied with and which is also "one of Yukio's special interests" (175). The revelation of both Karl's precious possession and his scholarly inclinations prompts Cass "to revise her knowledge of him: he was, after all, an educated man, and one with assiduous – bookmarked – intellectual passions" (175). For Cass, books and reading are markers of what, and who, she values.

These links established in *A Guide to Berlin* between books and value, readers and words, are open to question beyond the pages of Jones' texts. Why should books in particular, and the capacity to read them, be singled out as indicators of an individual's subjectivity, appeal and merit? Do all books "count" in the same way? And what does reading involve, anyway? These questions are debated in Jones' novels, too. They are put under particular pressure in *A Guide to Berlin* when everything Cass thinks she knows about Marco, and books and reading, is called into doubt by his actions to protect Gino. When the act of Gino's fatal violence against Victor occurs late in the narrative, and Karl organises the disrespectful disposal of Victor's corpse into the icy Havel, a reconsideration of all that has come before, including the affect and intellectual weight afforded books and their reading, takes place.

Up to this point, reading had mattered greatly to Cass. In their original encounter outside the (rebuilt) apartment block where Nabokov and his family took rooms, Marco's seduction of Cass into the group, and eventually into bed, involves an undisguised appeal to the importance of reading and writing. He asks her – rhetorically, of course – "Who cares about complication? Who cares about Nabokov?" Cass part-playfully replies, "Who indeed?" (15). Cass cares, and she insists on reading as a precious pursuit, one that might even evidence an individual's authentic temperament and worth, as her perusal of the spines of her lover's books suggests. That Cass assumes to determine and decipher her new lover's inner life by means of his books might explain why she can barely disguise her displeasure at Marco's post-coital imputation that she has misread Nabokov's short story "A Guide to Berlin" (1925).[9] In significant contrast to Kępiński's fading bourgeois apartment, Marco's place is stylish and full of books. On entering her new lover's apartment for the first time, Cass notices right away a "wall of bookshelves, stacked full, to which Cass was immediately drawn ... She stood scanning the titles of the books – a habit she always succumbed to – lost in hasty calculation of his intellectual tastes and predispositions" (179). Marco also has on his wall a Rembrandt print that, far from being mediocre as the artworks in Kępiński's apartment are judged to be, resonates with a memory from Cass' childhood and seems to affirm the pair's new affinity.

---

9   Vladimir Nabokov, "A Guide to Berlin", in *The Stories of Vladimir Nabokov* (1925; New York: Random House, 1997), 155–60.

Cass' habit of gravitating towards shelves weighted down with books in an effort to gather something of their owners' cerebral inclinations is also shared by Walter Benjamin, who Jones subtly references in *A Guide to Berlin*. It is Benjamin's reading of Paul Klee's monoprint *Angelus Novus* that Marco summons to instruct Cass on the apparently correct interpretation of "A Guide to Berlin"; it would be no surprise if Cass were to find a volume by Benjamin in Marco's bookcase.

Jones has written explicitly about Benjamin's thoughts on book collecting in a short newspaper article on the occasion of her then recent move from Perth to Sydney.[10] Faced with the need to pack up her books for the journey, Jones turns to Benjamin's personal essay, "Unpacking My Library", as a companion. Benjamin's essay begins with the event of his joyful reunion with his volumes "after two years of darkness" (and presumably after the divorce from his wife, Dora, that sees him now moving to a new apartment).[11] Unlike Jones, who is putting away her books temporarily, Benjamin is writing in the act of "unpacking my library. Yes, I am."[12] The essay's interest in Benjamin's reacquaintance with his beloved books lies less with the matter of Benjamin returning the volumes to both the light of day and accommodating shelves than an understanding of the collector himself. For Benjamin, the unpacking of his library is an autobiographical excursion as speaking about his books finds Benjamin to be "speaking only about himself".[13] As Jones acknowledges in her article, in addition to the idea that personal libraries are as much archives of memory as they are physical assemblages, for Benjamin "any collection is a peculiarly external evidence of a self that may in other ways be private or inscrutable".[14] Furthermore, book collections are a reminder of the radical arbitrariness of the self. They suggest how "chance and chaos exist in baffling proximity … Book collection is an appearance of order; it is the ardent, precarious pretence of stability."[15] For Cass, hoping to catch something of her new lover's inner life, the books on the shelves in his neat apartment are a way to discern this complexity, which she presumes must exist because Marco loves to read.

Cass' belief in books as a sign of the authentic self and the credulity of the speak-memories that laced together the characters in narrative companionship are rendered radically uncertain following Victor's death and the worth of literature itself is called into question: "The most earnest and open story still meant nothing assured" (254). In her shock and mourning, reading and writing, which Cass had upheld as vital and necessary, now appear to her as "stupid and cynical" (256). Even as the last image of the novel is of Cass diminished and "simply sliding away" (260), the capacity of literature and interpretation to shape differently how the

---

10 Gail Jones, "On a Library of Memories", *The Weekend Australian*, 23 February 2008, 2.
11 Walter Benjamin, "Unpacking My Library: A Talk about Book Collecting", *Illuminations*, trans. Harry Zorn, ed. Hannah Arendt (1968; London: Pimlico, 1999), 61.
12 Benjamin, "Unpacking", 61.
13 Benjamin, "Unpacking", 61.
14 Jones, "On a Library", 2.
15 Jones, "On a Library", 2.

world is apprehended is nevertheless insisted on. While telling of her diminishment, the narrative voice pauses to relate '[t]he S-station names: Storkower Strasse and Frankfurter Allee. Ostkreuz, Treptower Park, Sonnenallee. So like a poem" (260). Strung together like this, the station names are aesthetically transformed. The novel therefore ends in some doubt about whether or not Cass is correct in her claim that "there was no trustworthy knowledge" and that what she had learnt from the Nabokov-inspired speak-memories is "the failure of any tale" (254). Cass is despondent about the capacity of books and reading to convey signs of value, but the narrative voice is more cautiously optimistic about the possibilities of written art.

As *A Guide to Berlin* makes clear, Jones' novels stage reading in complex ways, and certainly as something other than a functional skill. The response Lucy Strange has in Sixty Lights to her discovery during her passage to India of the library filled with novels by Charles Dickens, George Eliot and William Thackeray is additionally instructive in acknowledging that reading is seriously contemplated in Jones' writing. Lucy, it must be said, is in an especially heightened state when she reflects on reading. She is a young woman alone in the decidedly anomalous non-place of a ship at sea; adventure into the unknown lies just ahead; and she is experiencing sexual pleasure for the first time with Captain William Crowley. She is, however, also "tilting into a kind of translucency" and "feeling desolate" because she knows her lover "could not quite see her" (115). It is in this context, and with the discovery of the books, that Lucy is prompted to reflect rhapsodically on the fundamental nature of reading:

> She thought for the first time about what it meant to read a novel. What process was this? What self-complication? Reading was this metaphysical meeting space – peculiar, specific, ardent, unusual ... There were sight-lines, image tokens, between people and people, between people and objects and words on a page, that knitted the whole world in the purest geometry of connections. (114)

Lucy's contemplation of reading is not only philosophical; it also connects her imaginatively with her mother, Honoria, who is said to consider reading a figurative transportation: "the compartment Honoria inhabited was not this wood-panelled and glass-paned one, rattling along the road, but her own quiet space, with its own duration and propulsion. She travelled *Jane Eyre*. She was sped on by its melancholy and motivating desire" (12).[16] Whereas her sexual union

---

16 Honoria thinks of reading in similar terms to Jones' Eleanor Marx who, in the process of translating *Madame Bovary* in the short story "Eleanor Reads Emma", deems Flaubert's novel to be "ineluctably her self. *I am Emma Bovary*". It must be said, though, that the short story does also offer a salutary warning about over-identification; it is thought "impossible to contemplate the suicide by poison of Eleanor Marx without supposing that, in her extremity and her unalleviated misery, she may have recalled the suicide by poison of Emma Bovary". Before this unhappy end, however, Eleanor, like Honoria, also conceives of reading as a kind of travel, asking, "What is it, to read?" and answering with the suggestion, "They are paper wings you fly

with Crowley is fleeting, if euphoric, it is reading that Lucy sees as truly binding her to (unknown) others, in shared knowledge: "knowing, was the gift story gave her. She learnt how other people entered the adventure of being alive" (114). By Lucy's reckoning, reading involves the creation of community and an imaginative embracing of otherness, although *Sixty Lights* admits the possibility that reading might also create divisions.

This idea is made apparent when, not long married, Honoria measures her life against the great expectations her romance reading has inspired and finds wanting both her circumstances and her husband (rather than the novels themselves):

> What Honoria could not tell Arthur was that the world, since Italy, had been terribly disappointing ... books led her to believe that adventure was everywhere to be had, that catastrophes, coincidences and conjugal excitations abounded, that lives were melodramatically enhanced and symbolically under-written. After their metaphoric beginning – this man sliding on his belly into her carriage, the whole coach stalled to allow the generation of romance – their lives had become rather literal and prosaic. (61)

Honoria only has access to reading because, as a child, she waywardly trespassed one day into an ice cave, and another social class. The cave was located on the estate of Lady Rosamund Leonowens, and as "punishment" for the infringement committed – this is how Lucy likes to imagine her mother's coming-to-reading – Lady Leonowens sets about educating the young girl (31). She does so with such success that "within a year, with flair and precocity, she [Honoria] was reading to the old woman" (31). It is a shared love of reading that later draws an older Honoria into an intimate friendship with the English traveller, Miss Harriet White, while she and Arthur are on their honeymoon in Florence. And this arrangement sees Arthur become expressly "aware of a kind of exclusion" (33), and he unwillingly views himself as a competitor with Miss White for his wife's attention and affection.

If the promises of Honoria's reading leave her largely disappointed with the everyday realm she moves through as a married woman, for Lucy, the daughter of Arthur and Honoria, reading (and then photography) marks her out as largely separate and singular. She alone understands her need to take employment at an albumen factory in literary terms, evoking Dickens' writing to note that "her own situation was a kind of reversal" of the good fortunes that befall Pip in *Great Expectations* (102). This bookish disposition also means, however, that she is figured as quite unlike the women with whom she works but whom she longs to befriend: "The women at the factory knew that she could read and write ... and

---

on. They are spaces of mysterious black on white rarefaction. You travel through air to the last page ... You are carried along, a kind of symbol, a useless kind of symbol ... to some destination that is both precious and a total nothingness ... Think of it: how strange! What a peculiar absorption." Gail Jones, "Eleanor Reads Emma", *Fetish Lives* (Fremantle: Fremantle Arts Centre Press, 1997), 45, 55, 44.

was lodged for some reason in the wrong class and work" (102). And while Lucy continues to lean on literary points of reference during the narrative to understand the world and the places she and others occupy within it, her presumption that these are shared sites of knowledge is proven incorrect, at moments awkwardly so. When pressing her sister-in-law, Violet, for childhood stories and images arising from the time she spent in "the Grosvenor Foundling Home" (180), for example, Lucy's response to Violet's recollection of the sudden and unexpected appearance of seven crosses in one day in the nearby graveyard is to compare the memory to a scene in *Jane Eyre*: "Like Lowood School? Like the school in *Jane Eyre*?" (181). Violet confesses that "she had never read the novel *Jane Eyre*" and quickly apologises for what she feels are "the scant, ordinary quality of her images" that do not come close to meeting what she perceives as Lucy's aesthetic expectations, "some airy beam of light resting on a single cross, its shadow, its promise, its everlasting etc." (181). The narrative suggests that Violet's memory of the graveyard is nothing for which she ought to apologise as she regrets later that for Lucy "she could manufacture nothing beyond churned earth and the certainty of seven lost souls" (181). This sibilance on which the scene ends stresses just how upsetting Violet's memory is, and alludes to the possibility that the capacity for communicating deep feeling and traumatic experience is not limited to literary sources alone. Yet, to the extent that this insight rests on such a poetic device, the narrative and the literary intelligence it attributes to Lucy converge.

While *Sixty Lights* allows these complexities of reading, *Five Bells* also acknowledges different contexts in which reading, and meanings afforded it, are shaped. At one moment in that novel, Ellie fondly recalls her father reading in his electrical goods store:

> Sometimes out of boredom, or because they had little to say to each other, he would tell her the plot of the novel he was reading. There were inevitably hidden codes, or spies, or nefarious subterfuge, there were wild life encounters, there were beautiful but evil women, limply inviting, there were dashing heroes with whom they eventually entwined. Ellie loved these charming and slightly absurd meetings with her father.[17]

With their Cold War espionage, colonial nostalgia for undomesticated places and *femmes fatales*, the books Ellie's father reads are most likely not those read by Lucy in *Sixty Lights*.[18] What the scenarios of reading share across the two novels, though,

---

17 Gail Jones, *Five Bells* (London: Harvill Secker, 2011), 132–3. All subsequent references are to this edition and appear in parentheses in the text.
18 One wonders with interest at what adventure about being alive they might impart. Along these lines, Jones has written in her essay "A Dreaming, A Sauntering: Re-imagining Critical Paradigms" that: "In phenomenological terms both reading and writing operate in this way. We engage in spooky projections, we read and write across thresholds of actuality, even plausibility; we detach and attach with spirited mobility, gratuitous and energetic." The books Ellie's father

is the conviction that they are connective. The notion that acts of reading might be means towards understanding and reconciliation underpins Pei Xing's decision in *Five Bells* to read aloud each week to a woman, now named Dong Hua, who was once her prison guard in Shanghai during the Cultural Revolution. The unexpected encounter with the woman in Sydney has Pei Xing viscerally recall her trauma – "she felt a surge of nausea. The tapeworm in the gut. The body remembered its beatings" (117) – and voicing the wish never again to see Hua. The woman persists, however, and after telling Pei Xing of her reasons for her loyalty to the Red Guards, she apologises and asks Pei Xing for her forgiveness. Pei Xing is at first cynical and dismissive, but she then realises what Hua's saying of sorry admits: "But this woman, she thought more generously, was asking forgiveness, had surrendered herself to another story in which she was the villain. She had no reason to ask forgiveness if she believed she acted without choice" (120). Hua enacts an empathic ethics in terms that Pei Xing recognises. Hua has admitted herself into the story of another wherein she is confronted with the difficult knowledge of her culpability.

With no epiphanic moment announcing her decision but rather an everyday act of watching a young boy skateboarding in patterns, Pei Xing decides to forgive Hua. This forgiveness is couched in her repeated and dedicated reading to the woman, who is now paralysed by a stroke and living in a nursing home. Reading is both a metaphor for life – "Their reading was moving towards the inevitable conclusion" – and a sign of reconciliation: "On the table before them lay the novel they had shared … And they had been visited again by a kind of provisional peace" (122). That *Doctor Zhivago* (1957) is the novel Pei Xing remembers her father translating before his disappearance during the Cultural Revolution makes her reading of it to Hua, and what she declines to share with her former captor, all the more significant. Pei Xing does not read to Hua the last paragraph of Boris Pasternak's novel because she sees in it her family's own unresolved history: it "summoned the fate of her mother and her father; this was the proxy tone of unremarked death, the impersonal sweep of fate and the atrocities it acted … sometimes there was just this, a quiet disappearance" (197). As much as Pei Xing might conceive of reading as an ethical act, it also evokes for her private sorrows that she refuses to disclose.

Reading, beyond Pasternak's text, is nevertheless conceived of by Pei Xing as a sign and means of empathy and accord. Her grown son, Jimmy, argues with his mother about her weekly visits to Hua: "Why would a woman want to visit her former prison guard? Why reattach to that history? Why torment herself so?" (113). Jimmy gives little credence to his mother's explanation "that there were forms of forgiveness that make life go on, and forms of reproach that hold history still" (113). Pei Xing momentarily admits that her son's disbelief might be attributable to his

---

reads would seem very much to cross thresholds of actuality. Gail Jones, "A Dreaming, A Sauntering: Re-imagining Critical Paradigms", *JASAL: Journal of the Association for the Study of Australian Literature* 5 (2006): 18.

second-generation migrant identity, "happy young men and women, many of them students or like Jimmy, children of migrants who left China in the 1980s" (114). But she singles out his lack of reading as the reason underpinning what she sees as his misunderstanding:

> [T]here were things her son would never understand because he was not a reader. Reading had taught her that actors in history must find a logic beyond violence. When Jimmy was smaller they had watched action movies together; it was the one activity he had allowed her to join. Now she wondered if, seeking his company, she had also encouraged his ignorance. (114)

For Pei Xing, reading involves ethical learning and imaginative solidarity that eschew, and indeed reject, the forms of violence she has experienced: "how Comrade Peng had borrowed a pair of boots to kick her senseless on Mao Zedong's birthday. She remembered the blow to her face that had broken her nose and the sour taste of blood at the back of her throat" (118). Other forms of representation – the action movies Jimmy preferred as a child – are thought of as more ethically dubious and Pei Xing seems to suspect that they might even promote the witlessness she detects in her adult son.

This passing idea that childhood reading (or lack thereof) is formative is rehearsed in Jones' short story "Skiascopy (or, The Science of Romance)" in *Fetish Lives*. The story tells of a skiagrapher whose lover has left her, and left behind stories: "It is a peculiar aspect of her suffering that she seems to recall, and in detail, every single delicate instance of their mutual self-narrating."[19] One particular exchange, which occupies a significant part of the narrative and presumably the woman's memory, involves the two lovers in bed and exchanging accounts of the books "which were important in their childhoods" (62). For the lover, *The Book of Saints and Heroes* for years "bore terrible implications"; for the skiagrapher, living on a remote cattle station, a book that "told the story of Marie Curie" (65, 66) affords her not only an inspiration, perhaps, for her later profession but also the metaphors for her depression and loss – "This negative of touch" – and the aesthetics of her science of disease: "These skiagraphs ... are vulgar evidences of the loveliest things" (69). The memory of sharing stories about books read in childhood outlasts the relationship.

Such determined yoking of reading and childhood that "Skiascopy (or, The Science of Romance)" entertains, and the notion that reading might be a means by which people meaningfully connect, is something that Alice Black intuits as a child in *Dreams of Speaking*. Confined to a hospital ward having contracted scarlet fever, Alice finds companionship with another interned patient, James, as they read

---

19 Gail Jones, "Skiascopy (or, The Science of Romance)", *Fetish Lives* (Fremantle: Fremantle Arts Centre Press, 1997), 62. All subsequent references are to this edition and appear in parentheses in the text.

to each other in a shared bed from their "wondrous books" about fairytales and technology.[20] Their innocent act, however, is misinterpreted by a nurse – clearly, she is a poor reader of the situation – who violently wrenches them apart.

It is a proposal additionally raised in *Sorry* by Mary, the young Walmajarri woman who is also forced into separation, albeit in a very different way and context. At the hands of a racist government, she is removed from her mother and placed in an orphanage "[t]o learn to be a whitefella" (55–6), and then raped by the anthropologist father of the white girl, Perdita Keene, whom she looks on as a sister. Having learnt to read at the Christian-run institution as a child, Mary explains her hypothesis on reading to Perdita (who remembers and retells it when she is older and, fittingly, a librarian):

> Mary had a theory that when people read the same words they were imperceptibly knitted; that there were touchings not of the skin, and apparitional convergences. Some kind of spirit inhered in words that one might enter and engage with; there were transactions, comminglings, adjacencies of mind and of sense ... Mary extended to written words the forms of community she [Perdita] longed to express, just as, in their generosity, the creek people [Mandjabari] had bestowed on Perdita a relationship of skin. By this reasoning, too, David Copperfield was part of her and Captain Cook was part of Mary; and even in the world-weariness that reading sometimes induces, they absorbed irresistibly, naïvely, elements of the lives they imagined. A kind of family without limits. Occult relations. (73)

Perdita puzzles over this thesis as a young girl as she wonders if writing and reading might form a private communion or pact between authors and readers such that "[s]ince the first reader is the author, might there be a channel, somehow, between author and reader ... There are always moments, reading a novel, in which one recognises oneself ... might there be in this covert world, yet another zone of connection?" (145).[21] It is only when Perdita learns of Mary's passing that she understands the truth of her friend's proposition about reading.

The circulation of a book through the text, and through the hands of Perdita and Mary, affords this knowledge. Along with a letter matter-of-factly announcing Mary's death, Perdita comes into ownership of a book of saints that has passed throughout the narrative between herself and Mary, who first had the book because grieving parents had donated their dead daughter's possessions to the Aboriginal orphanage. The book then miraculously finds its way to Perdita, who is travelling

---

20 Gail Jones, *Dreams of Speaking* (Milsons Point, NSW: Vintage, 2006), 43. All subsequent references are to this edition and appear in parentheses in the text.
21 It is a notion Alice Black also comes to in *Dreams of Speaking* as she thinks, "There are texts ... even one's own, full of surprising and unexpected personifications. Texts that summon known faces to fit unknown stories. Novels that split open to reveal one's family. Tales that appear exotic, but drive one home. Recognitions. Returns. Ineluctable associations" (202). Alice has these thoughts while waiting in anticipation of the death of her friend, Mr Sakamoto.

with her mother as part of their wartime evacuation to Perth from Broome. They stop at the convent from which Mary had been expelled. It was here that Mary had first come into temporary possession of the saints book. On encountering the physical book she had been told of, Perdita, "[w]ith the manic enthusiasm that most child-readers display … opened the book at random, believing she could discover secrets by the mere focus of her mind" (122). As it happens, she does; the saint whose life she reads about uncannily recalls her aunt's name and unexpectedly provides Perdita with a consolatory narrative for Mary: "Her suffering was to be imprisoned, but she would also burst forth" (123). Perdita at that moment also determines to return the book to Mary, and "the reading, as Mary claimed, would knit them together. There would be a surrender to something as close as a kiss. There would be imperceptible continuities and inspiring revelations" (123). Perdita fulfils this desire, only to have the book unexpectedly returned to her when Mary dies in detention. As Perdita begins to read, "peering at what Mary had read", she comes suddenly to the knowledge not only of the truth of Mary's claim about reading – "The weight of what lay, interleaved, in any lives" – but also of her own answerability at not having said sorry to Mary for her false imprisonment (211). Perdita's sudden realisation that she has acted unethically confirms Mary's theory that books and reading forge meaningful connections.

Along with this concern with thinking about why reading might matter, Jones' texts also consider the pleasures and perils of writing. In the short story "Dark Times" in *The House of Breathing*, writing is rendered an unexpectedly dangerous act. An unnamed writer-narrator finds himself in prison. At first, he thinks he has been incarcerated for his work to expose local political corruption. Later, he is told that the reason, or ruse, for his capture is his "sexual deviance".[22] Evidence for this claim is a volume of love poetry he had written some twenty years earlier for an indifferent male lover. In retrospect, he sees himself as having internalised imperial values that his education had fostered. He had been "playing colonial-acting-English" (60) while studying English history abroad at the University of Cambridge with the desperate aim of becoming "an Englishman … specifically Percy Bysshe Shelley" (64). Before the disbelieving prisoner, the military captor orates from memory some lines from the poem, inexplicably translated into district dialect. While being led towards his torture, the unnamed narrator tries to recall the rest of the poem, only to have words fail him: "words which shift and change with no order or reference, which are anarchic and inconsequential" (67). The narrative halts before the anticipated torture, suggesting an inadequacy of words to approximate bodily agony.

In a different context, but with a shared concern about how writing might come to be yoked with violence, *Five Bells* has Catherine Healey, a journalist, travel to Australia having left Dublin to pursue her career following the murder of Veronica

---

22 Gail Jones, "Dark Times", *The House of Breathing* (Fremantle: Fremantle Arts Centre Press, 1992), 65. All subsequent references are to this edition and appear in parentheses in the text.

Guerin, an investigative reporter. As Guerin's death attests, and as *Five Bells* seems to be underscoring with its extratextual reference to this journalist and Catherine's concerns about her own safety as a reporter, being a writer in certain contexts can involve tremendous risks:

> It seemed that everyone in Dublin in '96 has an urban tale about Guerin. Someone had known her at school; someone else knew gossip or scandal. She was a saint or a complete bitch, or a fucking brilliant journo. Her image was everywhere. Her name was in the papers. But Catherine had never met or seen her, other than on television, and knew only in a remote way that there might be brave acts of writing, and that this murder on Naas Road, this silencing of one writer, would punctuate and determine the course of her life. (125)

In *Dreams of Speaking*, Alice Black is confronted by the violence of modern nation states and modern science told of by witness testimonials at the Atomic Bomb Museum in Nagasaki, where she travels to visit her elderly friend, Mr Sakamoto.[23] In Paris where the pair first met, Alice had been researching and writing her book on modernity, a project concerned not with the violence of modernity at all but rather its aesthetics.[24] Yet, her scholarly topic brings forth feelings about her chosen form that are worth noting because of their ambivalence. At one point, she enters a bookshop with plans to buy a novel that is "fashionable and new" (79) but ends up leaving with a copy of Henry James' *The Portrait of a Lady* (1881) because she finds herself overwhelmed by the status of contemporary books as flashy commodities "with expressionistic covers and virtuosic claims" (80). Later, however, when she is in a smoky internet café and is faced by the "galaxies of information" that

---

23 Mr Sakamoto is also a committed reader, and credits reading a life-saving capacity. He declares to Alice that "reading had saved his life. Not mathematics. Not money. Not travel. Reading. At a time, he said, when he felt blasted by images, words had anchored him, secured him, stopped his free-falling plunge into nowhere" (132). Tellingly, his first love was for a woman he met reading "a battered second-hand edition of Homer" in an Edinburgh bookshop (69).

24 Robert Dixon helpfully parses this idea of a poetics of modernity in his article "Ghosts in the Machine: modernity and the unmodern in Gail Jones' *Dreams of Speaking*", *JASAL: Journal of the Association for the Study of Australian Literature* 8 (2008): 121–37. This concern with the aesthetics of modernity is shared by the young girl in Jones' short story "Modernity" who intuitively detects something transcendental in the light of the first film she sees and whose projected images otherwise terrify her. Gail Jones, "Modernity", *The House of Breathing* (Fremantle: Fremantle Arts Centre Press, 1992), 11–19. Alice too is seeking aesthetics and value in the overlooked things of everyday modernity. Perdita Keene in *Sorry* sorrowfully recognises that her own experience of the everyday is specific, and relatively privileged (for all the hardship and violence it involves), when she comes to the realisation, "with startling clarity, like a punch in the ribs, one of the terrible, unassimilable anomalies of the world: … that there are people dying and – *at the same time* – there are people playing cards, sipping, as they do, from cups of sweetened tea" (82). Catherine in *Five Bells* also implicitly carries this knowledge as she "drank a glass of soy latte and picked at a flaking croissant" (49), and glimpsed the frontpage headline of a nearby newspaper that announced: "Another bombing somewhere. This much she knew, that there were always bombings" (50).

modern technologies provide (136), Alice promises herself that she will next visit a bookshop; the idea sets in train a lengthy meditation on books and her passionate feelings towards them:

> She loved the feel of books, their integrity as objects … Random flicking of pages, inscriptions, dog-ears. She loved – though it was a sin – to see books left open upside down, their bird shape accentuated in the keeping of a page … She loved second-hand bookshops for their presumption that any tatty volume mattered, and new bookshops, for their signs and neat rows of books, waiting to be opened for the very first time. Inherited books. Books as gifts. Books as objects flung across the room in a lover's argument. Books (this most of all) taken into the warm sexual space of the bed, held upon the lap, entered like another body, companionable, close, interconnecting with innermost things. Those bed books that chart the route between waking and sleeping, that are a venture of almost hypnogogic power. Those enticements. Adventures. Corridors of words. Capsules. Secrets. (136–7).

Perhaps to demonstrate to herself her (desired) difference from those others in the café who are plugging words into search engines, gambling and watching pornography, Alice understands at this moment her love of books as both a very unmodern preoccupation and a contradiction, given that she is researching and writing about modernity. If there is any irony in this scenario of bibliophilia, it possibly lies more with the fact that Alice is not often seen in the narrative as progressing her own book project, beyond returning one evening to her apartment "weighted with her papers and ideas" (104) and acknowledging that after their long conversations, she and Mr Sakamoto would part, "each to their own projects, each back to the silent production of words" (132). On her return to Perth (the time and place at which the narrative commences), Alice is nevertheless confronted by a near-complete manuscript written in "feverish excitement, contracted into purpose, engaged, absorbing the whole world" but which "now it seemed to her like so much litter" (6) because the friend with whom she had shared ideas about modernity has died.

If Alice's processes of writing her book are placed in the background of the narrative, then the stories and notes Mr Sakamoto gathers for his book are very much in the foreground as they constitute some of the narrative. Mr Sakamoto himself is researching and writing a book on the life of Alexander Graham Bell and he tracks "with biographical monomania all the flaunted public events and hidden private emotions", but determines his project, which he completes in manuscript form, to be "folly" (93). It is an assessment shared by Alice, who early on in the project fears her work "folly" (39). And in her grief at Mr Sakamoto's passing, she is ambivalent about her writerly endeavours: "The stacked pages of the manuscript glowed faintly in the dawn. She must send them, or dispose of them" (6). The fate of the manuscript is left unsaid and Alice's mourning casts all of the books she owns and has read in a negative light: "The spines of the books were a kind of reproach – a life lived too inwardly, too much alone, too given over to perplexity and complication" (5–6). Books can be a form of censure, as well as consolation.

Dreams of Speaking concludes with Alice quietly beginning to tell her sister, Norah, about Mr Sakamoto following his death. Or rather, what *Dreams of Speaking* turns on is the story Alice has deferred telling her sister from the first pages of the novel. "Another time … I'll tell you another time" (17), she replies to Norah's initial prompting: "So when are you going to tell me about Mr Sakamoto?" (16). A version of Norah's question also appears as the novel's penultimate sentence, and in terms of the story's chronology, these two similar questions are posed not long after each other. But in terms of the story's structure, Norah's questions bookend the narrative, with Alice beginning to tell her sister about her friend concluding the novel. It is as though speaking this story, which has already been told, might give respectful form to both Alice's grief and the memory of Mr Sakamoto. Alice declines to respond to her sister's first request because she is concerned that a telling-too-soon will disrespectfully encrypt her friend in the wrong words: "there was a kind of block to her feelings … and a superstition, perhaps, that she should not recover this man too soon by formulations of words. Against the waste of death, no language availed … She must wait. She must know. She must know exactly what to say" (17). As an author and as a friend, Alice is especially cautious about the capacity of words to curtail the complexity of the life she seeks to honour, and to approximate her own extra-linguistic feelings. What is offered up in response is the narrative in which these doubts about words are entertained.

This concern with attesting to a life lived is one that also preoccupies Anna Griffin in *Black Mirror* in an extended way. As a biographer, she is represented throughout that novel as grappling with how to write the life of her dying subject, a concern the novel's prologues introduce. There are two short passages that serve as preludes to *Black Mirror*. The first relates the aesthetic apprehension of Anna Griffin in an inclement London street: "And later, when Victoria is dead, she [Anna] will remember how on this day of their very first meeting she was so distracted she became soaked before she recalled her umbrella."[25] The second focuses on the once-celebrated avant-garde artist and from her window Victoria is simultaneously watching a woman, Anna, moving through the downpour towards her front door and thinking "*I am waiting for this visitor so that I can tell my story and die*" (3). The opening passages of *Black Mirror* therefore intimately link in images the women who are presently strangers to each other, and anticipate the unlikely intersections of their childhood memories of a Western Australian gold-mining town, which the narrative relates as it unfolds non-linearly. Furthermore, in their shared interest to represent the same moment from different positions, these sections of the text resemble both the malleable and multiple visions of the world that film makes

---

25 Gail Jones, *Black Mirror* (Sydney: Picador, 2002), 1. All subsequent references are to this edition and appear in parentheses in the text.

possible and the ambitions of the early twentieth-century avant-garde, two modern art forms on which the book repeatedly reflects.

What is especially striking about these incipient passages of a novel that is conspicuously, and in many ways painfully, marked by multiple forms of loss, trauma and grief – mothers are lost and mourned; the absence of loved ones is achingly palpable; the traumas of colonialism bring about a dissociation of affect and representation – is their thanatic preoccupations. In the first passage, which contorts time tellingly, Anna's future memory of her confused, damp state on that wet day centres on Victoria's death as both past and imminent. In the second section, death, or rather, the thought of an impending, inescapable and utterly individual death, surfaces almost involuntarily and is bound with both the advent of this visitor and story-telling itself.

The novel is concerned with proleptic mourning;[26] what the philosopher Jacques Derrida proposes as the law of friendship. Writing in the long shadow cast by Sigmund Freud's thinking on mourning and melancholia,[27] Derrida posits prescient grieving as predating specific friendships and bringing unique subjects into relations of affect and address; it is something half-articulated and already at work before particular friendships are formed and unique losses are inevitably suffered. He writes, somewhat pessimistically it must be said, that "the anticipation of death comes so indisputably to hollow out the living present that precedes it".[28] (Jones has also rightly recognised that the gothic tropes attendant to Derrida's thinking on mourning have been energetically taken up to a degree that runs the risk of eliding the specificities of "historical circumstances that warrant its clear expression as a preliminary to justice".)[29] *Black Mirror* pauses before this law and the hollowing out it seems to involve to enquire into how to testify to the integrity of a

---

26 In recent philosophical theory, there is a seeming impasse in thinking on mourning. One position stresses the ongoing responsibilities of the surviving friend to the unique friend lost in its efforts to reframe mourning in ethical terms. It turns on "an aporetic work of mourning that succeeds when it fails, which is to say that is cannot be resolved". Alessia Ricciardi, *The Ends of Mourning: Psychoanalysis, Literature, Film* (Stanford: Stanford University Press, 2003), 12. Another emphasises the imperative of psychological and emotional health for the surviving friend that a refusal to mourn purportedly threatens. *Black Mirror* signals a negotiation of these two positions as it works to reject >mourning's potential reduction of otherness to sameness while also attentive to those who suffer loss.

27 Sigmund Freud, "Mourning and Melancholia", *The Standard Edition of the Complete Psychological Works of Sigmund Freud*, vol. 14, trans. James Strachey (1917; London: Hogarth Press, 1953), 243–58; Sigmund Freud, "The Ego and the Id", *The Standard Edition of the Complete Psychological Works of Sigmund Freud*, vol. 19, trans. James Strachey (1923; London: Hogarth Press, 1961), 12–66.

28 Jacques Derrida, *The Work of Mourning*, eds. Pascale-Anne Brault and Michael Naas (Chicago: University of Chicago Press, 2001), 151.

29 Gail Jones, "Sorry-in-the-Sky: empathetic unsettlement, mourning and the Stolen Generations", in *Imagining Australia: Literature and Culture in the New, New World*, eds. Judith Ryan and Chris Wallace-Crabbe (Cambridge, MA: Harvard University Press, 2004), 161, 160. Derrida's turn to gothic tropes is clearly apparent in *Spectres of Marx The State of the Debt, The Work of Mourning and the New International*, trans. Peggy Kamuf (London: Routledge, 1994).

proximate life lived, and how one might live with loss. The novel is certainly attentive to loss and the ongoing responsibilities that the surviving friend might have to the unique friend lost. Yet, it also offers the possibility of redemption, of affirmation in the face of loss. In *Black Mirror*, proleptic mourning insists on Victoria's presence, on her singular alterity, at the same time that preparations are made for this friend to be vital within both Anna's living self and the novelistic biography Anna has been called on to write, which the novel itself comes to approximate.

It is for this reason that *Black Mirror* is committed to testing the conventions of biography. *Black Mirror* makes clear that writing a life is an ethical enquiry by means of two overlapping preoccupations.[30] The first resonates with enquiries into how one should live, which has also motivated much recent, and not-so-recent, engagement with the ethical in philosophical scholarship, including the work of Martha Nussbaum.[31] The second turns on the role literature has in responding to that question, with the working through of the ethics that *Black Mirror* enacts being both thematic – it features a writer grappling with such concerns – and formal in the sense that the narrative in which this effort is told loops around moments, memories and dreams so the effect is impressionistic rather than conclusive. Further, the novel is open to considering not only how one should live, but also how one ought to live (and write) in anticipation both of one's own death and the death of the other. It asks: how should one testify to the integrity of another life lived? Is the act of narrating an other's life a violation of that responsibility? Or, can it be an ethical testimony to being in the world?

Most obviously, the cogitations these enquiries encourage are of immediate interest to Anna, Victoria's biographer. And it is fair to say that biography, a genre that can impose a narrative form on an otherwise chaotic, fragmented and excessive life, is treated with some suspicion in *Black Mirror*. Early in the text, biography is referred to as a "meanly simplifying genre" (16), and later, when Anna is at work on her project, the demands the genre makes prove difficult to meet:

> There is a stringency to writing biography that Anna seems unable to observe. She had imagined a process of solidification, like the building of an identifiable face out of clay: the slow, careful achievement of feature and definition. But the more Anna knew of her subject the more imprecise she began to seem … She assembled her notes and transcriptions in a chain before her, and saw not the neat confirmation of a life, but its meagre supplement. Not attestation, but its barest trace. (155)

In response to this situation and "striving against the treason of images that Victoria has presented her with", Anna is said to "try to meet Victoria Morrell once again.

---

30 For texts that address in detail the ethics of life-writing, see Paul John Eakin, ed., *The Ethics of Life-Writing* (Ithaca: Cornell University Press, 2004) and James Onley, *Memory and Narrative: the weave of life-writing* (Chicago: University of Chicago Press, 1998).
31 Martha C. Nussbaum, *Love's Knowledge: Essays on Philosophy and Literature* (New York: Oxford University Press, 1990), 36.

Novelistically" (156). The novel, however, does not disregard biography in its entirety in favour of fiction or insist on discrete distinctions between these representational forms. Instead, it extracts from biography the question *par excellence* that motors this genre: who are you? And it responds to a rhetorical question asked in *Sixty Lights*: "Might there be a plot within biographies arranged entirely by affections?" (195). What the novel does with these questions is expose them to a critical opening in an effort to honour the subject addressed in this inventive form. The text lets the questions remain extended ones, without expectation of a final, definitive answer. In other words, the novel raises issues that resonate well beyond the boundaries of biography and speak to wider deliberations on ethics in which writing and reading might be cast as playing a pivotal part.

At a most private and vulnerable moment in the novel, which also entails an express element of tender voyeurism, Jones writes:

> Within just a month, Victoria has weakened. It is as if giving up her own stories depletes her of something vital. Yet she is an avid narrator, and looks forward to Anna's coming as though her life depended on it; this contradiction is somehow at the basis of their relationship. How it is possible, Anna asks herself, that Victoria wills her own fading, just as she comes so amply into being?
>
> Sometimes she watches the old woman sleeping and sees the delicate blue flicker of the process of her dreams. She persuades herself that biography is futile. Beneath closed eyes lies this woman's *inaccessible* complexity. (108)

The novel offers what might be termed ethical hesitancy at the very moment that Anna's reading/watching and writing of this dying woman recognises Victoria's alterity. Here, narrative gives life at the same time that it is posited as a menace, a threat to life. It is the impending loss of life, however, which requires both a witness to this immoderate activity of story-telling and narrating itself that, most crucially, is recognised as partial and incomplete, and indeed remote. Anna, the receiver of Victoria's stories (or perhaps the producer of them in the otobiographical sense that without her as listener, as witness, the accounts would not be told), suspends any demand for complete coherence of self and story that biography might claim with its arresting desires.[32] Creative attendance, in its interrogative mode, obviates such appropriative aspirations and points to an ethical encounter that asserts Victoria's unique presence, an insistence that appears, paradoxically, all the more pressing and impossible in the face of the older woman's imminent death.

The written narrative with which Anna is charged has been commissioned in the knowledge that Victoria is dying. In addition to the intricate ethical dilemmas that are set in motion by the social contract into which Anna as the would-be biographer is called, Victoria's proximate death also raises questions of how to

---

32 See Jacques Derrida, *The Ear of the Other: Otobiography, Transference, Translation*, trans. Peggy Kamuf, ed. Christie McDonald (Lincoln: University of Nebraska Press, 1985).

mourn. These are not separate issues. Like biography, mourning runs the risk of ventriloquising or internalising the other, of speaking on their behalf, of reducing the alterity of the subject to the same, to the self. And in the more specific context of *Black Mirror*, Victoria's impending death is linked inextricably to her petition for her life to be recorded and narrated by Anna. The detail to stress, though, is that her death is anticipated and, as such, it points to a wider concern of the novel that is obliquely referenced in its opening sections, namely that prescient grieving – proleptic mourning – might lie at the (ethical) heart of friendships.

Friendships, of course, are many things to many people – voluntary allegiances, means of social support and respect, relations of intimacy (and hence all too vulnerable to betrayals and exposures) – and it would be incautious to reduce such composite and involved social relations to any one condition.[33] Nevertheless, the various friendships and relationships represented in *Black Mirror* are relentlessly marked by the spectres of loss.

Not only is Victoria dying, with Anna as the immediate witness and mourner, but Victoria herself is haunted by her lover, Jules, to whom she was unfaithful and whom she suspects was murdered during the Holocaust: "When she was alone, Victoria thought often of Jules; over the span of absence his phantom arm still lay warmly across her breast, cupping her heart. Sometimes she resented this everyday haunting he had bequeathed her. The stories he left behind – an entreating outline – with no body to attach them to" (112). As a child, Anna recites personal prayers to protect her father from an always anticipated death in the depths of the dark mines in which he labours – "*Gentle Jesus kind and wise, Let my father be alive*" – and Griffo himself, her father, is imagined in life to have "the dismal appearance of a corpse" (126). This is a quality shared by Victoria's mother, Rose, who looks lifeless in "the only known photograph of Victoria's whole family" (166). It is an attentiveness that her own lover, William (the chauffeur who is also Victoria's father), carries on his grieving body when he learns of her death: "he became thin and spectre-like; his skin was blue and pallid" (220). Lily-white, the Aboriginal woman who Victoria's mother employs as a servant and who becomes the "outline that Herbert Morrell, mine-owner, desired" (178), suffers sexually and violently at the hands of both Herbert and his highly disagreeable son, Henry. Her trauma is unmistakable and Victoria feels her absence keenly: "Perhaps, after all, it was Lily-white I was missing. Am. Am missing," she tells Anna (227). Anna's own intimate relationship with Winston, her married lover from Jamaica who is studying the plays of Shakespeare for their representations of slaves, is also inscribed in a casual but nevertheless telling way by the knowledge of inevitable loss:

---

33 For some (very different) philosophical accounts of friendship, see Marilyn Friedman, *What are Friends For?: Feminist Perspectives on Personal Relationships and Moral Theory* (Ithaca: Cornell University Press, 1993); Maurice Blanchot, *Friendship*, trans. Elizabeth Rottenber (Stanford: Stanford University Press, 1997); Jacques Derrida, *Politics of Friendship*, trans. George Collins (London: Verso, 1997).

> Anna watches as he [Winston] fumbles with a box of matches.
> Let me, she offers. These things will kill you.
> In the long run, as Keynes says, we're all dead.
> Some consolation! (133)

Anna frequently engages with the everyday things – narratives, matches and cigarettes – that are imagined to harm the friends (Victoria and Winston respectively) for whom she develops an earnest, if at times tested, affection. And she finds little comfort in Winston's flippant reference to Keynes, which reduces everyone to the same in death and ostensibly serves as a solace of sorts. After all, just as Anna grapples with the ethical implications of imposing a genre on a life lived, the novel itself, characterised by shifts in narrative time, is distrustful of the elegiac mode, which conventionally works to resolve grief following the loss of a loved one by offering compensatory creativity.

The answers *Black Mirror* offers are presented in terms of an ethical unknowingness, of an ongoing negotiation with the interpretive challenge that the enigma of loss, of death, demands, and that addresses both the friend lost and the surviving friend. The trope of the black mirror that lends itself to the title of the text, to symbols in, and an instance of, Victoria's art productions, and to the name given to a series of stories that Victoria relates to Anna, suggests this hesitancy. Playfully but purposefully inserted into the narrative is a description of Victoria's black mirror painting that appears in an art exhibition catalogue:

> Black Mirror is in many ways typical of Surrealist pictorial art of the 30s and 40s, purporting to depict dream states as allegories of unconscious desire or meaning. This painting represents the treachery of art itself. … aeroplanes, giraffes, hourglasses and Eiffel Towers … are merely decorative, a random selection of images, suggesting Surrealist fascination with the principle of strange and meaningless conjunction. … The tone of Black Mirror is sombre, and it bears a clear indebtedness to the work of Salvador Dalí. (273–4)

This entry exemplifies the reductive nature of knowledge claiming to be authoritative and explanatory that the novel in which it appears is calling into question. Victoria's acerbic assessment of the artist Salvador Dalí, which occurs in the narrative just prior to the appearance of the catalogue (and counts this artist as another of Jones' characters who is familiar with Nabokov), clearly contests the interpretive claims that art history assumes to make on her behalf:

> Do you know what Nabokov said of Salvador Dalí? That he was Norman Rockwell's lost evil twin, wreaking vengeance on the world with bucket loads of shit. Or was it bucket loads of kitsch? I despised him, Salvador Dalí. That flabby world he inhabited. That moral deliquescence – (270)

The novel gives room to Victoria both to voice her experiences and intentions that she gathers as black mirror stories, and to exercise agency to withhold certain knowledges:

Victoria said:

I have several Black Mirror stories and I will give you three.
What are the Black Mirror stories, my Anna-lytical?
They are myself, unrecognisable. They are myself, writing disaster. I looked into a mirror and darkness looked back. (213)

With its insistence on opacity, the trope of the black mirror warns against any romanticised notion of reciprocal recognition, or indeed misrecognition, whereby one subject simply mirrors another. It also cautions against the assumption that one might be easily recognisable to one's self. As Victoria again recognises with her last breaths, the self is not easily or readily transparent: "*I looked into the mirror and darkness looked back*" (272). Further, the trope of the black mirror is linked with traumatic losses and memories that Anna is called upon to witness as biographer. These moments turn around the absent mother figures, Rose and Lily-white, and a long-lost sister, Ruby, a murdered lover, and a miscarried baby conceived by rape. Clearly, such losses and traumatic memories are not the "major historical events" that trauma theorist Dominick LaCapra privileges for "elucidating trauma and its aftereffects".[34] Rather, these are intimate experiences that are nevertheless resolutely specific and historical, and their ongoing impact is registered in Victoria's search for a sympathetic listener. Indeed, a sympathetic listener is what Victoria seeks rather than a biographer *per se*. It is with Anna that she reconstructs her life stories, however incomplete, and as she tells her stories, Anna too begins to relate partial accounts of herself, of memory, of shame, of possibility. In so doing, both women enter into what the novel proposes as ethical forms of understanding and responsibility.

Trauma theory suggests that for disturbing memory to be assimilable and "worked through" by the traumatised subject, communication must be achieved through an encounter with a sympathetic listener.[35] But as Jones herself has prudently warned in her non-fiction work, there is a need to be vigilant about "epistemological sublation" that "invests heavily in a pathological characterization and ... implies multiple victims to the point of misrecognition" when making reference to these claims which have gained popular currency "in ethics, theology, legal studies, pedagogy, and literary studies, to name but a few" in recent years.[36] The novel refuses to intimate that compassionate recognition is absolute in a way

---

34 Dominick LaCapra, *Writing History, Writing Trauma* (Baltimore: Johns Hopkins University Press, 2001), ix.
35 See Cathy Caruth, "Trauma and Experience: Introduction", in *Trauma: Explorations in Memory*, ed. Cathy Caruth (Baltimore: Johns Hopkins University Press, 1995), 3–12.
36 Jones, "Sorry-in-the-Sky", 161–2.

that might suggest that the listener reduces or assimilates the other, and their stories, to the self by having Victoria withhold from Anna her other black mirror stories. This gesture suggests that her life exceeds any account that she or Anna may give to it. Further, it signals a reflexive activity that is both a reconstruction of the self and a "rhetorical context for responsibility".[37] For Anna's part, in asking the question – who are you? – but by letting it remain open (rather than demanding a closed circuit), there is a recognition of both Victoria's trauma and alterity. What emerges is an acceptance of the limits of knowledge, which implicates the women ethically in each other's lives, and deaths, as the penultimate scene in the novel suggests.

Having returned home to the gold-mining town with Victoria's ashes, Anna re-encounters her father and experiences an inexact yet unmistakable feeling of loss:

> Grief was this strange folding in, Anna reflected, this recursion of something dark tucking under like a wave. Already Victoria's face was vanishing. Already silence was easier than words. Anna took her dark fold, this irrevocable reshaping, this crypt inside and walked past her father, out into the noisy night. (294)

It is significant that Anna is then immediately represented amongst the bones of the dead in the Parisian catacombs. She moves "through the ancient tunnels as though in another body, and not in a grave" (300). The spatial ideas of inside and outside that the metaphor of the crypt makes clear in both passages, and that mourning conventionally entails, are complicated here.[38] In this domain of the dead through which the living move (the inverse of prevailing understandings of mourning that imagine the living as a vault for the dead), the most important and pressing of ethical bonds is forwarded: a recognition of the reciprocal responsibilities of the living and the dead. With an obligation to let live the alterity of the lost friend, that friend is carried hesitantly, rather than cannibalistically, in the living friend as memory, while the dead, as an inspired body, envelop the living – a haunting, unsettling and persistent presence.

Further, it is this experience of grief, of mourning, that seems ultimately to reanimate rather than paralyse Anna as she "marches past waste and elimination and follows in the breezy wake of the young people ahead of her" (301). Mourning is by no means neatly resolved in *Black Mirror*; it is ongoing and aching, and the dead continue to issue ethical challenges to the living. This refusal to mourn, to overcome loss, which the novel takes seriously, is not an incapacitating melancholia, however; it is affirmative and redemptive, a hard-to-describe folding out (as well as folding in) that allows Anna to begin to see the world intensely and anew. With respect to her once spectre-like father, Anna notes: "Without his cloak

---

37 Judith Butler, "Giving an Account of Oneself", *Diacritics* 31 no. 4 (2001): 31.
38 The crypt is also a suggestive trope central to the mourning work theorised by Nicholas Abraham and Maria Torok, *The Wolf Man's Magic Word: A Cryptonomy*, trans. Nicholas Rand (Minneapolis: University of Minnesota Press, 1986).

of dirt ... my father is like Lazarus, returned from the grave" (283). At her loss of Winston, who returns inevitably to his family in Jamaica, Anna is now said to face "the night without imagining loss and deficiency" (292).

Affirmation and hope are made possible in the novel not by exorcising ghosts of the dead, of the lost, but by entertaining them, however unsettling, painful and confronting this may prove to be. And this approach to loss is particularly important in relation to the text's concern with ethical responses to the claims of the past. In its formal and thematic preoccupations with memory, the novel is highly responsive to Australia's colonial past in the contemporary present. Hence, it is significant that *Black Mirror* concludes, albeit inconclusively, with the image of the site at which Lily-white buried in quiet ceremony not a body – for this is not a grave—but rather the life-sustaining placenta "she gave birth to with her daughter, Ruby" (301). It is Ruby, Victoria's sister, to whom Anna gives the older woman's ashes on return to the gold-mining town. In turn, Ruby offers Anna, the wary biographer, a gift of narrative that both sets in motion other ghosts of the past that have been hitherto suppressed, and confirms the interwoven lives of Victoria, Anna and Ruby. And the imagining of this special site is one of redemption – a recovery of the land – in the face of "all the mine-work and despoliation that is everywhere around" (301). The scars of settler capitalism are perceptible on the land and the wounds its agents inflict are appallingly and traumatically apparent with the partial blinding of Lily-white by Henry Morrell: "Her wounding had fixed her forever in a moment of distress, and left her there, marooned" (193). This site, and the positioning of its image at the end of the novel, is meaningful. It determines that the (effects of these) acts and contested histories will not be laid to rest and recognises that there are additional narratives still to be told, or indeed withheld, in so far as the place is "both the unregarded and persisting monument of countless other stories" (301). Unlike Herbert Morrell, the inveterate collector-colonial-capitalist who obsessively seeks to possess, in the form of private property, objects, cultures and people from across the globe, the novel deliberately acknowledges the limits of its knowledge and reach.

The loss, trauma and grief that mark *Black Mirror* are palpable. There is a profound sense, however, that the recurrent processes of mourning that keep alive those who are lost are imperative, ethically and politically, and do not necessarily deaden the survivors. Rather, each unique occasion of mourning solicits active, critical responses and representations that leave open the question of how one should live and represent others in the face of multiple, impendinglosses. *Black Mirror* approximates the "novelistic vision", with its persisting ethical enquiries, that Anna is seeking and which Jones' texts and their interests in books, reading and writing, also pursue.

4
Image

In "The Veil", a short story in *Fetish Lives*, Gail Jones writes of "Magaretha Geertruida Zelle, aka Marguérite", aka the classic *femme fatale*, Mata Hari.[1] In just a few pages, Jones tells of Zelle's childhood in the Netherlands – "too pretty to be popular and too imaginative to be ordinary" (104); her living in "the Indies" as a result of a desperate and ill-advised marriage to a Dutch colonial army captain (106); the poisoning of her children and a subsequent divorce that saw Zelle move to Paris and play into Western fantasies about the sexualised East by working as an exotic dancer; her alleged spying for the Germans; and her unambiguous execution by a French firing squad. In other words, Jones sympathetically sketches the mythology that has built up around, even displaced, Zelle's life story and experience, and allows her subject an internal life – tellingly in parentheses – that legend otherwise denies:

> (Later she will read these poems [written by her mother to her father] to a few selected lovers, but they will be bored and stroke their moustaches, or roll their gazes to the ceiling. They treat her mother's words as mumbo jumbo. This loss will repeat and repeat, and cause her to invent all her feelings.) (105)

In presuming to imagine this life, Jones' short story is also alert to how Zelle has been persistently represented, particularly through the mass circulation of images both still and moving. There are the *cartes postales* (historically photographed mostly by Paul Boyer and Lucien Wallery) that readily transported Zelle's sexualised image to places and men she herself never saw while she was alive, "lying available on her belly, naked but for a diadem and a long string of pearls" (110). And after her death, there are the movies. The titillating appeal of an exotic dancer who used her powers of seduction to extract state secrets from her lovers was not lost to

---

[1] Gail Jones, "The Veil", *Fetish Lives* (Fremantle: Fremantle Arts Centre Press, 1997), 105. All subsequent references are to this edition and appear in parentheses in the text.

generations of film producers, and cinema is presented as holding out a promise of Zelle's celluloid return and rescripting:

> In a black and white movie of 1932 Greta Garbo resurrected Mata Hari as a figure of luminous star quality, inaccessible and sublime ... She was a woman of lit close-ups and whispering intensities ...
> In a 1964 movie, scripted by Francois Truffaut, Jeanne Moreau played Mata Hari, in sixties quality colour, as sardonic and intelligent ... Metaphorically Jeanne Moreau winked at the camera, as though she found her Mata Hari role somewhat ludicrous and embarrassing. Nevertheless she was modern and sexual; she knew how to have a good time.
> In 1984 Sylvia Kristel played Mata Hari who was sulky, impassive and with no star quality at all ... This Mata Hari was blank and horizontal, a figure not unlike the iconic postcard that robbed a woman of all her animate dimensions. (111–12)

To this list of films Jones adds another whose title – "The Veil" – playfully recalls that of the story in which this new movie is being related. "The Veil" the film does not yet exist; it is to be "produced sometime in the future with one of the current pantheon of famous faces" (112). And in this film-to-come, Jones writes, Mata Hari "will be all these women and none, for she remains veiled over in a kind of nimbus of mythic unknowability" (112).

As it entertains the idea of yet another film with Mata Hari as its subject (and object), the narrative wonders at the capacity of cinema to represent the existential elements of Zelle that the story "The Veil" presents as constituting her truer self: "We must remember that she knew herself best when blurring into the future, with her hair blowing backwards and her face stroked by international wind," Jones writes (112–13). That such a description calls to mind an artful photograph or film still is surely not accidental. Earlier in the narrative, Jones offers the possibility that writing of Zelle necessarily evokes images: "Perhaps it is a dream we are entering, this inconsistent federation of pasts and futures. Perhaps it is a movie" (106). With these mergers and tensions between realms of images and the written narrative suggested, it is significant that the filmic version of "The Veil", which the narrative "The Veil" foretells as its conclusion, is the story's beginning.

"The Veil" the story begins matter-of-factly with "a middle-aged man probably named Claude – he was paunchy, balding, somewhat phlegmatic in manner" – who rides his bicycle "to the rifle range at Vincennes" and proceeds to shoot "one of twelve well-aimed bullets into the body before him" (101). The film version of "The Veil" is similarly cast as "the story of the soldier Claude, who rode his bicycle to Vincennes on the morning of October 15, 1917, to discover that his task, absurdly, was to shoot down a legend" (113). And the detailing of it at the story's end returns to where the narrative began, therefore posing the possibility that the story just read is (a version of) the film projected for the future. It also says something about the capacity of both film and written narrative to rearrange conventional chronology.

What is ultimately shown in "The Veil" is not a woman stripped down to a "jewelled breastplate" (110), her body exposed, as the alleged spy's infamous performances would have her. Instead, the coalitions of visual representations that continue to fashion Mata Hari/Zelle are revealed.

This determined entanglement of written narrative, bodies and images that "The Veil" enacts is the subject of this chapter. Of particular interest is the role that images in the form of dreams, art (in the conventional sense of pictorial or painterly forms), film (and other moving images) and photography have in Jones' narratives; of how they might be constitutive of the self and relationships with others, and what part they might play in imagining loss, and also love. Of additional concern are the effects of the dialogues between written narrative and images that are entertained in Jones' texts, if indeed it can be said or assumed that the two representational forms are distinct in the first instance. After all, "The Veil" proposes that they may not be so radically separate. That the well-known etymology of the word "photo-graph" turns on the notion of light-writing – with photography being a major preoccupation of Jones' work – only underscores this caution and invites further contemplation of Jones' writerly interest in the image.

The persistent presence of images in Jones' stories involves the staging of altered or heightened perception; reflections on meaning making; and meditations on the responsibilities involved in witnessing in representational forms the fact of existence and rescuing, perhaps, otherwise disappearing things and moments. These ideas are announced in Jones' short story "The Reincarnation of Madame Tussaud" in *Fetish Lives*, and are apparent in much of Jones' subsequent work. In this story, a woman tells of her grandmother, Pearl, "an amateur portraitist of considerable skill" whose talents are redirected by circumstance to the mechanical painting of mass-produced ornaments.[2] In her later life, she develops a mania for sketching, which is propelled by the belief that "her artistry was an act of preservation, that although everyone would die, their drawn doubles were vouch-safe and would persist forever and imperishably. Until world's end. Amen" (25).

Pearl's obsession is motivated by loss – her father is hideously disfigured in war by a landmine, and then suicides; she births a still-born son; her husband returns "cadaverous" from another war (32) – and she understands herself as "re-populating the world, creating everyone's mirror other" (24). Yet, she is condescended to and regarded as a "loon" by her relatives (43). But Pearl's motivating insight into art's complex relationship with human mortality is conceded in the end as the narrator gazes upon a portrait her grandmother made of her as a teenager and admits, echoing the earlier prayer (without the solemn ratification "Amen"), "that I have the look of a young woman who, preternaturally, will live on forever. Forever. And ever" (43). And Pearl's intuition of the image's

---

2   Gail Jones, "The Reincarnation of Madame Tussaud", *Fetish Lives* (Fremantle: Fremantle Arts Centre Press, 1997), 24. All subsequent references are to this edition and appear in parentheses in the text.

persistence, its relationship with time, is one that is apparent in the three novels discussed in this chapter, *Sixty Lights*, *Black Mirror* and *The Death of Noah Glass*.

Each of these texts has an explicit interest in differing forms of the image. Lucy Strange, the protagonist of *Sixty Lights*, has a particular commitment to nascent photography; *Black Mirror* features an artist who has gained late-life recognition for her Surrealist paintings; and *The Death of Noah Glass* tells of an art historian – who specialises in the paintings of Piero della Francesca – and his two adult children, one of whom is an artist and the other who finds herself employed by a blind man to translate into words the moving images of cinema. While the role images have in each of these novels will be discussed in some detail, the novels can be broadly said to entertain, if not share, Pearl's insights about the image. Nearing her death, Lucy Strange accedes that "These images would endure. These would gloriously outlive her."[3] In *The Death of Noah Glass*, a mourning Martin Glass wishes to memorialise his father in images that are implicitly understood to persist in the face of death.[4] In *Black Mirror*, Jules Levy, Victoria's lover and a photographer, similarly determines that "the photograph retrieved something from death, something unidentifiable but nevertheless essential".[5] Victoria herself proclaims at one point early in the novel that "*Vanished things …. are the basis of all art*" (33), but it is a proposal that is immediately, if soundlessly, contested by her biographer, Anna Griffin, who "silently disagrees" (33). *Black Mirror*, as well as other instances of Jones' writing, grapples with what images might do or mean. And these roles and significances are cast into relief, and complicated, by the fact that such hypotheses and explanations are explored in words and narrative.[6] Jones' texts enquire into the representational possibilities and limitations of images and writing respectively, as well as what they might achieve in concert, when it comes to their engagement with material worlds and bodies. As such, they also examine how images might be figured in ethical relations.

The notable presence of various forms of visual art in Jones' narratives is something on which the author herself has commented. In an interview she gave on the publication of *The Death of Noah Glass*, Jones related her original interest in the visual, telling her interlocutor that "I began as a painter, not as a literary person … In everything I've written, there are images and words in contention."[7] Cass

---

3   Gail Jones, *Sixty Lights* (London: The Harvill Press, 2004), 239. All subsequent references are to this edition and appear in parentheses in the text.
4   Gail Jones, *The Death of Noah Glass* (Melbourne: Text, 2018), 313. All subsequent references are to this edition and appear in parentheses in the text.
5   Gail Jones, *Black Mirror* (Sydney: Picador, 2002), 114. All subsequent references are to this edition and appear in parentheses in the text.
6   W.J.T. Mitchell has pointed out that it is ostensibly the job of art historians in particular to "master the field of representation" by means of words. W.J.T. Mitchell, *Picture Theory: essays on verbal and visual representations* (Chicago: University of Chicago Press, 1995), 9. Jones suggests that is the task of writers to complicate that presumption.
7   Steve Dow, "Gail Jones and the Art of Words", *The Saturday Paper*, 10–16 March 2018, https://www.thesaturdaypaper.com.au/2018/03/10/gail-jones-and-the-art-words/15206004005912

Turner in *A Guide to Berlin* offers a similar autobiographical sketch (although there is no implication meant in this coincidence that the author and Cass are one and the same). Cass relates to the speak-memory group gathered in the conspicuously bookless Kępiński apartment in Berlin:

> I studied painting at first, then I studied literature. I wanted to be an artist. All that I saw and knew needed an analogy of some sort: I wanted the world fixed and intelligible, not flowing away behind me … I wanted images to stop, for my quiet inspection. I needed for some reason or justification to look more closely. … At art school my eccentricities were valued for a time, but then I became tiresome to others, and to myself … I fled art school to London … then returned, moved to Sydney and turned my attention to literature. … Then I left, I simply uprooted. Travelling revives the intensity of images. It recovers curiosity.[8]

As Cass tells the group, her interest in images is imbricated with movement. Her initial aim to be an artist is bound up with a desire to momentarily still the world, and thus be afforded clarity and comprehension, with the concentration that images are imagined to offer ironically illuminated through the physical travel Cass has undertaken. While Cass is displeased at her speech-memory account of herself, determining it to be "thin" (167), her soliloquy nevertheless goes some way to confirming Jones' reported claim that her writing stages words and images in contention. After all, Cass' speech arguably suggests less a disputation between two representational forms than a continuum of Cass' vocations and commitments.

What Cass also points to in her speak-memory is the notion that the image involves an affective force, and a way of seeing the world anew. This conceit is something that many of Jones' other protagonists experience and intuit, and Jones' texts often establish and emphasise the seductive strangeness of images by having characters view them for the first time. For the young girl who visits the cinema in the short story "Modernity" in *The House of Breathing*, it is moving images, rather than Cass' preferred still ones, that have a profound metaphysical impact. And an experience of enlightened shock is similarly had by Perdita Keene in *Sorry* when she too goes to the cinema. In that novel, Perdita attends on her birthday with her foster mother a screening of Alfred Hitchcock's *Rebecca* (1940). Like the girl of "Modernity", she has never before watched a film and the experience is overwhelming. The movie affords Perdita not only a dreamlike encounter with images that "so easily transported [her] into the lustred world of stories told in light" but also ontological upheaval.[9] Whereas other viewers at the end of the film screening calmly collect their belongings, resume their previous poise and leave the cinema without fuss or

---

8   Gail Jones, *A Guide to Berlin* (North Sydney: Vintage, 2015), 167. All subsequent references are to this edition and appear in parentheses in the text.
9   Gail Jones, *Sorry* (North Sydney: Vintage, 2007), 177. All subsequent references are to this edition and appear in parentheses in the text.

comment, Perdita's response is suggestively singular. She is thrown into a new sense of being such that when "the town hall clock chimed just as they stepped into the street … [i]t announced the new girl she had become after her first visit to the cinema" (178, 179). For these characters, first-time encounters with moving images are transformative of both their sense perception and their sense of self.

The cinema and the moving images it screens are also subjects of interest for many of Jones' protagonists for whom films are familiar. The accounts provided of their experience suggest that it is anything but habitual, however. In Jones' novels, going to the movies is an act that sets in train meditations on desire and subjectivity, and holds out the possibility of temporary succour. In *Black Mirror*, Victoria Morrell takes refuge in a cinema in Paris at a time when she is despairing of fascism's increasing hold on prewar Europe and inconsolable that Jules has left her because she "flirted and fucked around" (148). The darkened auditorium holds erotic possibilities, with Victoria hearing around her "couples making love" (148). It also invites self-absorption, with Victoria choosing to sit "in the front row, so that she could believe that what appeared was for herself alone" (147). Further, the cinema is a site for the projection of her unhappiness – "A box to pour her sadness in" (147) – that allows for momentary self-forgetting. This idea that cinema allows for a disremembering of the self is also figured in *Dreams of Speaking* when Alice Black, still deciding if she is going to write on movies as part of her book on modernity, goes to see a film (also in Paris) with Mr Sakamoto. The occasion affords an extended meditation on the everyday experience of watching a film, which is rendered anything but ordinary:

> What happens in a movie theatre? There is a transitional phase between the real and the screen, in which one views ironically, with everyday scepticism. Then at some point one falls head-long into the screen – there is an occult coalescence, a portal, a transfer, where the evidence of the senses is suddenly hijacked into fakery and exaggeration. It is a kind of release of self, a benign absorption.[10]

For all this serious philosophising, it is a community of laughter – the pivotal on-screen laugh of Greta Garbo, playing the titular character in the film *Ninotchka* (1939), is matched by the expression offered by the community of disinhibited viewers – that draws Alice away from her sadness at having just intervened to protect a woman from being beaten in the Paris Métro. Cinema enlivens and co-opts Alice's senses, with the result being that the comedy leaves her feeling as though she had been "cleansed" (83), and with a renewed sense of what movie-watching entails: "The screen carried fantasies writ large, but also bestowed games, gestural repertoires and collective stories; bestowed, moreover, a few images that stayed a lifetime, as if produced in intaglio. It was not mere absorption, but

---

10   Gail Jones, *Dreams of Speaking* (Milsons Point, NSW: Vintage, 2006), 82. All subsequent references are to this edition and appear in parentheses in the text.

some kind of transaction. Not loss of self, but some fictive complication" (84). Watching a film is not mere spectatorship or an exercise in being entertained, the novel suggests. Rather, it is a relation between images and viewers. And it is one that takes on an ethical significance in that it subtly forwards a theory of images that emphasises their strangeness and calls for a response to them.

It is this fictive complication on which Jones' texts and their preoccupations with images turn, even as, or perhaps because, later in *Dreams of Speaking* Anna catches herself, with some dismay, conjuring "prepackaged imaginings" she has received from film to filter her grief at the death of a boy she has only watched – as though a movie character – from her apartment window (110). Jones' novels are alert to how images can take on this utilitarian function as conduits for established social meanings and serve as substitutes for authentic feeling. But they are also cast as catalysts for revelations. Perdita Keene in *Sorry*, for example, comes to some truth when she glimpses a photographic image of a soldier in a newspaper that tells of the war raging in Europe, while she is playing cards in outback Western Australia. The moment is said to be transformative, a "rupture in the texture of her life" (82–3), and has an ethical force. The image presses Perdita to realise that "This was a man whose job it was to kill, and somewhere, behind the image, were the corpses he had made … And the day after the photograph he would kill or be killed. … She thought to herself: *I am ten years old, there is a world war going on, I am playing cards*" (83). Perdita is prompted by the image to recognise not only the man's horrific circumstances and likely death but also those who lie outside the photographic frame and her own, relatively safe, circumstances that the photograph draws into relations of correspondence, understanding and difference.

Jones' texts can therefore be said to be alert to "a whole fugitive empire of images" that has meaning and currency "with or without the frame" (178). Within their narrative worlds, images might furnish pleasure and connections; offer reprieve and solace; and reveal life-altering truths. But they can also infiltrate, distort and deceive. Indeed, Lucy Strange in *Sixty Lights* views with some disgust a magic lantern show screened at the Childish establishment where her brother, Thomas, is employed. Unlike others in the audience, including her sister-in-law and brother, who regard what they are seeing as a form of light entertainment that nourishes nationalist feeling, Lucy is affronted by deceptive visions of empire that rest on effortless binaries which pose the English as defenders of civilisation and Indians as murderous barbarians. She has only recently returned from India, and she knows the projected images are untruths. But even as Lucy is critical of the thematic scenarios portrayed, she also internalises the camera-in-reverse machinations of the technology that produces them, and suggests other visions these might afford. On leaving the show, Lucy pauses before the light thrown out by gas lamps on the London street and notices, as though a revelation, "another kind of magic lantern, another visual effect" and her own imbrication in its logic: "She was bound to this contradiction: between the material and the ethereal incarnation in light" (186). Lucy is wedded to both the substantial and abstract aspects of the image, to the point that she sees as though a magic lantern show, or as might a photograph.

For all these possibilities, Jones' texts return to an idea contemplated by Pei Xing in *Five Bells*, namely that "Perhaps love rested more in images than in words."[11] The "perhaps" that marks Pei Xing's thinking suggests a hesitant proposition. But, it is one that is central to Jones' narratives and their interest in images, and is a counterpoint of sorts to much contemporary theorising on photographs that insists on the image's essential relation with death. Eduardo Cadava's claim that "Photography is a mode of bereavement" is exemplary and symptomatic of such an apprehension.[12] For Cadava, it is the enigmatic image of ruin that captures his imagination:

> The image tells us that it is with loss and ruin that we have to live. Nevertheless, what makes the image an image is its capacity to bear the traces of what it cannot show, to go on, in the face of this loss and ruin, to suggest and gesture toward its potential for speaking. In other words, the fact of the image's existence – and here I refer only to an image worthy of the name "image," to an image that would remain faithful to the ruinous silences that make it what it is – ruins the ruin about which all images speak – or at least seek to speak.[13]

Elsewhere, thinking about photography's relationship with time, Cadava confirms that "Death, both the word and the event, is a photograph that photographs itself … A photograph therefore speaks *as* death, as the trace that passes into history … Yet, speaking as death, the photograph can be neither death nor itself. At once dead and alive, it opens the possibility of our being in time."[14] Jones' writing is attuned to this understanding of the image; a quote from Cadava's work serves as epigraph to part one of *Sixty Lights* – "There has never been a time without the photograph, without the residue and writing of light"[15] – which Lucy Strange embraces. In Jones' texts,

---

11   Gail Jones, *Five Bells* (London: Harvill Secker, 2011), 45. All subsequent references are to this edition and appear in parentheses in the text. By contrast, as he witnesses his young daughters' faces flickered by television images, their backs turned to him, Mr Sakamoto in *Dreams of Speaking* held steadfast to a belief "in the superiority of words over images" (72).

12   Eduardo Cadava, *Words of Light: Theses on the Photography of History* (Princeton, NJ: Princeton University Press, 1997), 11. Roland Barthes' thoughts on photography, in the midst of his mourning for his mother, have been highly influential in shaping this stance. Roland Barthes, *Camera Lucida: reflections on photography*, trans. Richard Howard (New York: Hill & Wang, 1981). Cadava's writing on photography is also indebted to Walter Benjamin's reflections on history and the image, including the 1931 essay, "A Short History of Photography", *Screen* 13 no. 1 (1972): 5–26. In that essay, Benjamin draws links between photography's capacity to illuminate the unseen and the invention or discovery of the unconscious.

13   Eduardo Cadava, "*Lapsus Imaginis*: The Image in Ruins", *October* 96 (2001): 36.

14   Cadava, *Words*, 128.

15   Cadava, *Words*, 5.

though, images and the language of images (in particular that of photography) are asked to picture not so much death as love.[16]

The image Pei Xing is referring to when she poses her thought is not a material photograph, and it is one that is certainly bound up with loss as well as love. It is a vision of her father, Chang Yong, that she remembers from childhood and which is not entirely of the sort that is aligned with Lucy Strange's resolution in *Sixty Lights* "to know the world by its imagistic revelations" (86) and Anna's awaiting as a child in *Black Mirror* of visions as "another kind of knowledge" (73). For these two characters, such moments of vision are intuitive and secular, and the sense of some passing illumination they afford arises from unexpected experiences with the everyday. Anna stands with her uncle before a salt lake that seems to her tremulous and prismatic, and the two are "subordinated by awe, by loveliness, by who-knows-what" (74). And while Lucy keeps a written journal of all the special things she sees and the photographs she has not taken, for Pei Xing it is the absence of words – "There was no memory of him speaking at this time" – that singles out this memory as an image, and one that is "quiet, folded" and "entirely her own" (45). It is of her father but not at his customary place at the desk, working on his translations. Instead, he is reclining, smoking and thinking, and the image she affectionately recalls is "of the great man at rest" (44). This seemingly simple and private moment is recast by Pei Xing as an image to give it its poignant political charge. Pei Xing expressly remembers her father as a proud owner of a "Box Brownie camera" (45). And with this camera, he had taken a "series of cheesy photographs" of his friends "posed before various London landmarks"; the camera was also used to take photographs of his marriage to Nan Anyi (45). As Pei Xing quietly relates, "None of these images survived the Cultural Revolution. None of their group" (46). With her parents and their friends killed, and their images destroyed, Pei Xing's thinking of her father in terms of a remembered image-not-taken casts her memory as camera-like, resistant to the political will to annihilate but also a reminder of it, as well as a sign of her enduring love.

This turn to the image to represent the love for, and loss of, a parent is a recurrent motif in Jones' novels. In *Sixty Lights*, Lucy Strange makes the counterintuitive claim that she has always been a photographer; she has a particular fascination with light and the image, and a commitment to looking intently and contemplatively at the world. She comes early and tellingly, however, to this knowledge and photography following her mother's death:

> Nothing summoned her mother's face. Nothing was intelligible. Lucy will spend the rest of her life looking intently at faces. She becomes, at this very moment … a

---

16　Lyn Jacobs offers an account of the role of photography in Jones' writing, which also argues for the affirming effects of the image. Lyn Jacobs, "Gail Jones' 'light writing': memory and the photo-graph", *JASAL: Journal of the Association for the Study of Australian Literature* 5 (2006): 191–208.

photographer. And every photographic ambition will turn on the summoning of a face and the retrieval of what is languishing just beyond vision. (46)

Lucy affords photography a questing propensity as well as extra-visual powers; the photograph might recuperate the unseen, and Lucy's devotion to it in this way is founded on the loss of her mother. In *The Death of Noah Glass*, visual art is also called on to think about love and loss. At the beginning of the narrative, on the morning of his father's funeral, Martin Glass begins to conceive loosely a new project, one that recognises the unlikely commonalities between a mass-produced consumer item, his daughter's doll house, and one of his father's favourite artworks, Piero della Francesca's *The Flagellation of Christ* (late 1450s). By the end of the novel, this vague design is replaced by the idea to transfigure his father into "artful terms: *The Death of Noah Glass*. This is how he will convert his father to art and place him in the world of images. He will … start again, tomorrow, with something new. Something new for Nina" (313). What Martin is primarily concerned with at this moment is how, or if, memory, grief and love might concentrate in the image. Martin imagines that he will make this painting for his daughter Nina, further suggesting that this is a gift of love. It promises to loop his daughter into the network of difficult affections that attention to the image nurtures in this narrative, and in this family. This final image-to-come, in a novel so preoccupied with conceiving of time multifariously, further gestures towards a future time, and affords Martin a way to mourn his father.

Another of Jones' artists, Victoria Morrell in *Black Mirror*, is attracted to "the Surrealist promise of *figuring out*" (227) because she is privately striving in her artwork to reclaim from forgetting her mother, who suffered a fiery, accidental death when Victoria was a young child and who the artist cannot recall as an adult. Yet, Victoria is not the only character in that novel for whom images serve as affective registers. Her lover, Jules Levy, is a photographer, and while Victoria contrasts her preferred art form with his, their visual interests – played out formally in the novel's narrative structure – coalesce in suggestive ways for thinking about representations of love and loss.

The stylistic features of each of Jones' novels are important to note in this regard. The title of Martin's proposed painting is also that of the narrative in which the project is entertained. And it raises the question (much like the film imagined in the short story "The Veil" with the same title) as to whether Martin's artwork can hope to, or want to, approximate the complexities, both formal and thematic, of the story just told. *Sixty Lights* also entertains its thematic interests in the visual in its form. The novel itself enacts a mode of conceiving of narrative that is discontinuous rather than sequential. The sixty chapters that comprise the novel bring to mind the notion of prose snapshots, which suggests an affinity between the text's subject and its style that is not simply artful but also purposefully attentive to the photograph's fragmentary form and its possibilities for story-telling. And *Black Mirror* stages from its first lines its entanglement with, and indebtedness to, various forms of the image with its introduction of Anna as an artwork:

> As a painter might see it:
> The rain has made her luminescent and she is a pillar of shine.
> She pops open her umbrella, holds it close above her, and is transformed into a domed shape, darkly vertical. The air is suddenly pale; it bears the appearance of onion skin.
> *How translucent the sky is. How awash and water-coloured.*
> For some reason this is the way she imagines herself, as a modernist composition in a hypothetical artwork, caught in the possibilities of the elements and their visual trickery. (1)

These initial sentences make clear that the narrative is seeking to approximate in words the form of the still image, and that the female character described in this way shares this effort to see the world, and herself, imagistically. Lucy Strange in *Sixty Lights* also entertains this way of seeing: "It is like sexual hunger … to wish always to see things like this, to see more intensely, more zealously, more unrealistically. To wish everything into a state of stunning exaggeration" (121). But this painterly introduction to Anna is immediately coupled with an alternate view. That perspective is Victoria's, and she is said to see the same moment cinematically, as "a movie she is endlessly unspooling. This screen, its slick flickerings, a new face represented" (3). In this manner, she casts herself not as a "hypothetical artwork" as does Anna, who has modernism on her mind. (She is about to meet the famous Surrealist artist and subject of her intended biography.) Instead, she regards herself a viewer of herself filmed "in the sly act of gazing" at Anna's approach (3).[17]

That the visions of the two characters are indebted to the forms of painting and film respectively seems apt. Anna thinks of herself in terms of a still image, "stalled by her own nervousness and chilly apprehensions" (2). And Victoria is expressly positioned both as viewer of "the wet woman crossing the street" and cinematically timeless: "she could be any age; she could be fifty or twenty-one" (3).

More than these affective and temporal ideas that the characters' conjuring of images involves is the implication that their self-fashioning and self-conscious acts of looking (at themselves) as images connect them before their initial encounter, which takes place some pages later in the doorway of Victoria's London apartment. Here "Anna stood in the rain, waiting to be admitted. … It was one of those taut peculiar moments in which strangers, having passed the flurry of effusive first greeting, are halted before each other, in a pause of true estrangement" (17). The

---

17 Paul Genoni offers a reading of *Black Mirror* that places it alongside other Australian texts also interested in representing modernist women. Paul Genoni, "'Art is the Windowpane': novels of Australian women and modernism in inter-war Europe", *JASAL: Journal of the Association for the Study of Australian Literature* 3 (2004): 159–72.

novel does not seek to overcome entirely the estrangement Anna and Victoria encounter at their first meeting. Instead, it proposes from its beginning that thinking in images might be a way that the complexities of the characters' separate but overlapping affective relations and histories might be suggestively represented, and their otherness to each other, and others, might be respectfully maintained.

This idea that images might serve as connective ties is underscored by Anna. Following on from their first meeting (the telling of which is returned to across the chapters), Anna is perplexed by her subject's reluctance to speak: "Victoria was polite, evasive and having second thoughts; she dismissed her visitor after only twenty minutes" (35). She determines to write to Victoria, telling her that the two of them grew up in the same mining town: "*We share images*, she will write. What could be more intimate?" (35). Anna is sincere in her conviction that this as yet unrevealed connection will introduce an element of her own life story to the already faltering professional relationship she wants to establish with her subject: "she wanted to relocate herself as the twelve-year-old girl who had pressed a library book of reproductions against her chest as though claiming a lover" (35). She is aware at the same time, however, that her appeal to shared images, which she hopes will attract and sustain Victoria's interest, calls on the tricks of her writing trade, on a form of linguistic cajolery: "Seduction, she thinks; so much depends on the right words" (36). What this admission suggests is the complicated relationships between words and images that *Black Mirror* pursues.

Within the world of *Black Mirror*, images not only proliferate but are highly contested by its characters. Jules in particular is scathing of the Surrealist aesthetic his lover celebrates, declaring it unambiguously "*bête*" when he first happens upon it when attending the 1936 International Surrealist Exhibition with Victoria in London (67).[18] It must be said that Victoria, too, has her doubts about the art movement with which she comes to be associated. In her first encounter with the Surrealists, " Breton, Ernst, Desnos, Man Ray", she is discomforted by their casual insistence that she serves as a synecdoche, "*L'Australienne*", and silently disagrees with Breton's universalist proclamations: "We are all Australians. All bodies are black" (19, 21, 23).[19] Later, when Victoria hears Breton speak at the *Au Chien Qui Fume* extolling "revolution in art and sexuality in all things; he spoke as though the marvellous alone would defeat Hitler and collage would demoralise the bourgeoisie", her assessment echoes that of Jules and is blunt – "Bullshit" – although she also admits that "[s]he was fascinated and appalled" (144–5).

---

18   James in *Five Bells* is reminded of an acerbic assessment of Surrealism given by a woman he once met at a party, namely that it "was an adolescent taste, something for lonely teenage boys wanting to do violence to the order of things" (102). The paintings of Magritte, however, persist in his imagination and give some semblance of shape to the losses he experiences.

19   Robert Dixon reads Breton's appeal as revealing of Surrealism's compromised cosmopolitanism, "a production of imperialism, racism and sexism". Robert Dixon, "Cosmopolitan Australians and Colonial Modernity: Alex Miller's *Conditions of Faith*, Gail Jones' *Black Mirror* and A.L. McCann's *The White Body of Evening*", Westerly 49 (2004): 126.

Surrealism is the obvious aesthetic signpost in the novel and it marks out Victoria's claims to experimental modernity in which the novel also has a (critical) formal interest. With her adherence to Surrealism's tenet of convulsive beauty, Victoria sees "the beauty of things in dislocation" (86), an aesthetic the text approximates with its persistent juxtaposing of dreams, memories, projections and the present. Yet, Jules' admonishment of it is a recognition of some of the limitations or criticisms that might be levelled at Surrealism's signature features and figures that the text adopts and who populate the text. At the same time, however, Victoria is equally underwhelmed by her lover's photographic enterprises. Like the photographer Victor Browne, to whose studio Lucy Strange is apprenticed in *Sixty Lights*, and who specialises in "vain posturings; the stiff fictions of a happy marriage" (142), Jules' main subject is weddings, much to Victoria's aesthetic consternation:

> Jules Levy was a photographer from Lyon on a working holiday in London. He specialised in weddings. Most of his time was spent snapping at garlanded brides with orange-blossom and fussing mothers, stiff-looking grooms who fiddled with button-holed carnations, bridesmaids with laps full of cascading flowers. When Jules showed Victoria his photographs she was at once dismayed by their sameness, by the eradication in his images of love's specificity. (38)

For Victoria, Jules' wedding pictures are the negative outcomes of art in the age of mechanical reproduction.[20] If Victoria is derisive of these uniform images, it is nevertheless Jules' pictures that support the couple financially during their early years together in Paris when Victoria was at best "a fringe Surrealist, selling nothing at all" (40). As the art catalogue relates it, Victoria "established a reputation as a painter of dreams", only to be forgotten during the mid-century and then rediscovered "in the late seventies … which both consolidated her fame and established her as something of a cult figure in the London art scene" (16). This status is signalled by the reproduction and circulation of her own photographic image. Anna first came to learn of Victoria and her artwork through images. When she was younger, Anna had found in the library of her town's Mechanics' Institute a catalogue from one of Victoria's early exhibitions, and the painter herself had been known to Anna first through photographs, although the biographer is pleased to observe on their initial personal encounter that "the woman … unlike her photographs, was multicoloured, discomposed and vigorously animated" (17).

---

20 While she concedes that Jacob Webb's paintings contain a "gentleness", Lucy Strange in *Sixty Lights* is similarly cautious about the aesthetic register in which her soon-to-be lover paints: "Jacob specialised in a kind of prettified counterfeit, depictions of ladies in ruffled hats, children in neck bows, gentlemen with barrel chests and watch chains and solid leaden postures. … there was also a pastelly unfocused quality to the paint that made everyone appear more decorative than human" (231). As with Victoria, this instructive aesthetic point of difference does not deter Lucy from initiating amorous intimacy with the painter.

For all its claims to verisimilitude, this photograph is found wanting, as Victoria similarly determines Jules' wedding photographs to be.

It may be that Jules' photographs do not meet Surrealist expectations and do not immediately abide by Alice Black's ideas (and ideals) about photography in *Dreams of Speaking*, namely that "If there is a necessity to this technology, it is to abet troubled remembering and to drive us to other futures" (37). But Jules certainly entertains private theories about photography that would interest Lucy Strange in *Sixty Lights*, who recognises "all the positive and negative relations that combine to conjure a beloved face" (239). It is her mother's face that Lucy's photography impossibly strives to summon; Jules' love of photography is unambiguously yoked in the novel with his love for his mother. It was the vision the x-ray allowed that first enthralled him as a young boy when his mother took him to a store that had installed the device to entertain its customers.[21] And from that moment, which serves as his artistic origin story, Jules proceeded to take endless photographs of his mother and "every single thing around him" (113).

From these experiences Jules devises his photographic philosophy, namely that "photography takes its power from attention to shadow … Shadow is no reduction but the adjective of the image … Like ice whorling upwards, he said, from a skater's bright path" (138). The image he conjures to describe the interplay between shadow and light, which is central to photographic composition, is not just technical. The detail he tells to Victoria of his parents' courtship is of the couple skating "together in that quaint old-fashioned way, with the woman encircled, leaning slightly into the shape of the man's body. Together the new couple reinvented movement; they discovered the rapture of arcs and the simplicity of speed"; his father's early death in the war is marked by his mother giving away her skates (42). Jules' understanding of photography is linked with love and loss, with the image of blades on ice making the connection between his art form and his "inherited family tales" (41). And his linking of photography with the love he has for his mother is returned to him by Hélène Levy's dying request.

Hélène had been searching for her disappeared son since her release from a concentration camp, and on meeting her for the first time, Victoria is confronted by the duplicity of the image (and, by inference, the unspeakable horror of Hélène's experience). She is struck by how her lover's mother "looked nothing like the photograph that Jules had kept of her" (44). Her last wish is that she be buried with a photograph of her son as a sixteen year old, pinned with a yellow star over her heart. Despite Victoria's dismissal of her lover's wage-earning wedding pictures, Hélène's entreaty confirms her son's conviction of photography's affective charge.

---

21 In *Dreams of Speaking*, Alice and her sister Norah are similarly captivated by an x-ray photograph that showed Norah's broken arm, "an ivory lever, floating in a cloud of smoke … Nora and Alice both thought the photograph wonderful … it revealed the glossy frame of the inner body, the architecture beneath flesh, the taut structure of being … Both girls felt that they possessed a special knowledge" (177–8).

And when Victoria attends the funeral, it is not Hélène whom she sees when she looks into the open coffin. Instead, it is an image of Jules, "young and seductive, looking back. He was sixteen years old with a boy-smile and messy hair, and he peered from his rectangle, from his pillow of star, shyly eternal".(267). Given that Jules' whereabouts is unknown – Victoria believes he might have been executed by the Germans – the rectangular photograph is a testament to his past presence. With its shape mirroring that of the casket in which it is mournfully nested, however, this particular rectangle also suggests Jules' own entombment.

Photographic images in *Black Mirror* are attributed truths to which the characters might otherwise be unable to admit. In a far less distressing scene when Anna finds a photograph of Pablo Picasso and Victoria together, hidden among Victoria's belongings, this image goes some way to dispute Anna's suspicion about Victoria's autofabulation and her claim that she is, in fact, the subject of Picasso's painting "*Crying Woman*" (57). Not only does Victoria's determination sit at odds with received art history – as Anna well knows, it is Dora Maar, a photographer, who all the scholars say was the inspiration for *La Femme qui Pleure* (1937) – the biographer has had doubts that Victoria ever met the Spanish artist, with these misgivings expressly cast in photographic terms: "Her subject is as self-aggrandising as she is wedded to modest detail. She is unresolved and imprecise, like a photograph not properly taken" (58). The discovery of the photograph lends some weight to Victoria's otherwise audacious and unlikely declarations.

This attention to the importance given to images in *Black Mirror* for conceiving of characters and their relationships with each other is underlined by the appearance, and apparent artistic incomprehension, of one minor character, Mrs Dooley. Mrs Dooley manages the rooms where Anna and her lover, Winston Field, separately lodge while they are both temporarily in London. Mrs Dooley is kindly enough, reflecting on both her nephew who has made a home in Australia and her former boyfriend, who she understands long ago took his own life by drowning; or, perhaps he too started a new life in Australia. Either way, he is lost to her, and she nostalgically recalls him for Anna. But the memories which preoccupy her are not what interests her house guest.

Anna presents to Mrs Dooley a reproduction of Victoria's painting *Black Mirror* "and asked her what she thought" (99). By her own admission, Mrs Dooley is "not at all arty herself" (99); by contrast, Anna's thoughts fly immediately to artworks to make sense and consolidate what she sees, as when Victoria presents herself adorned in her feathers and "Anna was reminded instantly of those paintings by Max Ernst, in which women have the peaked and almost monstrous heads of birds, and flounces of iridescent feathers streaming like cloaks down their backs" (129). That Mrs Dooley does not have these cultural reference points to call on is reinforced when, pressed by Anna to offer her thoughts on the artwork, she admits that "That French stuff is all double-Dutch to me, lovey" (101).

For her part, "Anna cannot understand why she [Mrs Dooley] has not commented at all on the images; the woman-on-fire, its symbols, its curious mirrorings" (100). Her disbelief at her landlady's disinclination to notice, let alone interpret, the images that have captured her own imagination since she first saw them in an art catalogue as a mining-town schoolgirl, momentarily admits how art, and knowledge about art, can circulate in the text, and beyond, as a form of cultural capital, albeit with a different motivation to that shown by Herbert Morrell, Victoria's father. Morrell, a wealthy mine-owner, has a habit of thinking about art and artefacts as uncritical extensions, and signs, of mercantile acquisition and colonial proprietorship. Anna seems unable or unwilling to comprehend that Mrs Dooley might not share her art interests, perhaps for reasons which are suggested in *Five Bells* by another diasporic Dubliner. In that novel, Catherine Healy identifies Irish class structures as contributing to her sense of feeling "ignorant, stupid" and distressed by the "sanctimonious tone of galleries" (161). She singles out "her childhood in the [Dublin apartment] tower, with too little private space to see her own life clearly" as that which has "left her depleted in her capacity to appreciate visual art" (175). In *Black Mirror*, Anna's assessment of Mrs Dooley does not seem to extend beyond the landlady's aesthetic incomprehension.

That Mrs Dooley also comes later, unexpectedly and explosively, to nominate Anna "Lady Muck herself, fuckin' whore more like, call yourself as white as driven snow and a book-learning lady, fuckin' black men like there was no tomorrow" (253) suggests a half-conscious awareness of the "book-learning" origins of Anna's artistic pursuits. That Mrs Dooley's critique is couched in racism, however – which she herself explains as a form of displacement: "It's just that I was saving you, like. For my nephew in Australia. You'd make such a lovely couple" (254) – arguably blunts her insights and leaves Winston, not Anna, packing "his things" and leaving the boarding house (255). Anna herself is largely unruffled by both Mrs Dooley's outburst and "the woman who has newly and flamboyantly abused her" (254). She immediately casts Mrs Dooley and her vitriolic flare-up in the aesthetic terms to which Victoria lays claim, and from which Mrs Dooley is excluded. Recalling Victoria's determination that it is she who is the true subject of Picasso's painting, Anna sees Mrs Dooley as "A crying woman. Another woman shattered by the bombshell of what is hidden inside" (254). In so doing, she pictures the older woman as an image in a way that Mrs Dooley would not do, and would not understand.

The novel also poses other questions about the possibilities and limitations of images for forging affective connections and expressing inner lives. While Anna thinks that by revealing that she and her biographical subject share images an intimacy between them will necessarily follow, it is a photograph that decisively punctures Anna's affair with Winston. Earlier in the narrative, Anna considers the threshold of the image when reflecting on her developing relationship with Winston, determining that "Images, outsides, do not suffice. Images do not tell their love-making propinquity or the intimate hallowing of their mutual time. Every artist knows this: the mendacity of images" (120). And yet there is one photograph that tells Anna a truth she would prefer not to know.

Having retreated to the library following Mrs Dooley's bluster, Winston is found by Anna not reading, as she expects, but rather "gazing at a photograph and talking to himself" (256). It is a picture of his wife and son in Jamaica, and a picture of love: "They had brilliant smiles and faced the camera with an aspect of jubilation, as though offering up to the photographer their hearts and souls. Behind their heads was a hibiscus, massed with huge yellow blossoms: trumpeting love" (256). While the narrative does not admit Winston's inner thoughts, the implication is that the photograph of the family he has left behind carries an irresistible affective pull which will propel him back to them, "no question" (256). For Anna, however, the photograph serves to signal "the rent distance that had opened between them", and she immediately imagines her unreciprocated love and the future they will not have together in terms of the reversed order of the photographic negative: "She was a woman in love with a man whose image she bore away, reversed into false whiteness, held in frail promise, as the imperishable negative of some photograph not yet developed" (256). The photograph serves to divide Anna and Winston; or at least it points out that Anna's desire for a life together is an impossible fantasy, one that is undercut by the reality of Winston's life elsewhere, which the photograph admits.

If Winston's photograph tells of a future in which Anna will have no part, then another photograph in the text is also imagined to carry premonitory powers. This image is said to be the only known picture taken of the Morrell household and it has, at the back of its scene, a trace of Victoria's father, William, who worked as the family's chauffeur. In the foreground is both the man who presumes he is Victoria's father and Victoria's mother, Rose, who is pictured as foretelling her own death: "She has one year to live and her eyes seem to know it" (166). The photograph self-consciously exposes the conventions that have a role in creating ideas, and ideals, of family: "everyone, even the children, has achieved the requisite immobility, posed stock-still and unblinking … for the man with his head beneath the cloth" (166). And the narrative within which this image is told, which approximates Anna's determination to write imaginatively of her biographical subject, points to a gap between that perceived ideal and reality. The fictive account Anna is experimenting with, which the novel itself realises, seems to approximate a truth more faithfully than the photograph does.[22]

If the narrative at this moment underscores the duplicity of the family image, then elsewhere the photograph is held up as evidence of sisterly camaraderie. Victoria tells Anna of a photograph taken in Leicester Square of her and her younger sister, Frances, whom she meets later in life and whose father was also William. Victoria points to the image as proof of their affective ties:

---

22 Marianne Hirsch writes of the ways in which photographic conventions frame families ideologically. Marianne Hirsch, *Family Frames: Photography, Narrative and Postmemory* (Cambridge, MA: Harvard University Press, 1997).

> [Y]ou can see the solidarity of feeling that existed between us, the Surrealist show-off, madly feathered, and the prim-and-proper housekeeper with the handbag clutched anxiously over her crotch. We are both smiling radiantly. And we both share a glorious and sisterly likeness. (222–3)

Further, the two women's shared interest in the image underscores their unlikely affinity. Immediately following Victoria's reference to this photograph is the artist's remembrance of Frances' desire to be "an extra in a Hollywood movie … her face carried forward into history in some incidental, irrefutable and time-defeating way; not important or even speaking, but incorrigibly visible. I loved her when she told me that" (223).[23] The thought of the photograph leads associatively to Victoria's memory of her sister's modest yet immortalising filmic aspirations, and it is the two women's commitment to the visual in its variegated forms that, to Victoria's mind and in terms of narrative sequencing, conclusively binds them.

This abiding interest of the narrative in images is not only attributable to Victoria's profession and aesthetic preferences. Intangible memories are cast as images, so that Victoria "carries into adulthood an image of herself after bathing, still wet, spreadeagled, sleeping very peacefully with her burnt face in the sun" (202), and Frances remembers her father as a "long shape in a winged armchair, and a certain, but definite, circlet of embrace. It was a memory Flora [her mother] maintained she was too young to recall, but Frances insisted was true. The shape of him, she said. Just the shape of him persists" (223). It seems therefore apt that Anna likens Victoria's recall to film, her willed meeting with an internalised past which becomes more urgent as death approaches:

> Towards the end … Victoria's *liaison* was with her avatars, her own other selves, and she met them in an excited time-lapsing rush, the way, Anna thought, one sees film of petals quickly opening in a magical pop, or storm clouds skidding across an inconstant sky, or the polished sun rising or falling with the confident bounce of a tennis ball. Victoria was racing through her history, swift as an animation, colliding with herself. (276)

While Anna is able to conjure this pleasing analogy, there are limits put on what words can convey. The brutal murder of Victoria's first lover, Louis Bell, by her brother has the artist despairingly wonder, "What words can tell this. Violence is somehow beyond my language" (236). And the image, too, is found wanting in the face of loss. The first black mirror story Victoria tells her biographer concerns her incapacity to remember her mother, and the inadequacy of art, in both its written and visual forms, to console, resurrect or represent:

---

23 In distinct contrast, James' teenage ambition in *Five Bells* to be a movie extra is "a symbol of his accurate sense of mediocrity" (34).

> I once tried, like the artist Brauner, to paint with my eyes closed, believing this act might recover the lineaments of her lost face, or at least its vague aspect, or intimation; but there was still no consequence and no true icon. I tried too, like the poet Desnos, to speak Surrealistically at will; I imagined that a word-link, unconsciously chanced upon, would somehow reconnect us. But all contrivances failed. Art is the windowpane, the barrier, against which we press our searching faces. (215)

If art is conceived of as external to the self and possibly possessive – Victoria's chalk-drawing on their apartment wall of the shadow cast by Jules asleep has the artist feel as though "I'd trapped him, that he was mine" (263) – then it is in private recesses that some hope of respectful retrieval is made possible. The unbidden impressions and images that emerge during sleep allow Victoria to recover Louis and also Jules: "I dreamt again of darling Louis Bell … It was a reclamation. It was a return of something lost … I dreamt frequently of Louis and Jules, often in conflation, and could see them again beneath my eyelids, youthful, sexually present, ablaze with optimism" (244). And with Victoria's accidental discovery of a secret diary her mother kept, she both loses again and finds anew her mother: "I both found and relinquished my mother for the very first time. The journal summoned an admixture of recovery and grief: I loved her, and I wept" (230).

The diary itself is an admixture of image and words. To record her socialist politics and to conceal her passions for William, Rose devised her own system of pictograms, "her cuneiform disguises, embossed with ampersands" (229), which Victoria learns to understand. In so doing, Victoria comes to know something of her own story, as well as her mother's, which is other than that which the surface of the posed Morrell family photograph relates.

The pictograms Rose develops might be thought of as the representational register that *Black Mirror* itself enacts, or at least gives some consideration to. The novel is interested in part in how words and narrative might approach visual forms, engage in *ekphrasis*, to consider how new knowledge and understandings might come into being. It is therefore not incidental that Victoria thinks and sees like an imagist poet from a young age. (In *Sixty Lights*, there is a suggestion that "communing with images" is something done from infancy, with Lucy Strange's baby daughter, Ellen, imagined to respond "to all she had incomprehensibly and vividly seen" (170).) The novel intimates that Victoria had always been a Surrealist: "She was a child who knew that horizons swung and that the look of things converted, and understood that marvellous conjunctions reconfigure the ordinary as excitement" (174). But her precocity is such that as a child she also imagines the appearance of a powdered face emerging from a brothel in terms lifted from Ezra Pound's rhythmic, paratactic Imagist poem, bobbing "like a petal on a wet black bough" (197).[24] And this interest in conversions and conjunctions is suggested

---

24 This line of poetry also drifts into the thoughts of Catherine in *Five Bells* (14). Ezra Pound, "In a Station of the Metro", *Poetry* 2 no. 1 (1913): 12.

formally by the way in which the narrative is plaited with shifting points of view and dreams recollected; the present time of Victoria and Anna's developing relationship and their respective pasts that come to overlap in their telling; as well as the use by Jones of past and present tenses.

The effect is one of collage, which is also faithful to both the aesthetic preferences of Surrealism and how memory-images are cast in the text as subject to varying intensification and velocities: "Victoria's childhood, like all others, has jarrings, arrested moments, bright distillations, and then long grainy spaces, fast-motioned and faint" (181). There are also designs that recur through the text, which additionally suggest that the narrative is less driven by the literary convention of plot than by a consideration of how repeated patterns – visual motifs and shapes – might contribute to the creation of meaning and the forging of connections.

While they might be aesthetic antagonists, Victoria and Jules share an image repertoire, for instance. Victoria herself comments on the recurrence of hands in her paintings (and also draws attention to their abundant presence in the novel): "those hands are one of my important symbols. You see them everywhere throughout my paintings. White hands. Cameo hands. Hands like thin clouds on the verge of erasure" (219–20). And Jules jokes at one point to Victoria about his first attack of tachycardia beneath the piano his mother was practising on with one hand: "*Single-handed* … I learnt about mortality with an accompaniment, single-handed" (115). Hands are poetically imagined as asterisks and starbursts throughout the novel as well as signs of the dirty, dangerous labour that Anna's father, Griffo, undertakes underground in the mine tunnels and shafts. That "the palm of his hand decreased in size by almost half; there was also some paralysis" is the disfiguring consequence of an industrial accident, and not some marvellous Surrealist reconfiguring (282).

Another painterly shape that carries particular charge within the novel is the rectangle. The rectangular image of a youthful Jules pinned to his mother's chest in her coffin is devastating, but also recalls Victoria watching Jules develop photographic images he has taken of her, "reversed, whitened, immobilised, etherealised, shrunken and wholly contained within rectangles", with the darkroom quickly becoming a location for seduction (115). This form also comes to frame an earlier passionate relationship, with Victoria musing that her mother's lover "must have known her best through the rear-view mirror – a lover in a glass box, small and rectangular" (216). And if the novel can be said to imbue this shape with such meaning and implications, it also casts triangles as smiles; the shape of torn fabric; and signs of predatory sexual desire. References to flowers abound, and kisses conjoin the characters. Anna relates her film matinee-inspired attempts at passionate physical affection as a young girl; later Victoria is said to have "dreamt of a network of kissing of which she was the centre" (150). One of the few memories Anna has of her own lost mother is "A gentle enfolding. A good night kiss" (282), which resurfaces when Anna returns to the town in which she and Victoria lived as children, and receives from her stepmother an understanding, affectionate kiss.

For all these correspondences, the respective responses Victoria and Anna have to the pictograms in Rose's diary suggest that if the text might be said at all to resemble those hieroglyphs, with their shared weaving together of image and word, then keeping alive what these forms do not tell, and cannot tell, is also of concern for *Black Mirror*. Whereas Victoria comes to decipher and understand her mother's writing-image code, Anna does not. She happens upon the journal while sifting through Victoria's belongings, and "could not resist peering inside" (151). What she finds, however, is not immediately apparent to her: "Small fragments were legible, but for the most part it was written in an unfamiliar script; it looked furtive, illegible. Only ampersands, their filigrees, were at all familiar, but connection was clearly the least of its meanings" (151). While *Black Mirror* considers what words and art might relate both in coalition and separately, it is also alert to how readers and viewers might varyingly respond to these interests, as Anna's incomprehension at this moment (as well as Mrs Dooley's earlier non-concern with Victoria's paintings) demonstrates.

It is Jules, the photographer, who implicitly learns of another complex interplay between image and word, which he remembers as an adult while visiting the "trickster" Surrealist exhibition with Victoria (135). As a child, standing before a Monet painting, he comes to appreciate that any meaning of art might not be readily apparent; that words are called on in an effort to interpret art; and that those words are not simply or only utilitarian but are themselves open to aesthetic resonance. When looking in incomprehension at a "painting of the Gare Saint-Lazare", Jules' mother, Hélène, explained to her son that:

> this was a painting of the effects of steam; the obscured train at the station, hidden almost entirely by clouds of blotchy paint, was the consequence of an artist enchanted by steam.
>
> That was what she had said: *enchanted by steam*.
>
> The mystery, Hélène, continued, is not that everything we see is altogether clear; some things present themselves as nebulous instances of the beautiful.
>
> *Nebulous instances of the beautiful.*
>
> Jules still remembers his mother's words because it was an occasion of understanding. (135)

The moment is such that Jules retains it as a singular image of his mother: "He still remembers, too, exactly what his mother was wearing: she wore a tawny belted dress with a white lace collar, and shoes with sequences of buttons, covered in leather. She carried a coral pink embroidered handbag, which rested at her hip" (135–6). And the repetition of these lines underscores that they are lodged in Jules' memory, and insists on their poetry. Further, this emphasis suggests that understanding might arise with the aesthetic meeting of image and word, an idea to which *Black Mirror* with its interest in art and writing (and its own poised prose) is committed.

If mothers are tied to various images in *Black Mirror*, *The Death of Noah Glass* has a particular interest in the visual inheritances a father bequeaths his children.²⁵ Noah Glass' special attraction to the paintings of Piero della Francesca "became a language they shared, as other families shared television, or tales of cheery outings" (74). While Martin and Evie tire of their father's loving lecturing on the topic, as adults the discussions about art the siblings have with their father, and between themselves, shape their affective relationships.

Their father's death prompts intense contemplations of these connections, which come to be understood in terms that derive from their shared interest in the image. Reflecting on the bond between her father and her brother soon after their father's funeral, Evie turns in part to the metaphor of the mirror to explain this relationship to herself:

> We have just endured, she thought, the funeral of our father and my brother is still as he was, negligent, self-centred, without a clue. He is still the cocksure adolescent bound for fame and glory, still contesting his father's authority. They were so alike, father and son, that they loved each other in self-confirmation. The equation of what they were was a tangled knot. They had mirrored each other's expressions, taste in women, in food, an admiration of all things Italian and for stories of miracles and saints. (19)

Whether imagined as a knot or a mirror, Evie's sense of being excluded from this relationship is clear. She admits adoring other twinned images, however, namely the diptych by Piero della Francesca of the partially blind Duke and Duchess of Urbino that was "always hung so that the couple faced each other" (201). She has a particular fondness for these images because "They'd been in the Uffizi with Noah, triangulated with the Duke and Duchess portraits before them. This capacity to make images live was the circuit their father had created" (238–9). (Her brother's recollection of the moment is somewhat different: "Noah's painterly topic that day was concealment. He was telling his children that concealment was also a function of art" (242).) Not only does Evie realise that "She understood what it was she was feeling, a kind of resentment that Martin had been loved more. It surprised her to name it for the first time. *Martin had been loved more*" (19). She makes the point to herself, perhaps unconsciously, by covering the mirror in her guesthouse room "as they did in traditional rituals" and also because she "liked the idea that she prohibited her own reflection" (30–1). If Evie refuses in her grief to admit her own image, elsewhere in the narrative it is her young niece, Nina, who is her playful double. Both Nina and Evie are represented in the novel as content with their

---

25 Evie Glass comes across a previously unseen photograph of her mother, of whom Evie (like Victoria) has no memory except for "the astonishment of not finding her there, of searching the rooms of their cold house, of crouching in corners waiting … in case stillness might summon her mother back" (63).

inwardness, and this affectionate, sensuous identification between them is made apparent in a brief but telling moment that rests on the image and act of mirroring: "She bent over Nina and kissed her, making her lips pudgy and fishlike. Nina screamed in pleasure and with her two hands, held Evie's face, distorted her own in a mirror of the fish lips, and returned the kiss" (219). If Evie enjoys this solidarity with her brother's daughter, then the narrative also supports, but equally contends, Evie's notion that Noah and Martin share an intimate understanding about images, and concedes her conception of them as paired reflective surfaces.

When Noah shows his son a postcard of a Caravaggio painting, *The Crucifixion of St Peter*, Martin's first response is playfully reductive. "Pissed-off St Peter" is how he describes it to his father, who senses that "his son seemed to understand what he had glimpsed in the brown light of that Roman church" (109). Yet, this relationship between father and son is also underwritten by the extra-textual, Old Testament-decreed guilt that Noah carries at both having administered alcohol to his son as a child, and the thought that his actions – undertaken while mourning his wife, the children's mother – might have had some role to play in his son's later addictions. This knowledge, which his children barely discern, weighs heavily on him and his relationships with his son and daughter. That Noah entrusts Evie with understanding the clue to the art heist in which he is implicated is only one instance in the novel suggesting her grief-stricken revelation might be more complicated than she can imagine at that time. And while she does not make the connection expressly herself, Evie, like Noah, has an interest in immaterial images, studying *acheiropoieta* as an adult but also thinking of movies as a child as being "just there, huge visions mysteriously unfabricated. It was a kind of natural magic" (125). It seems Evie, like her father, has always been thinking about images.

Initially, though, Evie's thoughts about her father and brother afford her to be (self-) cast in the novel as an outsider of sorts. Not only does the image of their mirroring have the effect of refusing her presence in their relationship; she lives at some physical remove, in Melbourne, from her Sydney-based father and brother, and has all but abandoned her professional interest in the miraculous image for a job at a bookstore. Or, as she tells her soon to be lover, images continue to interest her but "[s]he had not spoken like this [about them] for a long time" (125). When Evie is compelled to travel to Sydney to attend her father's funeral, however, she is also drawn to contemplate images again. The room in the guesthouse where she first stays before relocating to her father's apartment offers an unpromising glimpse of them. Here a "television hung from the ceiling like a black dead eye" and Evie reciprocates the gaze as she "watched the screen, unseeing. American crime drama … There was a female body, prone, and a fabricated tension. There was a babble of law language and a mishmash of cop threat" (36). It is into this kind of plotline that Evie and Martin have just been incredulously thrown, which might explain Evie's distracted disinterest in the program at that particular moment.

This uneasy relationship between the image and the real that this early scene in the novel relates is echoed later in the narrative (although temporally speaking it occurs prior to Evie finding herself in the Sydney guesthouse). Elsewhere in the narrative, the uncle of Noah's lover, Dora, calls on cinema to explain to a stunned Noah that the art heist he is proposing "will sound to you like the movies" but is, in fact, an everyday reality – "art theft happens here all the time" (173). Dora has a similar concern with how cinematic representations can act as a frame of commodified reference for others' apprehension of her reality, casting it as touristic souvenirs along the lines of "lurid T-shirts fashioned on the *Godfather* theme, with Marlon Brando silk-screened into a surly death's head, all eye-pit and shadow and distinctive skull" (251).[26] This cultural branding plays on Dora's mind. She earlier relates to Noah the violence and fear evoked by mafia members who murdered her male relatives and suggests her heightened awareness of how cinema has come to structure perception and ways of knowing: "'I know what you are thinking,' Dora said. 'That we are a brutal lot. You are thinking *The Godfather*. Don Corleone. You are thinking clichés'" (108). (Another character, Antonio, evokes the same cinematic reference to explain to Martin Palermo's shadow economy: "There were still Mafiosi in Palermo, still Cosa Nostra. But not, he insisted, like in *The Godfather*" (116).) Dora is half-right, even as Noah protests that her assumption is a misimpression. He quickly changes the subject to other images, those of Caravaggio that Dora studies as an art historian. As she tells him: "It is our compensation. Everywhere in Italy you will find the marvellous preserved in old images. I chose Caravaggio because he knew how these elements went together, because he was a man of violence" (108). For Dora, some images – those of Caravaggio – relate a truth that others empty of any aesthetic or political charge. The printed t-shirts are a case in point.

Dora might be suspicious of the ways select images circulate to turn material violence into kitsch, although one character's kitsch object is another's votive, as suggested by the silver ears Martin's elderly landlady in Palermo gifts him to ask for the "restoration" of his daughter's hearing. However, as Evie's time in Sydney stretches out in her waiting and grief, her fascination with the image is renewed. She needs a job, and responds to an advertisement calling for an assistant to provide descriptive audio for a "*blind movie viewer*" (120). Evie casts herself as eagerly participating in "a new kind of cinema; she would not allow any silence to go unchallenged" (127). It is a venture that has commitment to the idea that the description might keep pace, and faith, with the flickering of moving images.[27] The

---

26 One wonders what she might have made of Catherine in *Five Bells* thinking about Italy through the cinematic lens of Michelangelo Antonioni, "In the pallor of the world seen in black and white, Italy was a country of languid desire and unhappy women ... Emptiness, suspension, a vague searching that led nowhere" (166).

27 This new cinema is anticipated in *Dreams of Speaking* in an abbreviated form, wherein Alice remembers seeing with her former lover "the 1964 Japanese classic *Woman of the Dunes*" (163). Alice's recall of the tale of physical and existential entrapment is impressively vivid and concludes with the melancholic observation that "in the end there is no release, only the grim beauty of the black-and-white cinematography and the weird seduction of so stringent an

project sees Evie describing Alfred Hitchcock's *Marnie* (1964), with the narrative striving to approximate the action of telling – "The opening shot focuses on a canary yellow handbag, being held by a dark-haired woman, who is walking away from the camera" (149) – but also allowing for Evie's private editorialising: "'Blood red,' said Evie. 'Marnie is afraid of blood red.' … She resisted commenting: *bleeding obvious!* Such a clunky device" (150). If the job demands of Evie, and language, an accurate approximation of what is on screen, it also makes her newly aware of both the limits of her vocabulary, of her "attraction to metaphors of sight and light" (125) with their socially embedded values and ideas of images, and vision itself.

Present before Benjamin, Evie first believes herself to "speak from a position of invisibility" (124), and finds some relief in that situation. Benjamin challenges this presumed hiddenness, thought to be granted by his blindness. At dinner, he lets Evie know that he understands she is staring at him: "'People go quiet. They like to see if I'll knock over my wine. You develop a feeling for these things.' And with that forgiving remark they relaxed again" (201). Evie is not as occluded as she thinks she is, and her meetings with Benjamin prompt her to consider "the instability of vision" (127), which she discusses with Martin via Skype. Tellingly, the vision this technology affords is voluntarily cancelled to redress the power she feels is exercised by her brother's gaze: "What a relief the dark screen was – no huge brother-face to incite or command her" (163). Evie's wish to be unseen is partly understandable in the context of the persistent looking her male relatives exercise. Not only did Martin have a habit of watching and drawing his sister (specifically while she was asleep) when they were younger. At their father's funeral, her brother's eye is caught by an attractive woman and he then presumes to see himself as he believes (or hopes) the woman would: "The air of grief would make him appear mournfully seductive" (9). Noah is a little less self-involved, but for all his awkward hesitation he nevertheless has an occasional habit of looking upon Dora in terms that might otherwise serve as titles for paintings: "Her silhouette was beautiful: *woman smoking*" (108). In contrast, Dora is said to meet Noah "as he was, and granted him the benefit of the doubt, that he might be more than he seemed in the simplified economy of appearances" (167). His aesthetic image of Dora is resolutely shaken when she and her uncle later propose the art heist. When Noah looks at Dora, who "would not meet his gaze" (172), what he sees is not "*woman smoking*" but rather a woman who "sat with him not in fondness but as if assisting a business deal" (173). Noah has some difficulty reconciling the ideal image he carries of Dora with the reality of her situation, which is enmeshed with her care and concern for her beloved uncle and their shared history of violence.

Shielded from her brother's persistent and omnipresent looking by a blackened computer screen, Evie's summoning of "eighteenth-century philosophers preoccupied

---

allegory" (164). Alice is not relating the film to a blind man, but like Evie in *The Death of Noah Glass*, she has faith at this moment in the capacity of words to approximate filmic pace and vision.

with vision" and scientists specifically interested in experimenting with "the subjectivity of seeing" (127) is a way to further the novel's interests in the image and technologies of vision. The conversation with Martin has Evie talk about "these guys, with their romantic faith in our bodies as intelligent organisms. Sightless sight. Images without screens. What it might mean to have visions" (164–5). These exchanges go some way towards reconciling the siblings. Following Evie's move to Melbourne "they had become strangers to each other" (11), but there is a sense of new connection between Martin and Evie as they Skype-speak. The subjects discussed are themselves compelling, if somewhat alarming. They discuss Jan Evangelista Purkyně who "ran electric currents into his own eyeballs, and did little drawings of what he saw, diamonds patterns, mostly, and lines that looked like filaments and zapping electricity" (164). They talk also of Johann Wilhelm Ritter, admired by Johann Wolfgang von Goethe, whose poetic theory of colour perception took issue with Isaac Newton's objectivist *Opticks* (1704),[28] and who "fitted a contraption to his eyelids to hold them open so that he could expose his eyes to direct sunlight for up to twenty minutes at a time" (127). The conjuring of these exploits, which are pursued in the name of subjective visual phenomena, certainly aligns with the novel's wider interest in various types of images and the visions they produce.[29] Evie, for example, relates to Benjamin the conceit of *Blue* (1993), a far more recent film by Derek Jarman, who was "almost completely blind, suffering from AIDS, and nearing death" (177). As she tells of it: "There is just one image, a blue screen … But the soundtrack is extraordinary … Images come into being, as it were, from the hypnotic effect of contemplation alone … It's about losing sight, but not losing vision" (177). And what the siblings' conversation also submits (ironically, or pointedly, enough, given that the discussion about them is facilitated by an information technology that deals in abstract data and pixels) is the notion of human perception and knowledge located in bodily experience.

This idea is a telling one for Evie to raise as it was a turning away from corporeality that introduced her father to art as a child. At the leprosarium for Indigenous patients where he lived in his younger years, the sight of the people suffering around him, "his selfish revulsion" (43), has him "gripped by flinch and recoil; he could not imagine touching anyone but his mother" (42). This reaction is foundational to his ongoing shame at "his boyhood cowardice" (43), and it leads him to seek out distractions from the realities of the colonial infirmary that he only half-intuits. The racialised fear of contagion that saw Aborigines compulsorily interned is not something of which Noah, as a child, is fully conscious. And he certainly does not see it reflected in the book he turns to as an escape: "*Great Art Museums of the World*" (45).

---

28   Johann Wolfgang von Goethe, *Theory of Colours*, trans. Charles Lock Eastlake (1810; London: Routledge, 2019); Isaac Newton, *Opticks; or, A treatise of the reflections, refractions, inflections and colours of light* (1704; London: G. Bell & Sons Ltd, 1931).
29   See Nicholas J. Wade and Josef Brožek, in collaboration with Jiří Hoskovec, *Purkinje's Vision: The Dawning of Neuroscience* (Mahwah, NJ: Lawrence Erlbaum Associates, 2001).

In distinct contrast to his shunning of human touch, Noah is said to have "stroked the glossy paper and studied the legends to the paintings as if his future life depended on it" (45).[30] At boarding school, Noah turns again to images, moving ones this time, to cast himself, in a form of screen memory to distance himself from his disgrace, in the role of a celluloid saviour modelled on Charlton Heston in *Ben-Hur* (1959): "He too had looked at rags that might be people, and his fear and revulsion could be reworked into a ripping yarn" (49). Later still, when Noah comes to find in Piero della Francesca's *The Nativity* (1470–75) that future life his book of images pre-empted and protected when he was a child, a breathless, tumbling description is offered of the painting. The account attests to the painting's humanism, far more so than the revolutionary linear perspective it ushered in, and arrives at the observation that the image marries "[t]he mundane and the divine … in seamless coalition" (70). When Noah steps outside the gallery in London following this revelation, his body and senses are unusually alert: "He smelled wet wool and exhaust fumes and cigarette smoke … he was cold and alone and a foreigner in London, but he also felt an astounding relief. It was almost joy, a joy such as he rarely felt again looking at a painting" (71). Later, he remembers that moment as one in which "he'd come alive with inception and changed the direction of his life" (78). Noah insists on privileging art's immateriality. Yet, this image which he internalises – the event of Martin's birth has Noah expressly recall Piero's *Nativity* – nevertheless elicits a corporeal response that counters Noah's childhood turn to the image as an escape from the bodily realities brought to bear by the ongoing legacies of settler colonialism in Australia.

Noah dedicates his adult life to the study of images that are determined to be "great" by measures which are not always apparent and are certainly changeable.[31] Martin, who makes art, queries the systems of value in which images circulate by giving passing thought to the way in which the knowledge about images his father has imparted to him is not neutral. When reflecting on the Swiss scientist and mountaineer Horace-Bénédict "de Saussure … he invented the cyanometer, a little pie chart to estimate the shade of blue of the sky", Martin looks out of the window in Sydney and determines "How false was European knowledge. No Prussian tint out there: the sky was *cerulean*. A different pigment entirely" (23). (Martin's focus on blue also connects him and his thinking in colour with his sister's account for Benjamin of the film *Blue*, and with much of the text that is suffused with this hue expressly linked to the paintings of Piero della Francesca.) Despite the various

---

30 In *Five Bells*, James also lays claim to a never-realised future by means of an art book gifted him at the age of fourteen by his mother. Titled *Lives of Modern Artists*, the book suggested the possibility of "making meaning without needing a single word. The promise of Europe and of shadowy spaces, of a life grievous but endurable, the record of which might exist in a gallery somewhere, detached and valuable, impersonal and illustrious, stylish, pure" (34).
31 The works of Piero della Francesca were rediscovered and revalued in the nineteenth century; the museums showcased in Noah's childhood book would not then have recognised indigenous images as art.

shortcomings his sister attributes to him, Martin is certainly aware that the image carries social values and encourages particular ways of seeing the world. His own paintings command significant prices and are markers of taste, as Evie suggests when she sees an early painting by Martin on Benjamin's wall. The presence of the painting is a sign of both her new employer's class status and his artistic discernment, which Evie shares. She recognises hanging in Benjamin's apartment her brother's work, pieces of which she has been gifted from the same series, as well as other "paintings by various Australian artists" (148).[32] These are characters who move with a quiet confidence through the world of images that subtly distributes forms of cultural capital. Benjamin seems to part-acknowledge this effect when he responds with humour to Evie's account of "Our veneration of images. Our wish to see them as impromptu, and separate" (125). He tells her, "This may be difficult to sustain when we're watching *Die Hard* … Not much veneration there" (125). What Benjamin's interest in popular film underscores is that engagement with some images might afford immersive pleasure as much as Evie determines that others demand regard at a respectful distance.

For all this discussion about images in *The Death of Noah Glass*, an additional concern is raised as to what it might mean, what might be involved, in seeing others in terms that bring to mind the image. And this disquiet is expressed not through words but through witnessed acts of bodily violence. Among Noah's shames is his inability, or refusal, to go to the aid of a man he sees being beaten in the streets of Palermo. The scene sets up the two men involved in the incident as antagonists, even though, or perhaps because, they are both dependent on religious pilgrims for their livelihood. The Italian bus driver who inflicts the blows transports to one of the city's cathedrals the faithful, who dutifully take photographs of religious statues on their phones and buy postcard images of Santa Rosalia from an impoverished Indian street vendor, who is the victim of the violence. (The pilgrims' seemingly unthinking creation and consumption of images contrasts significantly with the affective response of Evie, an atheist, to the image of Christ for sale in the shop window opposite the same cathedral: "she couldn't bear it … the tortured body of a man … even here, in reverential show, the body was dreadful in its wounding" (269).[33] The impression left by way of these contrasting responses is that

---

32 Evie's financial situation is of some (perhaps patronising) concern to her brother, who resolves early on in the narrative "to find out … if she needed any help, or money. He'd noticed with a pang her cheap and unflattering clothes and the first threads of grey in her dark wavy hair" (12).
33 A similar distinction is found in Bruno Latour's thinking on idolatry and iconography, which Jones writes of in an essay remembering Veronica Brady. Gail Jones, "Dark Places: The Movement of the Image (Thoughts on the Work of Veronica Brady)", *Coolabah* 22 (2017): 10–18. What Latour proposes in his discussion are models of reading images. He determines that idolatry rests on the assumption that full attention to the image will afford access to the truth. By contrast, iconography involves an approach to art that acknowledges its implied, inexact and manifold possibilities. Bruno Latour, "How to be Iconophilic in Art, Science and Religion", in *Picturing Science, Producing Art*, eds. Caroline A. Jones and Peter Galison (London: Routledge, 1998), 418–40.

travel photography conventions can entail a dulling effect.) While others around Noah feebly protest the viciousness of the bus driver, Noah does not and his apprehension of the horrific scene approximates the still images that seem to be the touristic end in themselves for the pilgrims:

> He watched in guilty fascination as the man became smaller under the boot, squirming, a figure of pain, his face bloated and contorted, his jaw working with no words. Blood spurted from his nose.
>
> This was what was possible – the reduction of one man's life to bodily distress, time abolished in the crux of a spectacle. This knowledge made Noah hostage to his own paralysis. (168)

Noah forms this image directly following the narrative account of the pilgrims' interests in the circulation and possession of saintly images. One implication encouraged by this associative link is that the vendor is cast as an unsuspecting martyr whose persecution, undocumented by the quasi-permanence of the image, might be lost if not for Noah's recognition of this "figure of pain".[34]

Noah's position as witness is more complicated than this reading would suggest, though, as his inaction – "he did nothing to intervene" (168) – overwhelms and undermines his aesthetic apprehension: "He could have acted – he could have been the one to seize the driver's arm and pull him from the man turned creaturely with pain and submission" (168). Noah is pursued by this memory of the man and his own failure to respond to the man as a figure *in* pain. The scenario finds its ethical response in the narrative when Martin is beaten by unknown assailants, only to be surprisingly found, and tellingly assisted, by Veeramani, himself an immigrant who runs the internet café Martin frequents in Palermo.

What these doubled scenarios lend themselves to is the notion that while the novel insists on the complicated, multifaceted meaningfulness of images in their many forms and contexts, there are limits to the ethics they might be asked to enact. This is especially so, the narrative suggests, in the face of the facticity of bodily vulnerability and physical violence that permeates the text, from the respective beatings of the nameless vendor and Martin, to the killings of Dora's father and two brothers by the mafia and the absence of another brother, "an anarchist and a writer who disappeared about the same time. We never saw his body" (107). Evie intuits the violence that art itself might be charged with committing when she glimpses the image of the wounded Christ for sale among other "ecclesiastical paraphernalia" (269). It is an insight that underscores her father's humiliation at encountering the beaten man as a figure of pain, a spectacle observed from a distance

---

34 Susan Sontag, whose early work *On Photography* Jones acknowledges as an influence for her writing of *Sixty Lights*, is also concerned with how the ubiquity of the image might obstruct regard for the suffering of others. Susan Sontag, *Regarding the Pain of Others* (New York: Farrar, Straus & Giroux, 2003); Susan Sontag, *On Photography* (New York: Farrar, Straus & Giroux, 1977).

rather than being recognised as another human needing the protection and care he does not extend.

Lucy Strange in *Sixty Lights* grapples with a similar concern from the novel's first pages when an image comes unbidden to mind, mid-night. She may or may not be asleep, but the memory of the image, or indeed her concern at thinking in images, propels her into alert wakefulness. Whereas the incident Noah witnesses takes place in the streets of Palermo, Lucy recalls a scene in colonial Bombay where she is living with Isaac Newton.[35] The events she remembers also involve an Indian man (unlike the impoverished immigrant in *The Death of Noah Glass*, this man is at work in the city on a construction site), and issues of class and colonialism complicate any assumption of easy cross-cultural understanding or identification:

> This is what she had seen, earlier that day. An Indian man had been climbing the bamboo scaffolding of one of the high colonial buildings, with a large mirror bound to his body by a piece of cloth ... when some particular gust or alarum that carried the dimension of fate caused him to misjudge his footing and fall through the air. Because he could not release the mirror, but clutched at it as though it was a magic carpet, he landed in the midst of its utter shattering, and was speared through the chest. The quantity of blood was astounding. It spurted everywhere. But what Lucy noticed most – when she rushed close to offer assistance along with everyone else – was that the mirror continued its shiny business ... She simply could not help herself: she thought of a photograph. (3–4)

Unlike Noah, who is stalled before the violence he sees, Lucy rushes to assist. But both characters are distraught by their fascination, which is distilled in their common turn to the image to apprehend what they have witnessed. This troubling is signalled for Lucy when her thoughts return during the night to what she saw: "And only later, in deep night, did Lucy rise in distress ... and seeing before her this man who was horribly killed" (4). What she comes to see, after some delay, is the appalling, unexpected death of the man when at first she had called to mind a photographic image.

This impulse and its unsettling implications are rehearsed again, and recast, when this initial scene is later returned to. Importantly, this moment, and Lucy's memory of it, are related following a conversation she and Isaac have about art and religion. Both declare themselves to be atheists, with Isaac quick to acknowledge that (as with Evie and Martin Glass in *The Death of Noah Glass*) his lack of faith

---

35 Lucy is first introduced to Isaac by way of a miniature image, with her uncle presenting to Lucy a daguerreotype of a man "dark-faced and phosphorescent in his glassed-in square ... fixed in a doleful closet of perpetual night" and proposing that she travel to India to marry him (106). On Lucy's leaving of India, he in turn gifts her a miniature painting, surprisingly erotic but also suggestive of the elusive emission of light that her shipboard lover, William Crowley, had identified as bioluminescence and which Lucy determines is "in every living thing" (171). Their friendship is conducted through images.

does not lessen his appreciation of holy works: "the art achievements of sacred expression that seemed in themselves, and of themselves, transcendental … Mystery adheres only in art" (156). Lucy's proximate question: "But what is art?" is left unanswered by Isaac, but the immediate retelling of Lucy's witnessing and late-night remembering of the Indian man's death is a partial response (156). One provisional answer to the question Lucy poses might subtly lie with the patterning this moment evokes, with its recollection of the novel's first scene. The response given by this repetition is that art can be thought of as that which assumes the capacity to arrange and rearrange events so that connections and meanings might be actively made by means of associations and patterns. Another answer, however, focuses on Lucy's thinking about photography, which in the world of the novel has a contested status as art, with Lucy's mentor, Victor Browne, conceiving of it as strictly a science and Lucy herself privately contesting that categorisation.

The second time Lucy is pictured remembering her witnessing of the man's death (which is, in effect, the same moment that opens the novel; Lucy does not herself twice remember the event on different occasions although the doubled scene is not replicated in exactly the same way across the narrative), she again admits that "What in retrospect disturbed Lucy was her fascination … The mirror and the blood were an irresistible combination. Lucy could not help herself; she thought of repetition; she thought of a photograph" (156). It is not only that Lucy is rehearsing here her lifelong habit of thinking about the world in photographic terms; the implication is that the light-reflecting surfaces of the fragmented mirror recall for Lucy, highly attuned to photographic seeing, the flash of the camera and the partial, replicating vision photography affords. Curiously, though, the sight of the man's bloodied body being removed and the remaining trace of the accident, "a field of drying blood, sprinkled with sparkles of shattered mirror", conjures a seemingly puzzling phrase: "*Blood in bucketsful*" (157). This short string of words, which sits incongruously with the description that comes immediately before it, emerges unexplained in the narrative but it has the effect of lacing Lucy's witnessing to another sensory experience from childhood, one also founded on specific loss. On returning illicitly to their home, where both of their beloved parents have recently died, Lucy and her brother Thomas as children encounter a foul stench "of mutton and dog mess" and happen upon "a bucketful of water – *purple blood in bucketsful*" that kindly Mrs Minchin had left for the dog (24–5). So, by association rather than any conscious willing, the man's death brings to mind for Lucy her parents' deaths, and her initial, irresistible thought of photography comes to see Lucy pause before what she poses as the limit of the image.

The death Lucy witnesses might instantly conjure in her mind a photograph. But when she reflects on this response to the accident and her experience later at night, she recognises, in delayed reply to her own questioning about art, that death also retains its own mysteries. She determines that what she has seen is unspeakable – "Lucy did not speak of the accident to Isaac" – and also unrepresentable: "There was the mystery of art, but there was also this mystery, the slash of mortality …

Lucy could not record or exorcise the death by mirror" (157). Lucy is said to have "stored it [the man's death and unsettling aesthetic response to it] as a secret, as an untaken photograph" (157), while the narrative voice tells without extravagance of the unexpected violence the man suffered: "a long spear of glass entered his chest and another cut an artery in his arm. Blood spurted everywhere and the man died almost instantly" (156). Lucy's acknowledgement that any photographic image, taken or not taken, might fail to record or exorcise the death she has witnessed takes on further significance when her encounters with other ways of summoning the dead by means of images are considered.

As a child, Lucy accompanies her Uncle Neville to a medium, "Madame d'Esperance, whose special talent was for summoning the tragically dead" (92). Lucy is immediately suspicious of the medium's claims and talents, but her uncle, in his ongoing grief for Lucy's mother, is enthused and wants to believe that the conjured apparition is "the revenant Honoria Strange" (94). Lucy is enthralled by the image. But unlike her uncle, who is utterly convinced of the apparition's sincerity, Lucy also knows "in her heart of hearts that this was not her mother, and imagined devious trickery and hidden contraptions" (94). Even as Lucy realises the fraudulence of the image, it stays with her as a persistent memory: "She could not forget the anonymous image stretched like a sail upon the ceiling, or Uncle Neville's impassioned sobbing, given up for what he truly believed was his younger sister, recomposed above them, bright and imperative" (96). For all her knowledge of the fakery of the image her uncle accepts as real, Lucy's understanding of the photograph comes close to her uncle's hopes that the image might endure after death, and carry something of the lost presence. With this idea in mind, Lucy's conjuring of a photograph when faced with the Indian man's death might be thought of as extending to him her private photographic belief, and wish, for remembrance.

In a letter she sends to Isaac from London, she writes about the metaphysics of this absorption in the image, wondering if "*Perhaps we are not part of all we have met, but of all that we sensationally and passionately notice*" (198). In the same letter she also conceives of photography as something loving, and physical: "*A kind of honouring attention. I think of photography – no doubt absurdly – as a kind of kiss*" (200). Her appreciation of the manifold possibilities of photography is heightened as Lucy reads her approaching death on and through her physical body: "At night she was assailed by imaginings of her own inner body. She imagined her lungs like honeycomb, fretted into unsupportable organic sculptures, lacy with their own death-dealing dissolution" (189). Lucy thinks about her condition and corporeality quite unlike the doctor who curtly confirms her suspicions with one word: "Consumption" (188). And the knowledge of her impending death has Lucy's thoughts turn to a coming time when she not only imagines that "doctors would have an apparatus to photograph the inner body" (189–9), but those images will also be a form – compensatory, perhaps, given the disease and death they could predict and detect – of visual poetry:

To light the dark. They would present patients with crimson images of their hearts and lungs; they would show the skeleton in all its fine ivory architecture … They would even, Lucy imagined, photograph the brain, and these photographs would have a lyric and lambent quality: they would be like pods of loveliness, like newly discovered planets, remote, elaborate, drifting on glass plates like secrets still unbroken. (190)

What Lucy imagines here is the body as a darkroom where images of the inner world are produced and projected. It is an interiority devoted to images. She also anticipates future technologies of otherwise impossible seeing beneath the skin's surface that might realise this magic-lantern-like display. Her prognostications and poetics are confirmed by Mr Sakamoto in *Dreams of Speaking*. He tells Alice Black of how Magnetic Resonance Imaging conjures corporeal secrets, otherwise hidden from human vision, "a three-dimensional image of the interior body can be built … Water, waves, magnetism, image: it is a kind of poetry. A physical *haiku*" (167). And Lucy additionally wonders if death might not be an emptying out but rather a meeting of accumulated images, an "accession of vision from all the times and images she had known … She was already becoming pure space, a chamber of images" (220). The narrative then accedes to this fantasy, or hope, moving through a series of image-moments that suggests Lucy's metaphysical imaginings. And it is an idea to which the novel returns, with Lucy's moment of dying presented in photographic terms: "a slight tilt of vision, as when one tilts a daguerreotype in its box … an abyss of light" (246). Lucy is without religious faith, but she tutors her lover in photography with words that carry the sacred. She shows him the shimmering effect of halation and determines that this technical error might be understood as "the loveliest accident. It shows us the force of radiance, its omnipresence" (240). Jacob responds by conjuring complementary ideas, saying that "What you describe others would call the Holy Spirit" (240). The light Lucy anticipates on her deathbed is not the sign of some heavenly afterlife but rather the very substance of photography, which carries with it the promise of its own form of modern immortality.

In preparation for her own death (the pierced worker in Bombay presumably never had this opportunity), Lucy had taken photographs of those people she adores because of her commitment to the idea that these images have a kind of permanence, or at least endurance, that extends beyond her own lifetime: "These images would endure. These would gloriously outlive her" (239). She also understands them as signs of her love. Additional to these images are two photographs of Lucy herself that survive her death, although Jacob is largely dissatisfied with them. He wishes both for more photographs and ones that represent his beloved more faithfully. It is not so much her features he longs for, although these he desires to see rendered because he fears his memory of them will soon be replaced by the posed image of her alongside Isaac taken in a far-away photographic studio. It is "her luminosity" he desires (248). He wonders (in a similar way to Martin Glass, who considers an artful memorial to his father in *The Death of Noah Glass*) if he might, in paint, perform a resurrection of her, as he once did his father, but feels the task is impossible, both in his grief and in the knowledge that art has its limitations.

That Jacob is thinking of art in these terms at all, that the image, both painted and photographed, might be an honouring form of restoration, resonates with an idea captured in the inability, and unwillingness, of Lucy's family to dispose of the other photograph taken of her. This image is one in which she appears as a ghost, thanks to her movement at the moment of the camera's exposure, which both aligns her with, and exposes, the visual trickery of Madame d'Esperance. This premonition is disturbing to others but the dying Lucy contrarily considers it to be beautiful and "her gift" (236).

Lucy's way of seeing resonates with a perception of the image attributed in the novel to her father, Arthur Strange, who is otherwise given little narrative attention. Early on in the novel, and while on his honeymoon in Florence, he requests of his cherished wife that she have her profile cut by a craftsman working with thin black paper.[36] On its completion, Honoria's new friend, Harriet White, is repulsed at the resultant silhouette: "It's rather morbid … I don't like it at all" (37). Harriet views the cut paper as an image of death, as tomb-like and mortifying. Arthur, however, silently disagrees and sees in the image "This token. This sign" (37). Arthur's understanding of the image as a "figure cut into pure light" – his conception of it as an affirmation, rather than a mode of bereavement – anticipates his daughter's fascination with, and understanding of, photography (37).

That the photograph of a ghostly Lucy might be thrown away as waste points to its material quality.[37] The photograph is, after all, an impression printed on albumen paper, which Lucy once worked to manufacture. That Lucy's bereaved family cannot bring themselves to do so, however, suggests the emotional charge the photographic image carries in this text. Lucy nominates her photographs "[A]rt-in-the-age-of-mechanical-reproduction", drawing from and foreshadowing Walter Benjamin's political theory of reproducible art (239).[38] But in the world of this novel, the photograph is felt (irrationally, perhaps, but nevertheless powerfully) to be somehow private and close. It is a part of, or connected to, or stands in for, or even is, the person pictured. And this impression intensifies when the beloved is no longer present. The photograph is a verifying representation.

---

36   Arthur thinks of his love for his wife in aesthetic ways that Noah Glass would appreciate. On looking at Honoria's face, the word annunciation comes to mind as "All over Italy he had seen images in which the passage of spirit was rendered in a faint dotted line, a love-corridor, a dedication. Something in these particular images had moved him: the affirmation of imperceptible connection" (36).
37   The advent of digital photography in a time beyond Lucy's own questions, or at least complicates, the physicality of the photograph which Lucy's family confronts.
38   Walter Benjamin, "The Work of Art in the Age of Mechanical Reproduction", *Illuminations*, trans. Harry Zorn, ed. Hannah Arendt (1968; London: Pimlico 1999), 211–44.

Even as this claim is made for the photographic image in *Sixty Lights*, Jones' writing cannot be said to settle on any one final idea of the image. Instead, it is concerned to represent and honour the multiplicity of its forms and attributed meanings. The persistent presence of so many images in Jones' work is an acknowledgement of their affective power and their capacity to prompt intellectual excursiveness and ethical considerations. In dreams, on canvas and paper, and flickering on screens, they also are signs of aesthetic appreciation, of love and the elegiac, and that which might be difficult to comprehend.

5
Modernity

Following her return to London from Bombay, and grieving for her Uncle Neville, Lucy Strange in *Sixty Lights* experiences anew the judder of mid-nineteenth century modernity:

> Lucy now found her own culture a shock. After almost eight weeks in England, she was still thinking of India and feeling misplaced and dislocated. The radical modernity of London disturbed her – the clutter, the heavy clothes, the trams, the bells, the cash registers and the lampposts. … Standing on the corner of Oxford and Regent Streets she looked at the stream of people flowing by with their heads down and their coats pulled against the cold wind, and felt as they did: embattled, quashed, and by something as imprecise and irresistible as wind.[1]

Lucy's apprehension of the centre of empire is nested in her mourning as she reflects that "These may be … the forms that grief takes, this sense that everything is unmitigated and out of kilter" (184). Her quickly paced catalogue of the city environment imparts an impression of speed and discomforting clamour; even the weather seems to be in the service of its modernity, with the wind signalling alienating currents and force. Modernity is imagined in this scenario as that which pushes unrelentingly forward, clanging as it does and cowering those in its path, with Lucy's thoughts concurrently running in different directions. Yet Lucy is not immune to the impact of the modernity she hears and observes, her vision augmented by the camera she wheels around the city streets. Gail Jones' description of her character's perceptual encounter with the modern city as a shock suggests that

---

[1] Gail Jones, *Sixty Lights* (London: The Harvill Press, 2004), 184. All subsequent references are to this edition and appear in parentheses in the text.

the new technologies she notes mark radical changes in the realms of both everyday life and the senses.[2] Lucy's is an embodied aesthetic response to modernity.

Across Jones' texts, characters are often tasked with thinking about, and perceiving, modernity. The inventory of prewar modern Paris that *Black Mirror* details, for example, converges, aptly enough, on the eye of the visual artist Victoria Morrell:

> She bore in her eye the principle of convulsive beauty: together and correspondent existed typewriters, aeroplanes, purple hyacinths unfolding, the fur collars of large women trapping droplets of water, cigarette smoke, velotaxis old men weighted by sandwich boards, telephone receivers (ringing loudly or sitting silent), café names writ effulgent with electric lights, marble columns, kerbside garbage, gargoyles on the verge of effacement, the lit faces of patrons leaving a crowded cinema, lampposts, stairwells, wind-blown hair, the dark and deadly-looking night-time canyon of the Seine.[3]

The Surrealist principle of convulsive beauty that Victoria personifies carries its own updated, avant-garde designs on shock.[4] And as Victoria's gaze skims across seemingly unrelated elements and ephemera that comprise Paris, the effect is an impression of perception. What Victoria beholds is less an individual gaze than a modern way of looking, which seems to have undergone something of a transformation in *Dreams of Speaking*. When Alice Black first encounters Tokyo at the invitation of her friend, Mr Sakamoto, the solid lampposts and columns that were among the structural elements of Victoria's vision have given way to burnished exteriors that reflect back viscous visual perception: "Curved surfaces reflected people as jellyfish. There was fluted steel, trapezoidal glass and plasma-screen messages, escalators aplenty, virtual and actual realities."[5] Although the senses

---

2   Shock is a now-familiar trope for thinking about modernity. Walter Benjamin, for example, turned to it to describe new modern experience, which he saw registered in the poetry of Charles Baudelaire. He was making the point that sense perception is historical. See Walter Benjamin's essays "On Some Motifs in Baudelaire" and "The Work of Art in the Age of Mechanical Reproduction", *Illuminations*, trans. Harry Zorn, ed. Hannah Arendt (1968; London: Pimlico, 1999), 159–62, 216. Benjamin takes his cue from Karl Marx's aphorism that the senses are a human accomplishment: "the forming of the five senses is a labour of the entire history of the world down to the present". Karl Marx, *Economic and philosophic manuscripts of 1844*, trans. Martin Milligan, ed. Dirk J. Struik (New York: International Publishers, 1964), 141.
3   Gail Jones, *Black Mirror* (Sydney: Picador, 2002), 87. All subsequent references are to this edition and appear in parentheses in the text.
4   See Rita Felski, "Shock", in *Uses of Literature* (Oxford: Blackwell, 2008), 150–85.
5   Gail Jones, *Dreams of Speaking* (Milsons Point NSW: Vintage, 2006), 161. All subsequent references are to this edition and appear in parentheses in the text. Sydney, early at night, is thought of by Catherine Healy in *Five Bells* in similarly lustrous, mediated terms: "Restaurants were like televisions, boxes of fluorescent encounter and hyped possibility. Everything, every surface, appeared glossy and over-bright." She also regards the art gallery she visits as machine-like, run on a particular frequency and to a tight social script: "The gallery seemed also to have within it a hidden hum, as if circuits were at work in cables and grids, and

might be felt as privately experienced, their representations in Jones' narratives suggest that they render bodies open and vulnerable to others and the world.

This exposure is evident in *The Death of Noah Glass*, a novel overtly interested in visual art; it is Noah Glass' favourite Renaissance painter, Piero della Francesca, who introduced to seeing and Western art the convention of perspective. Yet, amid its concentration on vision and visual aesthetics, the novel also makes sense perceptions felt by the presence of two minor characters – Nina Glass, who is deaf, and Benjamin, who is blind. The "buzzing world" (61) that so enchants Alice and Mr Sakamoto in *Dreams of Speaking* is loud, frightening and alienating for young Nina when she receives cochlear implants at the end of the novel. Her experience of initial hearing and speaking is wholly frustrating, even violent: "The boom of sound, it assaults her, and here is her own heavy tongue, fat as a slimy slug."[6] By contrast, the descriptive audio that Benjamin is seeking when he advertises for someone to speak movies promises to bring about a new model of perception. Nina's aunt, Evie Glass, applies for the position and comes quickly to nominate the endeavour "a new kind of cinema" (127), which Benjamin anticipates when he identifies himself as a "*blind movie viewer*" (120). Benjamin cannot see; he is not literally a viewer, although his insistence on taking part in an audience with film summons that term's etymological roots – a state of hearing or condition of listening. His call, though, is for a co-mingling of senses. Beyond an individual body, this new perception emerges through the modest staging of an ethics that involves trust and truthfulness. Benjamin declares to Evie that their first screening together will be a "good test", to which Evie replies, "Of me or of you?" (148, 149). The question goes unanswered directly, but is perhaps addressed by both Evie's growing understanding that Benjamin's blindness, which she has earlier idealised, is not a "deficiency or loss" (310) and her determination that "she wants independently to know him" (311). The mingled perception she and Benjamin create does not mean that each relinquishes their separateness and specificity, and it is imbricated with a technology of modernity – the cinema.

Adjunct to her narrative worlds of modernity, Jones has signalled an explicit interest in the senses.[7] In an essay on Michael Ondaatje's novels *In the Skin of A Lion*

---

    technicians, invisibly efficient, were twiddling knobs and keying symbols behind the scenes to keep the electric lights low, the temperature moderate, and the atmosphere one of a lost city newly discovered with all its indecipherable artefacts." Some of the art she sees in this murmuring place is equally alienating; she is "confronted by a sequence of objects that might have been constructed by robots. They were of space-age substances and undetectable handiwork. They had a technological sheen and a kind of high unheard frequency." Catherine is confused, and unimpressed, by this particular exhibition. Gail Jones, *Five Bells* (London: Harvill Secker, 2011), 172, 161, 160. All subsequent references are to this edition and appear in parentheses in the text.

6 Gail Jones, *The Death of Noah Glass* (Melbourne: Text, 2018), 308. All subsequent references are to this edition and appear in parentheses in the text.

7 This interest in the senses is not contained to texts explicitly addressing modernity. The *Fetish Lives* short story "Touch (The Births of Walt Whitman)", for example, imagines the birth of its

(1987) and *The English Patient* (1992), Jones reads these two texts as celebrating the "cohering perceptual phenomena" of skin that privileges

> the life of the senses in contradistinction to the life represented in words. Both are preoccupied by an almost Aristotelian version of sense experience: the five senses are not discrete, but somehow linked by a cohering perceptual phenomena (aisthesis) which indissolubly connects affect, sensation, and perception ... Moreover, in a conspicuously joint poetics, each uses skin to exemplify both irreducible presence and the opacity of character; each situates the body in contexts of blackness and darkness; each is a writing of the wound, preoccupied with damage; each reads identity as tending towards an ethics of gentle regard, allowing the autonomy of the other and inaugurating a politics of relationality, in which kinship with the dead, as well as the living, is implicitly assumed.[8]

Jones' claims are subtly alert to original meanings of the term aesthetic, which involved a faculty to sense intensely, rather than any judgement,[9] and they self-consciously take their cue from Michel Serres' thinking about the senses. Serres provides the essay with its evocative epigraph: "The body is constructed as books are composed, its pages come together like pieces and patches ... sewn entirely from the skin."[10] And his sensorial interests might be thought of as contributing to what has been termed the "sensory revolution" in historical studies and anthropology in particular. This "sensorial turn" has presented itself as a response to scientific models which locate the senses within individual neurological and cognitive processes. Sense studies offers an alternative to this mode of apprehending the senses, with Mark M. Smith suggesting that it is "a way of becoming attuned to the wealth of sensory evidence embedded in any number of texts".[11] It is committed to investigating how the world is differently experienced through sense perception, and has also taken to task the ways in which modernity's

---

    titular character as an assemblage of sensations; for the poet's mother, taste is foregrounded: "Someone brushed at her mouth with a cloth soaked in water. Fluid had never tasted this sweet or this pure." Gail Jones, "Touch (The Births of Walt Whitman)", *Fetish Lives* (Fremantle: Fremantle Arts Centre Press, 1997), 126-7. And the infant's benediction by an elderly slave woman is made in a gesture of touch and song: "Her black soft hand was his first precise touch ... Prayers whispered in Dutch, the tongue of her early masters, were offered to contradict the bitter hug of mortality" (127–8). Sense perception, the short story proposes, is what gives access to the world and knowledge of the body: "He will carry forth in all his years the slave woman's caress ... As a birth-day gift she gave him the esteem of his body" (128).

8 Gail Jones, "A Poetics of Sense: Michael Ondaatje's *In the Skin of a Lion*", *Moving Worlds* 10 no. 2 (2010): 58.
9 See Robert Jütte, "The Senses and Aesthetics", *A History of the Senses from Antiquity to Cyberspace* (London: Polity Press, 2005), 142–56.
10 Michel Serres, *The Five Senses: A Philosophy of Mingled Bodies*, trans. Margaret Sankey and Peter Cowley (London: Continuum, 2008), 227.
11 Mark M. Smith, *Sensing the Past: Seeing, Hearing, Smelling and Tasting, and Touching in History* (Berkeley: University of California Press, 2007), 5.

knowledge systems have compartmentalised perception into discrete registers – sight, hearing, smell, taste, touch. The sensory approach seeks to understand corporeal existence as dynamically related to the world through complex and interconnected sense perceptions, giving rise to the concept of intersensoriality that has become central to sensory studies.[12]

Serres' work is exemplary in this regard. He insists on thinking about, and experiencing, the senses as intermingled;[13] the senses belong and work together, he submits, and are a threshold of understanding. He also signals a profound disagreement with the phenomenology of Maurice Merleau-Ponty, which is determined by Serres to be foolishly bodiless.[14] (This is quite a provocation given that Merleau-Ponty's philosophising is roundly credited with restoring to the philosophy of mind the sensory plenitude of the body.)[15] Serres' turn to the multisensory is also a renunciation of systematic analysis. His prose matches his subject in that its style is one of exploration, rather than examination. He suggests that "the sensible is open like a star or almost closed like a knot to every direction, mobile in all dimensions and sweeping over the entire neighbourhood", with this stellar poeticism necessarily resisting any effort to pin down his ideas.[16] He expressly writes against such a dictate: "Do not seek to know how to look at a landscape – compose a garden instead. Learn the aesthetic error of submitting everything to a law: levelling the local produces boredom and ugliness."[17] Serres' call to abandon reading for trampolining might not have immediate appeal for Jones' characters who are committed to the ethical possibilities of reading and literature, however. And his notion that language prohibits the connections to the world that the senses afford as creative forces is up for debate.[18] What Jones does

---

12   David Howes, ed., *Empire of the Senses: the sensual culture reader* (Oxford: Berg, 2004). This multisensory turn has its counterparts in contemporary neuroscience and psychology. These disciplines have suggested that sensory modalities previous thought distinct interact complexly.
13   Music has a special place in Serres' work. Its non-linguistic register makes it especially appealing and it incorporates all the senses, Serres suggests.
14   It is also an intervention in much theorising on the senses. Taking their cue from Enlightenment ideas that yoked vision with knowledge, scholars who have addressed the senses largely (although certainly not exclusively) privilege sight. See, for example, Rosalind Krauss, *The Optical Unconscious* (Cambridge, MA: MIT Press, 1993); Jonathan Crary, *Suspensions of Perception: Attention, Spectacle and Modern Culture* (Cambridge, MA: MIT Press, 2000); Maurice Merleau-Ponty, "Eye and Mind", in *The Primacy of Perception*, trans. Carleton Dallery, ed. James E. Edie (Evanston, IL: Northwestern University Press, 1964), 159–90. Martin Jay's encyclopaedic work takes issue with this alleged obsession with vision. Martin Jay, *Downcast Eyes: The Denigration of Vision in Twentieth-Century French Thought* (Berkeley: University of California Press, 1993).
15   Maurice Merleau-Ponty, *Phenomenology of Perception*, trans. Colin Smith (London: Routledge, 1962).
16   Serres, *The Five Senses*, 304.
17   Serres, *The Five Senses*, 239.
18   See Steven Connor, "Introduction", in Michel Serres, *The Five Senses: A Philosophy of Mingled Bodies*, trans. Margaret Sankey and Peter Cowley (London: Continuum, 2008), 9.

perhaps value, though, is Serres' "shapes of thought" about the senses,[19] which "draws attention to the habits by which we speak of sense experience".[20]

Fiction is one form that lends itself to imagining the senses in the way that Serres challenges scientific and philosophical thinking, and its apparently objectifying appraisals, to reconceive of them. As Steven Connor, one of Serres' foremost interlocutors, suggests, "Literature gives the necessary supplement of sensory form to the senses themselves, allowing the senses to be perceived as well as conceived."[21] It is this supplement that Jones sees apparent in Ondaatje's work, and which is also evident in her own writings that imagine how modernity is not only comprehended intellectually, or symbolically, but also felt and perceived. In some of his reflections on the senses, Serres seems to think of modern technologies as hampering the true nature of perception with his sweeping claims that "Our technology is often like orthopaedics for a healthy limb, which, as soon as it is replaced or lengthened ... becomes ill or impotent."[22] Jones' writing, by contrast, is open to the modern making, elaborating and extending of the senses because, her narratives suggest, these give shape to ethical enquiry.[23] This chapter's interest in the ideas and technologies of modernity in Jones' writing, with a particular emphasis on *Dreams of Speaking*, therefore touches on the senses.

Of all Jones' texts, it is *Sixty Lights* that would seem to engage most overtly with what are now commonly understood as the defining features of (one version of) modernity:[24] the development of speedy transportation; the emergence of new

---

19 This phrase is Steven Connor's. Steven Connor, "Topologies: Michel Serres and the Shapes of Thought", *Anglistik* 15 (2004): 105–17.
20 Jones, "A Poetics", 58.
21 Steven Connor, "Literature, Technology and the Senses", in *The Cambridge Companion to the Body in Literature*, eds. David Hillman and Ulrika Maude (Cambridge: Cambridge University Press, 2015), 180.
22 Serres, *The Five Senses*, 68. Elsewhere, Serres argues differently, writing that "Through technologies, which I have said sail from our bodies, we broaden our reception to the entire possible empirical biocapacity." Michel Serres, *Hominescence*, trans. Randolph Burks (London: Bloomsbury, 2019), 113.
23 With this interest, Jones' work has much in common with the Romantic poets whom Lucy Strange favours in *Sixty Lights*. As Noel Jackson has suggested, "Romantic poets ... develop an understanding of sensation as a crucial resource of cultural representation and a vital conduit for imagining models of political consciousness, communicative ethics and social change." Noel Jackson, *Science and Sensation in Romantic Poetry* (Cambridge: Cambridge University Press, 2008), 6.
24 Jones' work is well attuned to contemporary debates over modernity, from Karl Marx to Bruno Latour, Partha Chatterjee and Rita Felski. Karl Marx, *Capital*, Vols. 1 and 2, trans. Ben Fowkes (New York: Vintage, 1977); Bruno Latour, *We Have Never Been Modern* (Cambridge: Harvard University Press, 1993); Partha Chatterjee, *Our Modernity*, Sephis-Codestria Lecture No. 1 (Dakar: South – South Exchange Programme for Research on the History of Development and the Council for the Development of Social Science Research in Africa, 1997); Rita Felski, *The Gender of Modernity* (Cambridge, MA: Harvard University Press, 1995). Jacques Rancière's understanding of modernity in terms of an aesthetic regime "of perception, sensation and interpretation of art [that] is constituted and transformed by welcoming images, objects and performances that seemed most opposed to the idea of fine art" also resonates with Jones'

communication technologies including the press, photography and cinema in its nascent forms; the growth of cities; the economic and cultural reach of British colonialism; the widespread production of artificial lighting; progressive politics; and theories about space, time and matter, which find expression in Jones' novel in words themselves: "Words circulated in the air like a new kind of energy, in waves and particles, focused and diffuse, showing and obscuring what might exist in the world" (100).[25] But, if Lucy's world is characterised by felt jolts and a noisy soundscape, then the technologies presented as new or immanent in *Sixty Lights* are no longer wondrous in *Dreams of Speaking*, and hence it is this novel that pauses to consider in some detail the senses in relation to the modern innovations Lucy anticipates. This shift is suggested by the observation Mr Sakamoto's daughter makes of her father and his "affection for storytelling and redundant technologies" (181). It is a regard also shared by Alice. Alice's hope for her book on modernity is that it might tell of "the extraordinary existence of the telephone … Xerox machines, neon lights, photography, astronauts" which otherwise goes unnoticed (60). These are things which are rendered both ubiquitous and near-obsolescent in the shiny, pixelated world she and Mr Sakamoto inhabit. Exemplary of this state of things is a photograph Alice recalls: "The photograph of an astronaut pretends to exist in the future … a figure beyond time itself. Now we know otherwise. Now this double-sized man, this cumbrous puppet, is almost antique … he is lodged so directly in past time that no amount of gadgetry unfixes him, or propels him forward" (36–7). What was once an image of futurity is determined to be irrevocably stuck in the past.

That Evie and Martin Glass communicate in *The Death of Noah Glass* by Skype rather than by the conventional telephone seems to confirm Alice's suspicions about the obsolescence of certain modern technologies in the early twenty-first century. The experience of talking by computer is novel enough for Evie to give extended thought to how Skype brings her and her brother into virtual proximity:

> There was a timelessnesss to Skype that Evie found compelling. She heard Martin's ring and was home to receive his call. At once, forward motion ceased and they were both in their screens, in the lucid waft of a satellite drift. She imagined beams dividing through space, connecting them in the shape of a colossal A. Martin sat back, so that his face was undistorted; Evie was loose-limbed and relaxed after her zesty swim. (235)

---

writing. Jacques Rancière, *Aisthesis: Scenes from the Aesthetic Regime of Art*, trans. Zakir Paul (London: Verso, 2013), x.

25 In the acknowledgements of *Sixty Lights*, Jones signals the influence on that novel of Lynda Nead's work on nineteenth-century London. Nead's study traces the rise of visual mass culture and its shaping of gendered experiences in the modern city. Lynda Nead, *Victorian Babylon: People, Streets and Images in Nineteenth Century London* (New Haven, CT: Yale University Press, 2000).

Far from provoking the shock that Lucy felt when confronted by London's radical modernity, this new technology – characterised in terms of waft and drift – has Martin and Evie pictured as equally serene, their bodies accommodating the technology that connects them across time and space. The attention Evie gives to Skype, which is later repeated by Martin when he notices Skype's glossy vision while seeing and speaking with his daughter, Nina – "her pearly face illuminated and too close to the screen … His daughter, glistening in weird light thousands of miles away and tucked into her silence" (100) – is striking alongside another telephone call in the novel. Martin does not think twice about speaking by telephone to a man he hopes has information about his father: "It was exactly a fortnight, but felt much longer when Maria handed him the telephone and he heard for the first time the voice of Antonio Dotti" (88). This experience of telephony is comparatively unremarkable.

The modern things that interest Alice and Mr Sakamoto in *Dreams of Speaking*, and are imagined to be on the brink of desuetude, also form the basis of ethical friendship in that novel. And both *Dreams of Speaking* and *The Death of Noah Glass* emphasise embodied senses and literature's capacity for feeling and perceiving modernity as bound up with ethical contemplations and convictions. Reading across Jones' novels, this concern with ethics and the senses is thrown into relief by specific renderings of modernity which determine that aspects of it are problematic and dispiriting.

In *Black Mirror*, for example, Victoria's father, Herbert Morrell, is offered up as a thoroughly unlikable colonial capitalist fixated on economic modernity:

> Dividends obsessed him. Apart from his tin mine in Cornwall and his rubber plantation in Ceylon, apart from his shares in railways, steel production and the building of sea-going ships, the goldfields seemed to offer the prospect of truly world-dominating wealth … He theorised and imagined his own capitalistic enhancement, and saw himself unoriginally as a kind of European monarch, with his subjects arranged in a reverent pyramid, midget-sized beneath him. (170–1)

The novel underscores that Morrell's glossy wealth comes about from the labour of poor men suffering from lung disease and tunnelling the earth. But Morrell himself wields associated signs of modernity (such as steam engines) to shore up his avaricious endeavours and to justify colonial possession and exploitation of the land, which he understands to be teeming with untapped resources. That he presumes possession of the mines in the first instance is because he upholds a version of modernity as the measure by which the land's custodians, the Aboriginal people, are found wanting:

> At the top of the list, at one hundred per cent, he placed Great Britain, Great Britain the incomparable. This was a nation he considered peerless in its qualities and achievements. He thought of steam engines, country manors and Westminster

Bridge … Other races and nations (for he mentally conflated them) fell way in the steep declension of imperfection … At the bottom of his scale were the Australian Aborigines, a people whom Herbert considered despicable since they were without markets, commodities and evidence of artistry, and moreover refused all the blandishments of Civilisation. (158)

Indigenous people are without the trappings Morrell attributes to modernity, so he can conveniently deny both their connections with the land and their humanity, a pervasive colonial legerdemain. Elsewhere, the narrative voice recognises that "[t]he indigenous people, the Maduwongga, had myths to account for the amplitude of the desert" (53), but Morrell is unable, and unwilling, to admit such knowledge.

Alice Black in *Dreams of Speaking* is certainly no Herbert Morrell, but she is given over to fantasies of modernity that expose her privilege, with the novel looking to two acts of travelling as a way to identify and examine possibly suspect encounters with otherness. The first involves a story that Alice relates to Mr Sakamoto on the topic of "misplaced technology" (112). She and her former boyfriend had gone venturing to a volcanic Indonesian island "trying to avoid the big centres, trying to set ourselves a challenge" by climbing to the summit (114). Alice and Stephen carry with them notions of escaping modernity. The trek is obligingly laborious and treacherous, although their guide easily navigates the terrain, and their projections are quickly dispelled once the pair reaches the peak. They not only find their guide relaxing and smoking; they also come across another travelling couple, resplendent in "lime-coloured Lycra and reflective sunglasses" (114–15). Moreover, the man of this pair is speaking into a mobile telephone, "looking like an advertisement", his words relayed across the world by satellite while in the village below "there was not even electricity" (115). The turn of Alice's mind to advertising on encountering the man suggests how modern media shapes her way of seeing and knowing, and the mirroring of the couples leads Alice to part-reflect on her thinking about modernity.

For Alice, the contrast she detects between herself and Stephen and the Lycra-clad pair is both farcical and an affront that conjures ambivalent feelings; the man on the mobile both ruptures her half-hearted idea that this place is untouched by modernity and is a sign of how the infrastructure of modernity is unequally distributed. Even as the village is pointedly said to be without electricity, it is presumably a stop-off on the tourism trail of which Alice and Stephen are a part, however much they might want to see themselves as separate from that industry.[26]

---

26 Alice is not the only one of Jones' characters who seeks to distinguish herself as a non-tourist. Victoria Morrell in *Black Mirror* thinks of wartime Paris as simulacra, a city anticipated and known by maps, and she is largely unimpressed by the "Famous spots on the map, touristic X-marks of simplified and summarised attractions, seen already by everybody and already over-encoded" (140). Her topography is intimate, sense-filled and fleetingly lit, "Not the blue-guided or Baedekkered *monuments illuminés,* but the golden colour of faces that emerged

Tellingly, any thoughts on modern tourism had by the local guide Alice and Stephen have hired is left unknown. It is Alice instead who is left with the enduring memory of how the gadgets of modernity emerge in what she sees as the most unlikely places, even as this specific place she visits is possibly not as isolated from modernity as she seems to want to think.

The second moment when Alice's presumption to travel has attention drawn to it is with a letter written by Norah, Alice's sister, which appears early on in the novel. The letter is one of many correspondences in the book, with the vast majority consisting of emails Mr Sakamoto sends Alice, telling of the biographies of modernity's inventors. Norah's letter is therefore quite unlike the others, and it registers the contemporary political context that Alice herself seems to give little thought to, busy as she is with the writing of her book. Norah makes this point offhandedly but also cuttingly, when she writes to her sister that "Perhaps you are sensible to be away, overseas, thinking of other things" (62).[27] What is told by Norah's correspondence is that while Alice is in Paris researching modernity, an unspecified war (most likely in Iraq) is occurring and refugees seeking protection in Australia are being held in detention centres. Norah writes to Alice of her own anti-war activities against government actions that involve "bombing the shit out of people they can't see. And that it will go on for years and years, with poor and powerless people invisibly suffering" (62). Norah is thinking here of individuals transformed into virtual targets, their deaths made collateral damage by militarised technologies whose extended reach and speed supersede ocular perception and human capacities. And her concern with the incarcerated children speaks to an "older" form of technology, the penitentiary system of the nation state, that dehumanises those people "held behind razor wire" rather than extending them hospitality (62).

---

    lit from any doorway ... The glint off a saxophone somewhere smoky. Light rays shot, iris to iris, in the electric moment of seduction" (140–1). By meaningful contrast, the invading German soldiers are rendered sense-less; they are said to have smuggled "their evil intentions like a species of tourist. They book-browsed on the left bank and followed guides through Montmartre. They purchased perfumes, and silk stockings and miniature models of the Eiffel Tower ... They also took a census of French Jews and deported them to death camps" (241). Their rapacious attitude to things that otherwise appeal to smell, touch and sight underscores the casualness and unthinkingness of their horrific actions.

27 Norah also seems to conceive of her sister's project on modernity as separate, both physically and politically, from the activism in which she is involved with her husband; together they attend rallies and send the refugees "phone cards and toys" (62). The gesture marks out a point of difference between the sisters that turns on the novel's abiding trope of the telephone. In another form, Jones' short story "The Ocean" sought to counter the pervasive vilification of asylum seekers in Australian political discourse. Gail Jones, "The Ocean", in *A Country Too Far: Writings on Asylum Seekers*, eds. Rosie Scott and Tom Keneally (Melbourne: Viking, 2013), 103–9. The volume in which "The Ocean" was published aimed to bring "a different perspective and depth to the public debate on asylum seekers". Rosie Scott, "Introduction", in *A Country Too Far: Writings on Asylum Seekers*, eds. Rosie Scott and Tom Keneally (Melbourne: Viking, 2013), 1.

Norah's letter underscores that while some versions of modernity might be founded on flows (of capital, of communication),[28] which Mr Sakamoto and Alice discuss, not all people can presume the same ease of movement, and certainly cannot realise the kinds of travel and border-crossings, that the central characters of this novel do without hesitation. Unlike the refugees of whom Norah writes, Alice takes for granted her ability to travel unimpeded; she seemingly has money, and definitely has uncontested claim to that twentieth-century invention – the passport.[29] She drops hers at one point in the Charles de Gaulle Airport and consciously notes "a royal-blue square with the kangaroo and emu standing posed in the centre. It was like a surrealist object, displayed in its oddity and drastically misplaced" (22). The emblem might well be idiosyncratic.[30] But the passport enables Alice to move freely across borders, as Norah recognises, in a way that others cannot presume to do.

If Alice's circumstances are held up as a modest but meaningful fault line of modernity, then Mr Sakamoto's raising of questions in that novel about the existential damage that might be wrought by the fetishism which takes hold of Herbert Morrell, points to another. Mr Sakamoto thinks of Japan as the "kingdom of modernity, the empire of signs, gadgetry, robotics, futuristic inventions" (153); he himself comes from a wealthy family and when questioned by a former girlfriend, with whom he is briefly reunited, as to why he is researching the life of Alexander Graham Bell, he tells her:

> I saw men of my age disappear into their possessions. They became their cars, their stereos, their new apartments. They totalled their wealth and drank whisky late at night in smoky bars, looking sullen, looking sad. I wanted something else. It took me a long time to figure it out. I wanted a project to remind me of the complexity of things, and of human endeavour … does that sound pompous? (149)

Mr Sakamoto's project comes to look urgent and necessary, rather than grandiose or self-aggrandising, given a meaningful digression that occurs earlier in the novel and which centres on the comparatively recent invention of the now ubiquitous barcode. Designed to eliminate human error and indeed human labour, as well as collect masses of data rapidly and therefore make redundant language itself,

---

28 The metaphor of flow is one that routinely constitutes descriptions and desires of modernity, particularly as it manifests as economic globalisation. See Arjun Appadurai, *Modernity at Large: Cultural Dimensions of Globalization* (Minneapolis: University of Minnesota, 1996). Emily Apter offers a critique of thinking about modernity in terms of flows in *Against World Literature: On the Politics of Untranslatability* (London: Verso, 2013).
29 The idea of protected passage in another's land is not new. The passport of the standardised type that Alice carries, however, is an early twentieth-century invention. See Amitava Kumar, *Passport Photos* (Berkeley: University of California Press, 2000).
30 Like many of Jones' protagonists, Alice has a distressing childhood encounter with a kangaroo, the memory of which remains. One of the things Mr Sakamoto determines to be resolutely "unmodern" is the kangaroo (21).

the barcode is, the narrative voice suggests, the "new language of capital" (46). Its debut on chewing gum packets is taken as representative of the value the novel attributes it: "consumption with no real purpose, repetition with no end. Anti-food. Mere product. Chewable America" (46). This passage makes clear that the narrative voice has little sympathy for the kind of capitalism that upholds consumption for its own sake and converts everyday experience, including the sense of taste, into algorithms of trackable, anonymous information that can be operationalised. *Dreams of Speaking*, and Jones' texts of modernity more broadly, seek to recast modernity in a language that reclaims the senses.

One trope that Jones' narratives call on to set in motion this imperative is that of transportation, and in particular the train. As Wolfgang Schivelbusch has shown, the nineteenth-century development of train travel not only saw the natural landscape radically altered but also sense perception, and human ideas of time and space, transformed.[31] Trains and the change in sense perception they ushered in have been abiding interests of studies on modernity and the modern literary imagination,[32] and Jones' novels evoke that tradition to suggest how sense perception might be brought into ethical thinking and living. Whereas Herbert Morrell in *Black Mirror* thinks of trains in pragmatic terms, as the basic infrastructure of colonial economies, Jones' novels more broadly conceive of trains (together with one other form of modern transport, the aeroplane) as exemplars of modern experiences of motion and sensation, as well as metaphors for modernity itself, that accrue complex attitudes and ambivalent feelings. In Jones' narrative worlds, trains afford the imaginative interaction of internal life and external spaces, and the representation of ethical contemplations and connections.

In *Sixty Lights*, for example, among the markers of new modern experiences and technologies that Lucy encounters in London is the beginnings of the Underground constructed by "workers emerging from a gape in the street" and who "had skin made of earth and looking like a fraternity of the underworld" (189). The Underground train system will bring changes to the structure, speed and patterns of everyday life and sense perception that Lucy herself foretells but will not live to experience. Its presence is acknowledged only in passing in this novel, which is preoccupied largely with the camera and its augmentation of human vision, and it also finds fleeting but meaningful expression in *Black Mirror*.

Early on in that novel, the biographer Anna Griffin enters the very Underground train system that Lucy sees being built, only to return to it, both physically and in thought, at various points throughout the narrative. Anna's

---

31 Wolfgang Schivelbusch, *The Railway Journey: Trains and Travel in the Nineteenth Century*, trans. Anselm Hollo (New York: Urizen, 1979).

32 See, for example, Matthew Beaumont and Michael Freeman, eds. *The Railway and Modernity: Time, Space, and the Machine Ensemble* (Bern: Peter Lang, 2007); Marian Aguiar, *Tracking Modernity: India's Railway and the Culture of Mobility* (Minneapolis: University of Minnesota Press, 2011); Nicholas Daly, "Railway Novels: Sensation Fiction and the Modernization of the Senses", *ELH* 66.2 (1999): 461–87.

thinking about the Underground changes across the narrative as she comes to some understanding about Victoria Morrell, her biographical subject, and her own family history. When Anna first contemplates the Underground, Lucy's recognition in *Sixty Lights* of the human labour that modern industrialisation relies upon is instructive to recall. As Anna rides the Underground a century and some decades later, the sensorial bodies Lucy had witnessed, with the evidence of their labour etched on their skin by dirt, are not even a memory. The claims capitalism makes on the tunnels these men built are signalled by the "billboards blur" Anna sees from the train window (96). Yet, Anna thinks of the Underground in terms that are very much like those that come to Lucy's mind and which also implicitly recall her own father's dangerous toiling in Herbert Morrell's mines: "In the underground men advanced against the earth itself, creating air, like little gods, where none had been before" (176). Anna conceives of the Underground as "these roaring, fearsome, pitch-dark tunnels. As she descends the steps she feels she is entering an infernal space" (95). And her experience of modern mobility that the speed of the train affords is an unhappy one; it sees her locked with other passengers "in a strange and lonely union" and offers little in the way of sympathetic community (96).[33] Later in the novel, however, Anna comes to think of the Underground very differently. Whereas once the trains had conjured feelings of alienation and melancholy, they later come to resemble for Anna

> strips of film. They slide past her in a string of fluorescent squares, speeding vision in lit sequences to a kind of profane illumination. Trains hurtle at the darkness and disappear with a roar. They bear, she reflects, a lovely transience. And when sparks arise in a spray at a curve on the line, Anna experiences a flash of genuine excitement. She knows she is now seeing as Victoria Morrell sees – this fleeting dazzlement, this random white flicker of ordinary time. (251)

This abstract perception is expressly coupled with Anna's physical sensuousness: "Her heart is pounding" (251). Anna's felt understanding of trains as cinematic is a gift of seeing aesthetically given her by Victoria Morrell, the Surrealist artist, as well as the broader avant-garde interest in creativity and sense perception that Alice Black acknowledges in *Dreams of Speaking*. In that novel, while travelling on a train, Alice expressly recalls the Surrealist train-cinema proposed by Henri Michaux:

> Along the route between Paris and Versailles, there would be placed a series of movable sculptures, activated by the speed of the train passing by. A superimposition and fusing of images would occur, so that the passenger would

---

33 The Underground has similar metaphoric, and melancholic, resonances in Jones' short story "Desolation". Confronted by her ashamed lover, Eleanor is prompted to think of the metro "carrying figures whose faces blurred … as they zipped into the underground night, like people dragged, fast motion, beyond any reliable identification". Gail Jones, "Desolation", *The Kenyon Review* 25 no. 1 (2003): 13.

see outside the window a "plastic" cinema, a spectacle of odd beauty and dislocated enchantment. (163)

Alice's thinking about Michaux's three-dimensional, large-scale kinetic cinema is not only suggestive of the ways in which Jones' novels, and Alice particularly in *Dreams of Speaking*, detect modernity's unexpected gestures everywhere. It makes apparent, too, the cognitive mechanics of film perception, with the train speed realising the motion that is understood as apparent when static images projected as film are viewed.

Modern visual perception that trains and cinema give shape to is also foregrounded in the first pages of *A Guide to Berlin*. Waiting for the arrival of snow in Berlin, Cass' isolation is established in the novel's beginning not only by means of the pervasive cold weather to which she is unaccustomed, but also by her viewing of Berlin through a grubby train window:

> The white sky was menacing. The plates of ice on the Spree, uneven and jagged, resembled a spray of shattered glass after a wartime bombing. There must have been old people, she thought, gazing through the grime of an S-Bahn window, who looked down at the river and the canals and recalled something blasted and asunder, piles of bricks, lives scattered, and a windowless episode in their childhoods. It would have been an easy connection, this shiny reminder of things broken, this pattern of severity and damage showing the forsakenness of the world.[34]

The next scene has Cass ascend from the underground U-Bahn, with the cityscape that greets her presented as meaningfully bitter: "She slid escalated into frosty air and the noise of the street, generously surrounded in her loneliness by so many sights almost meaningful" (5). Cass' grasping knowledge of her displacement and solitude, which both train rides suggest, is directly relayed through her senses: the frosty sting of the weather on her face, her surrounds just out of focus and the din she hears.[35] But what the novel introduces in its very first paragraph is the idea of visual perception shaped by modern transportation. Cass sees the sky and the Spree through the train window; what readers are presented with is the notion that these isolated images are brought into relation, as though a film, by the train's movement, which also gives rise to Cass' thinking about memory.

This yoking of trains and memory is also a feature of *Five Bells*. Whereas Cass' travels on the Berlin trains cast her as an outsider and observer, the trains in *Five*

---

34 Gail Jones, *A Guide to Berlin* (North Sydney: Vintage, 2015), 3. All subsequent references are to this edition and appear in parentheses in the text.
35 Cass' initial observations about Berliners is that they are cut off from the world as a consequence of their individualised modes of moving and living: "They rode in sealed cars. They shut themselves in offices. Whole apartment blocks seemed to have not a single person about" (4).

Bells carry somewhat different connotations. In *Five Bells*, Pei Xing delights in, but is also wary of, the orderliness that she credits Sydney's modern trains, which are momentarily stilled. Along with crowds that gather on its platforms, Pei Xing finds herself at Central Station. But her attitude towards the trains – the fact that she is even thinking about them in studied, extended ways – marks her out from those around her. These people, she understands, are orchestrated by largely unnoticed technologies that regulate human movement in a pleasing, systematic fashion. By contrast, Pei Xing attends to the gathering speed of trains as a metaphor for her immersion in memory. Punning on the place-name from which these trains depart and arrive, Pei Xing is determinedly neither central nor stationary:

> It was reassuring to see so many people in the world. So many legs moving, stepping upwards, to the modern command of sliding doors.
> *Central Station*. Pei Xing thought wryly that she would never be at the centre of anything, that her life would always be this circling around an irrepressible past. As the train accelerated away, so did her recollection. The world in a train-ride was conducive to her own speedy summonings. (76)

In the same novel, and with the near-exact same phrasing used by Pei Xing that invites connection and comparison, James similarly resolves that he too would "never exist at the centre of anything" (34). He also finds himself at Central Station, although his experience is distinct from Pei Xing's. Here he feels disoriented, and when boarding a train, he "wanted to cruise" (75), to experience his own speedy convening of thoughts roused by the train's movement, as did Pei Xing. This alignment of his consciousness with machine velocity is not to be for James, however, as he is jolted from the slipstream of his memories by an unexpected sign that appears before him. Unlike Pei Xing, whose inner life lets in modernity on her train-terms, James is without such reassuring rhythms that span internal and external experiences, and as the novel progresses, he is shown to be without any sense of the peace that Pei Xing has come to through difficult means.

It is in *Dreams of Speaking*, however, that trains have an extended role to play and this is because they are inextricably bound up with the characters' interests in modernity, their friendship and the narrative's concern with ethics and the senses. The revelation of the two main characters' common interests in modern things occurs when Mr Sakamoto and Alice are travelling in the same compartment on a suitably older train between Chartres and Paris, and have a shared experience of listening. They are drawn to each other initially because of their mutual recognition of a John Lennon song that might otherwise serve as background noise. Alice is drowsily watching her reflection in the window when "she heard music from somewhere"; for his part, Mr Sakamoto is represented as coming to wakefulness when he too hears the same song in the same moment: "The man sitting opposite Alice opened his eyes and smiled. 'Instant Karma,' he said. 'This song is called 'Instant Karma'" (58).

Mr Sakamoto's gloss might well be unneeded: Alice surely already knows the title of the Lennon composition. What his naming of the song works to underline is the fusing of the unmodern and the modern that will be the basis of the friendship it brings into being, an idea that is repeated and returned to in the novel. The lyrics Alice and Mr Sakamoto hear while together on the train suggest the notion of the eternal that the pair will come to discuss – "Yeah we all shine on / On and on and on on and on … " – at the same time that the song title's reference to instantaneity recalls the logic of modern capitalism, with its commitment to the invention of speed and constant newness (59). The storage of Lennon's voice by technological means, which separates sounds from the singer's body and allows for its posthumous and widespread diffusion, perhaps makes these recordings a product in the instant economy to which the song's title refers. (It is also this technology that comes to structure and extend the friendship between Alice and Mr Sakamoto.) Yet, the text confirms that all that is "wired, lit, automatic and swift" in this way does not easily or necessarily supersede and displace other things or times (47). Alice explicitly recognises this point when she relates to Mr Sakamoto the story of Arthur Stace who, after a "conversion experience", obsessively chalked the word "eternity" on the pavements of Sydney for nearly four decades (90). Mr Sakamoto appreciates the gesture and in it recognises what he values in poetry: "'Nuance' and 'eternity': these are the two dimensions of *haiku*" (91). He also refuses the more familiar notion that the "time of modernity … was despotic acceleration and unholy speed. The hunger for nuance and eternity infiltrated the lives of everyone, even the speediest executive" (91). The implicit conceit is that unmodern things exist alongside (and indeed beyond and within) those that might be more immediately understood in the world of the text as exemplifying modernity.

As Mr Sakamoto tells Alice, "The difficulty with celebrating modernity … is that we live with so many persistently unmodern things. Dreams, love, babies, illness. Memory. Death. All of the natural things. Leaves, birds, ocean, animals" (21). For the sake of playful argument with Alice, Mr Sakamoto presents the world in this binary way – the modern and unmodern. The difficulty he identifies, however, which might also be thought of as the simultaneity that undoes dualistic thinking, is what Jones' writing is alert to. The novel makes this point plainly when Mr Sakamoto encounters his former girlfriend, Clare MacDougall, after many years of distance and silence between them. He has unobtrusive hopes for reconnection, but Mr Sakamoto is instead wounded when Clare collapses drunkenly into collective nouns and binary thinking to accuse him (as a metonym) of "invading Edinburgh … You Japanese tourists. In hordes, every summer" (151). His gentle critique makes a principled point that upholds the necessity of respectful difference and distinctiveness, and highlights his role in the novel as a guide to ethical thinking and practice:

"It satisfies Westerners," he said quietly, "to see us as a collective, to make us uniform, to dishonour us in this way."

> Clare seemed not to be listening or not to understand.
> "We are no less specific than you," he went on.
> "Westerners! Thanks very much." Clare was leaning on the table. She tilted her glass.
> "I was making an ethical point," Mr Sakamoto said, "about how generalisation destroys." (151)

Clare fails to get the point and proceeds to insult Mr Sakamoto with taunts and stereotypes that her brothers once used (along with the physical assault) to signal their overt disapproval of their relationship. The only possible end to their meeting is that the two former friends "parted in acrimony" (152), and Clare's swift departure from the narrative affirms Mr Sakamoto's convictions as just.

As befitting the velocity of their subject and the mode of transport in which they first meet, Alice and Mr Sakamoto's shared interest in modernity sees their own friendship speed up. The two meet for meals, movies and lengthy discussions about modern objects and aesthetics, the "unremarked beauty of modern things, of telephones, aeroplanes, computer screens and electric lights, of television, cars and underground transportation. ... There had to be a lost sublimity, of something once strange, now familiar, tame" (18). These conversations accelerate their connections and affections. As Mr Sakamoto's daughter, Haruko, teasingly suggests when she meets Alice for the first time, "He once rang and said he had met a woman who talked as he did and was interested in food ... We thought he was falling in love. It was a shock to learn your age" (180). Their discoursing about modern things casts them as unlikely companions, and not only for the reasons Haruko identifies. Since childhood, Alice has identified with the figure she determines to be the loneliest of modernity, the astronaut:

> she saw herself a floaty astronaut ... There would be a silver visor reflecting everything, and she would be a shape, just a shape, in what had seemed to her always a sorrowful enterprise. ... Even as a child she saw on television how sadly astronauts moved, smitten by world-historical symbolism and the gaze of too many invisible cameras. ... She was seven when she began to see them in daydreams. They belonged to moments of dismay and quiet estrangement. Alone in their silent world. Completely alone. (3)

Alice's deep grief at the recent passing of her friend, Mr Sakamoto, intensifies her feelings of remoteness that she expresses in this manner in the first pages of the novel (although it is an emotional state only understood in retrospect as his death is not explicitly acknowledged at the book's opening). Her longstanding preoccupation with this space-traveller figure from childhood is established in the text and, importantly, it is understood by Mr Sakamoto. In response to her admission of other-worldly disconnection, he tells Alice of the astronaut carved into the walls of the New Cathedral in Salamanca where he had recently visited. Mr

Sakamoto is not quite sure how to read the inclusion of the image: "I thought it a sacrilege, a kind of puerile mischief. But after a while it began to look more and more acceptable ... almost a theological point – about the inclusiveness of creation ... I'm not sure, really" (112–13). While wanting to keep alive the ambiguity Mr Sakamoto wonders at, in the context of Alice's abiding affinity with the astronaut the figure suspended in stone rather than space seems less theologically weighted than determinedly fixed in existential drift. The meanings Alice affords the astronaut emphasise her separateness from, and her fascination, with the technologies of modernity that produce and circulate the images on which she rests her self-fashioning. Like the astronaut, she is seemingly lost and alone in the modern world she inhabits, but the glimpse of this figure's extraterrestrial vision she is given is momentary revelatory.

Trains are not the only forms of modern transportation that interest Alice and which *Dreams of Speaking* turns to in order to signal the changes in human perception that modernity ushers in. Aeroplanes also preoccupy Alice, although she has little interest in the places on the ground where they stop to refuel and allow passengers to board and disembark. The novel presents the space of the airport as a wholly unremarkable part of a modern traveller's experience. Here Alice and Mr Sakamoto "drank coffee in an inhospitable café, ringing with noise. Chrome and aluminium clanged about them. A child was somewhere wailing ... Electronically modulated announcements, generated by machines, boomed into the café, incomprehensibly" (153). The airport is presented as an impersonal place, gloomy, with Alice reflecting that "this was yet another characteristic of airports – to induce generic dejection and slap-dash conversation" (153). But its ordinariness is meaningful in that it provides a noisy contrast to the visually sublime experience Alice has in a cockpit of an aeroplane.

When first travelling to Paris, Alice, who suffers from insomnia as so many of Jones' protagonists do, imagines the aeroplane she temporarily inhabits to be a non-place, "a wearisome, dull, zombie imprisoning" (18), in which time warps and humans are rendered insensible.[36] The descriptions of light transmitted by the screens built into the seat-backs – "a posthumous blue washed over bodies, faces" (19) – afford a deathly association to the sleep to which the other travellers have succumbed and lead Alice to wonder at "what form of modernity this might be, and how she

---

36 Compare this tedious, early twenty-first century experience with that of Victoria Morrell in *Black Mirror* who remembers as a three-year-old, nearly a century earlier, flying for ten minutes only with her father in a biplane "constructed of struts and boxes" with "wing fabrics [that] tensed and relaxed, like the inhalations and exhalations of an ingenious automaton". The marvel of this mechanical respiration; the feat of flying itself; and the new visions it affords – "she gazed down upon the earth and saw it sliding away ... Ahead and below the shape of wings skimmed over the ground and Victoria understood that this was their own projected shadow, their inhuman shape cast over an altered geography. She was thrilled and terrified" – are seemingly disregarded, forgotten or simply not experienced by Alice and her fellow passengers (167).

might include it in her book" (18).[37] At the very least, it is a form of modernity Alice observes; her affective response to it is minimal, or at least underwhelming.

The section of the aircraft Alice temporarily inhabits as a traveller is represented as utterly distinct from the cockpit to which she gains access by displaying her university credentials and concocting a story about needing to do research for a hazily conceived project on flight. Whereas the films Alice watches mid-air are of "diverting inanity" (19), her senses are enlivened in the cockpit; vision is intensified: "Alice saw a curve of endless black sky, and far below, a carpet of uneven lights, profuse and lovely. Bright forms constellated and slid beneath them. Patterns of flash, ardent glows, electrified destinations" (20). What Alice sees is cast as supernal, which Alice herself recognises when she quietly confesses to the pilots that, as an atheist, she feels "like God" (20). This extraordinary sight has her newly enraptured; earlier, Alice had determined that aeroplane time was something only to endure: "The habit of detachment was useful in such situations" (18). In the front section of the plane, however, she is alert to velocity – "She was watching speed, watching modernity" (20) – and the conviction on which her true proposed project on modernity rests seems confirmed: "There had to be in the world of mechanical efficiency some mystery of transaction, the summoning of remote meanings, an extra dimension – supernatural, sure" (18). Alice exalts this supra-human speed of her contemporary times, and she is existentially exhilarated by it.[38]

On the ground, however, things are presented as radically different. Whereas the "circuits, sparks, powerful calculations" that Alice physically senses in the cockpit – "her old-fashioned heart was racing" – lead to rapturous contemplations (20), when located at the airport Alice is still and glum. Not helping her mood is the fact that she is about to say goodbye to Mr Sakamoto, unexpectedly returning to Nagasaki, and the half-gleaned realisation that the heavenly, omniscient vision she was afforded by the view from the cockpit is re-apportioned to the surveillance technologies that dominate the scene before her. Alice watches Mr Sakamoto as he enters "the exclusive zone of scanning machines, metal detectors and antiterrorist devices. He passed under the archway that somehow knew if he was carrying a gun" (153). The technology addresses Mr Sakamoto as a potential threat. But the gesture he makes is a quiet defiance of this figuring, and confirms his humanity: "He waved. Then he bowed. Alice also waved, and then bowed. The symmetry between them contested the turmoil all around … It was a single event of neat correspondence. It was humane and tender. It was like theatre, like art" (153). Mr Sakamoto's gestures, mirrored back to him by Alice, benevolently convey their resonances. The surveillance equipment

---

37　Alice has a very similar response to the Tokyo hotel room she occupies – "a hotel of crushing anonymity … It did not feel like Japan. It did not feel like anywhere" – and thinks of "funerals – their eerie systems of motorisation in removing dead bodies, their distended time" (160).

38　In a different context and with different transport, Anna Griffin in *Black Mirror* is similarly pictured as exhilarated by accelerated motion. As a child, she rides her bike recklessly: "Plunge exhilarated her. She closed her eyes and surrendered herself entirely to gravity" (56).

is not purposed to detect this relational embodiment, which is imagined in the novel as an ethics of "sympathetic vibration" (213).

Sympathetic vibration is a redolent metaphor for connection. But more than this suggestiveness, what the phrase catches is that modernity itself can be conceived of as a vibratory force, "in the form of radio waves, cinematic flickerings, railway shocks",[39] as well as the translation of soundwaves central to the workings of the telephone – the very modern technology that preoccupies Mr Sakamoto and which plays an important part in the novel. If vibration "crosses sensory thresholds in so far as it can be simultaneously palpable and audible, visible and audible", then it is this multi- or extra-sensory quality that opens out the novel's ethics of sensation and friendship.[40]

Mr Sakamoto first recognises this ethical potential of sympathetic vibration in his account of Alexander Bell's relationship "with the blind-deaf woman Helen Keller" (101) which is ostensibly centred on touch. Mr Sakamoto implicitly encounters the difficulty of trying to transform such sensations into language, and as he relates it: "Helen had touched his hands with articulate signs and expressed the spiritual rewards of her unchosen isolation. Alec felt that he understood. That there was a sympathy between them. An unremarked vibration" (101).[41] What Mr Sakamoto is proposing is an idea that the novel develops: that "vibration might allow a thinking about modernity without privileging the visual, or any other single sense",[42] and that this foregrounding of sensation might offer understanding and correspondence.

Very soon after Mr Sakamoto's telling of Bell and Keller's wordless communion, the narrative again forwards this idea of an affective force that extends beyond any one sense by having Mr Sakamoto relate his thinking on *haiku*, which he expressly links with "a fabric of knowing, he claimed, beyond vision, beyond hearing" (103). This ethical potential of vibration which Mr Sakamoto attributes to *haiku* takes

---

39 Shelley Trower, "Editorial: Vibratory Movements", *The Senses and Society* 3 no. 2 (2008): 135.
40 Trower, "Editorial", 135. In a related way, Constance Classen documents that the Surrealist artist Leonora Carrington understood bodily vibration to communicate an "attitude" towards modern life. Constance Classen, *The Color of Angels: Cosmology, Gender and the Aesthetic Imagination* (London: Routledge, 1998), 135. In *Black Mirror*, Carrington nurses Victoria after she is attacked in the street by an unknown man. She is said to be incarcerated subsequently in a psychiatric institution, "believing her belly was a mirror that reflected the details of war-time" (240). In this way, Surrealist artistry seems less the gimmick that Jules Levy, Victoria's lover, had first thought it to be and more the only available mode to express the felt reality of the trauma of Europe-at-war.
41 Historians of the deaf have presented Bell in ways contrary to how Bell thought about himself. As Jonathan Stern has suggested, "While Bell married a deaf woman and considered himself a friend of the deaf and a committed teacher … Bell developed an enduring interest in eugenics, which led him to advocate the full integration of deaf people into mainstream American culture … Concurrent with those beliefs was his stand against deaf people marrying one another and having children of their own. Bell understood deafness, fundamentally, as a human disability to be overcome, not as a condition of life." James Sterne, *The Audible Past: Cultural Origins of Sound Reproduction* (Durham, NC: Duke University Press, 2003), 39.
42 Trower, "Editorial", 135.

on a particular charge because it is to that poetic form he turned following his experience of the bombing of Nagasaki.

Along with trains, which have their own terrible roles in modern atrocities,[43] *Dreams of Speaking* is preoccupied with modern warfare and the roles modern technologies have had in both exacting destruction and death on unprecedented scales, and attending to that trauma. Mr Sakamoto is all too aware of the deadly devastation wrought by weaponised modern inventions. As part of their developing friendship and trust, Mr Sakamoto hesitantly relates to Alice a biographical outline, which touches on his wartime experience and saw everyone he knew and loved, apart from his mother, perish. He has kept the details of this dreadfulness from his wife and daughters, but they re-emerge, unbidden and mingled with other griefs in nightmares and visions, and he is admitted for a period to a clinic for those "who had seen what was unassimilable and been occupied by loss" (73).

Mr Sakamoto tells Alice of the numbers of people killed – "Almost 74,000 people in the explosion alone" – but refuses to let those terrible statistics represent the horror (68). Instead, in adherence to his ethical point that generalisations destroy, he names those near to him that died, his sisters and father, his English tutor, his biology teacher and "[h]is Japanese tutor, who had been in the mountains meditating by a stream, survived, but wished he hadn't and committed suicide two weeks after the blast. Poetry, said Mr Sakamoto, was no longer possible" (68). Furthermore, with his turn to Theodor Adorno's enquiring after literature's capacity to comprehend and represent the barbarity of the Holocaust,[44] which resonates throughout the novel, Mr Sakamoto references the "multidirectional memory" the novel stages.[45] Alice is also represented as implicitly responding to Adorno, for example, when she encounters on a train a woman who reveals to her "blue tattooed numbers" (80) after the two witness a beating of a third woman. Alice's mind turns not to poetry but to visual images: " Film footage played from somewhere. Visions pre-emptive. Photographs of disaster in hazy tones of brown" (80). This moment is a passing one, but it acknowledges the powerful role representational modes have had in creating a collective memory of the Holocaust. And it contributes, too, to Mr Sakamoto's implicit sense that the coming together of different histories and experiences of extreme violence might be understood as dialogic rather than competitive, with the hopeful possibility that unexpected forms of solidarity and accord might emerge.

Despite his apprehensions, Mr Sakamoto is said to find some respite from his terrors by turning to literature; *haiku* specifically, with its sibilant "solace of seventeen syllables" (74). With the rest of his world undergoing postwar

---

43   See Todd S. Presner, *Mobile Modernity: Germans, Jews, Trains* (New York: Columbia University Press, 2007).
44   Theodor Adorno, *Prisms*, trans. Samuel and Shierry Weber (Cambridge, MA: MIT Press, 1967), 19.
45   Michael Rothberg, *Multidirectional Memory: Remembering the Holocaust in the Age of Decolonization* (Stanford: Stanford University Press, 2009).

reconstruction, Mr Sakamoto reads "*haiku*, and English novels and European poetry in translation", and feels as though he is a "being from another planet" (69). This feeling of otherworldliness poetically converges with Alice's self-identification with the figure of the astronaut. Yet, the novel is circumspect about poetic correspondence taking shape around traumatic events and experiences.

These concerns emerge most demonstrably in the novel when Alice visits the Atomic Bomb Museum in Nagasaki. Alice has travelled to Nagasaki to see Mr Sakamoto, only to be informed that he has been taken gravely ill; she is forbidden access by the hospital to see him as she is not a family member.[46] This time, Alice declines to adopt the guise of the modern tourist, preferring instead to stay in her hotel room and read. She makes an exception, however, to see the museum and its exhibits, which are emphatically imbricated in the material and representational realms of modernity. Here the synecdoche of the atomic bomb, the mushroom cloud "photographed from B29 bombers," is played on a filmic loop and multiplied across six screens (185). It is a disturbing visualisation of military force that also realises the stalled time of an adjacent exhibit, "an exploded wall clock, halted at 11:02 on 9 August 1945" (185).[47] Photographs and statistics testify to "atrocity and ruin" (186), as do eyewitness accounts that have Alice fleeing the "documented death" (186), which returns in her dreams, and again when she wakes during the night. Whereas in sleep the accumulated images are a "messy spilling over", on waking they are harbingers of unwittingly internalised knowledge that seems imprinted on her senses (188). The blinking billboard outside her hotel room seems to prompt, or mirror, Alice's internal imaginings as she involuntarily remembers another set of flashes: "It was a photograph of the shadow of a man and a ladder, imprinted by the blast on a wall. A persisting shadow. That was all. An autograph of death" (188). What Alice recalls is a series of interwoven images; a photograph of the shadows made and photographed by the flash of the atomic

---

46 This conception of the family, a social unit founded on exclusion as much as inclusion, takes on a particular charge in the novel. Mr Sakamoto's retelling of the story of "The Bamboo Princess", which insists on reuniting its titular, moon-based character with her parents and recovered siblings, posits a particular fantasy about family that rests with his traumatic history but which his daughter resists: "I really didn't believe my father's happy family version. And I suppose I rather liked the idea she had a space to herself … that she was at home, and remote" (182). And in a "soap-operatic turn in her life" (212), medical tests of the modern, future type envisaged by Lucy Strange in *Sixty Lights*, determine that Alice is not at risk of cancer, and nor is she biologically related to her parents or sister. This knowledge raises unanswered questions for Alice about her sense of self and family.

47 Timothy Kazuo Steains reads this stopped clock as both speaking to "the relativity of time" and a rupture in national time. Timothy Kazuo Steains, "The Mixed Temporalities of Transnationalism in *Dreams of Speaking*", *Journal of Australian Studies* 41 no. 1 (2017): 33. In *A Guide to Berlin*, Marco Gianelli tells of another stalled clock, one that announces the exact time of the bombing of the Bologna train station, which saw his father fatally injured. He relates to the group gathered to hear his speak-memory that he once thought the monument "a glib and insulting thing", but has come to learn that "the world of objects stands there, mutely unchanging, to remind us that we are careless and inconsiderate of our own given time" (80).

bomb (a photograph of which is itself now multiplied and endlessly looping on film in the museum).

The idea of the bomb as a camera, fixing an image of a shadow on a surface as though it were negative film, resonates with ideas about modern warfare, the media and perception that appear in another of Jones' novels.[48] In *Sorry*, Perdita Keene views animated visions of war when she attends the cinema for the first time and sees the newsreels: "In gun-metal grey and white, armies marched at an angle across the screen, fighting planes dived upwards, politicians gesticulated."[49] Perdita determines that this cinematic vision, with its sped-up, edited images, seems to eliminate the distance that the newspapers, which had delivered to her family delayed war stories from afar, rendered as time: "The war was faster-moving and less melancholy than Perdita had imagined it. Sound-tracked for victory, the Allied troops seemed, more than anything, rather chipper and cheery. One saluted directly to the camera and posed as a hero, another gave a jubilant wave as he sped away in his Jeep" (176). Perdita's innocent apprehensions are an intuition Alice recognises; images can serve as weapons of modern warfare.

Such an aligning of technologies of perception with devastating conflicts on this scale is unimaginable to another of Jones' protagonists, Lucy Strange, in *Sixty Lights*. For Lucy, photography is a form of aesthetic devotion. When she is anticipating future technologies of seeing, she imagines the exposure of the body's internal wonders, not a melancholic remembrance of its surface blasted into shadowy silhouette that Alice sees at the Atomic Bomb Museum. What is recorded here is how modern weaponry perversely preserves the trace of the destruction it brings about, which conventional photography then records and circulates as a form of testimony and memorialisation. In this series of images, as Alice tries to guess at "what Hiroshi Sakamoto, as an eleven-year-old boy, had witnessed on that cloudy August morning", she recognises that "She was a stranger here, she knew nothing, she could only guess. She could not enter into Mr Sakamoto's experience" (188). Alice is confronted at the museum by the images of the catastrophe of warfare that Mr Sakamoto has survived but declines to speak of, and which marks their separateness.

Their friendship is shaped by this difference, and also on the shared recognition that modernity holds many contradictory narratives. Alice can read at the museum the "description of the effects of gamma rays and radiation" (186), which sets her wondering about the wisdom of allowing school children access to this horrific

---

48 Lydia Wevers has also noted that "As Alice and Mr Sakamoto's collage of potted histories suggests, the role of warfare and military innovation is implicated in many of the distinguishing developments of modernity." Lydia Wevers, "Fold in the Map: Figuring Modernity in Gail Jones' *Dreams of Speaking* and Elizabeth Knox's *Dreamhunter*", *Australian Literary Studies* 23 no. 2 (2007): 194. It is an idea developed in theoretical works by Paul Virilio. See Paul Virilio, *War and Cinema: The Logistics of Perception*, trans. Patrick Camiller (New York: Verso, 1989).

49 Gail Jones, *Sorry* (North Sydney: Vintage, 2007), 176. All subsequent references are to this edition and appear in parentheses in the text.

knowledge. As children, though, she and her sister marvelled at the aesthetic effects of radiation, albeit put to a very different purpose: to create a picture of the broken bone inside Norah's body. Mr Sakamoto singles out this capacity for living with, and honouring, such ambiguities as resolutely ethical. He tells Alice, "You are large enough to contain contradictions. We are all large enough – are we not? – to contain contradictions" (83), and he links this expressly with the co-existence of unmodern and modern things that unexpectedly but fittingly coalesce in the novel around the wind.

It is the wind that Alice yearns for amid her thinking about modern things. The Parisian swimming pool in which she has this realisation is rendered unnaturally blue, a "false Aegean, this jet-setter's hue", made worse by the artificial lighting that renders the surface of the water "oily" (139). Swimming laps, Alice is made to feel as though she is "going nowhere" in this fabricated, oleaginous space (139). Her memory of windsurfing serves as a counterpoint: "The wet body that rises and flies away, straight towards the horizon. The labour of muscles, straining and feeling tight for a pull towards the sky, and the flash of a sheath of light, suddenly descending" (140). Throughout the novel, Alice thinks of windsurfing, an activity linked with energising speed that is otherwise associated in the novel with the modern technologies Alice and Mr Sakamoto discuss. As Stephen and Alice walk through the streets of Paris and past tourists with "digital cameras and mobile telephones held out before them", Stephen recalls an earlier time together in Perth:

> "I remember," said Stephen, "sitting on the bank of the river with a book, watching you windsurf. You were unbelievably fast ... It was as if you'd been snatched by an invisible force."
> "I was," said Alice lightly. "I was snatched by the wind." (31)

Mr Sakamoto determines that "all the natural things" including the wind, presumably, are "unmodern" (21) and for Alice the wind is "pure vehicle" (209). But in the novel, wind is an elemental force that not only propels Alice across the water and recalls her to her kinaesthetic body; it is also harnessed as a metaphor for telephonic communication that, for all the technology it involves, also requires human breath: "The dark space of technology between mouths is a space of pure wind; it is a wind that snatches presences, an erosion, a loss" (32). The repeated use of the word snatch affords the wind a benign power. It also conjoins Alice's commitments to unmodern and modern things, and registers the subtle and complex registers of affect, sense perception and extra-linguistic territory that the telephone represents in *Dreams of Speaking*.

Of all the technologies that pervade *Dreams of Speaking*, the telephone is singled out as suggestive of the contradictions of modernity, as well as friendship and the ethics of sympathetic vibration. While Mr Sakamoto is well versed in the engineering innovations of Bell, the biography he is writing of the inventor is motivated by his own experience of telephony and his belief that "Only on the telephone could Hiroshi [Mr Sakamoto] utter his truths" (76).[50] Mr Sakamoto's love of the telephone is well known to Alice and is told in befittingly ecstatic terms:[51]

> The telephone is our rapturous disembodiment. We breathe ourselves, like lovers, into its tiny receptacle, and glide out the other end, mere voice, mere function. Wires, currents, satellites, electrical systems: these are the hardware we extend ourselves into, spaced out, underground, alive in the trembling skeins that arch across nations.
>
> Countless conversations are happening at once. Transecting the sky, like lines of flight, like the trajectories of ancient deities borne by eagles or dragons, sentences, words, syllables, sighs – all fly into airy enunciation, becoming messages, becoming text. (32)

Mr Sakamoto's rhapsodic ruminations formally model the reach and sensorial qualities of their subject. The friends first speak of this quavering quality when they are together in Paris; thereafter "Mr Sakamoto, … after departure from Paris … sent regular titbits on technologies and inventions. Since she had no phone, he said, he was obliged to e-mail", although he subsequently "missed hearing her Australian voice" and seeing "[h]er answering smile" (166). The emails serve as a foil to the telephone: whereas the telephone holds out tremulous possibilities, email would seem to sequester the senses.

Nevertheless, in the lengthy email that sees Mr Sakamoto end by writing of the unremarked vibration between Bell and Keller, he tells Alice that his enquiry into the telephone and its inventor lies not so much with the revolutionary engineering of the technology but more with its promise of intimacy. For Mr Sakamoto, the telephone "knits emotions" (93). Mr Sakamoto anticipates Alice's scepticism of this claim by adding that he is not speaking of "ringing the plumber, or making a dental

---

50   Characters in *Five Bells* also have telephones on their minds. The novel ends with Ellie reminding herself of the need to call James (who unbeknown to her has committed suicide), with the sound of the call never answered – "*must ring James, must ring James, must ring, ring …*" (216) – bringing the narrative to its conclusion. And Catherine too is anticipating making a call to her former and far-away lover, Luc, although in a way that complicates Mr Sakamoto's thesis that truth-telling and telephone communication are intermeshed. Luc and Catherine had avoided speaking by telephone, "thinking phone-calls were much too intimate" (130). But, on this one day that *Five Bells* represents, Catherine's yearning for intimacy has her contemplating telephoning Luc, an act that involves some self-conscious self-fashioning: "She must not ring too early and must not drink too much in the meantime, lest she sound boozy and needy, or maudlin and mean" (174). Or, more accurately, Catherine is all too conscious of how a telephone conversation can be taken as a truthful disclosure so is compelled to craft a self she wants Luc to recognise as authentic.

51   In his cultural history of the telephone, Steven Connor similarly suggests that "Talking on the telephone was more than having a conversation face to face; it was like being coiled alongside your speaking twin, their lips pressed to your ear, and your lips murmuring into theirs." Steven Connor, "Incidents of the Breath: In Pneumatic and Electric Ventriloquisms", in *Articulate Objects: Voice, Sculpture and Performance*, eds. Aura Satz and Jon Wood (London: Peter Lang, 2009), 76.

appointment" but rather thinking about "the realm of exclamation, confession, poetry, love" that the telephone apparently affords (94),[52] and which reaches towards an ethics of sympathetic vibration.

It is this affective, somatic realm that Alice expressly feels twice when she communicates with Mr Sakamoto by telephone. The first time in the novel that Alice rings Mr Sakamoto is when she runs to a Parisian public telephone box to relay her shock at learning that a teenage boy, whom she had been periodically watching from her apartment window, has been killed. Her grief-stricken words tumble from her mouth as she recounts both the boy's broken body and what she views as the disrespect shown him in death by the attending police. Later, she reflects on what she determines to be her "uncharacteristic will to disclose … a summoning of despair into language, and its release through the telephone" (107), an experience she sees mirrored, albeit with the emotional pitch inverted, in the conversations she part-witnesses more than overhears – she cannot speak Japanese – when Mr Sakamoto speaks with joy on the telephone with his uncle in Japan: "It was an experience of the strange tenderness of hyperbolic moments" (107). For Alice, who sees herself in the figures of lonely astronauts, "[a]lone in their silent worlds" (3), the notion that telephonic communication can invite disclosure is a disruptive, if not entirely unwelcomed, revelation.

This speaking takes on a different meaning at the end of the novel, with the second time Alice unexpectedly hears the voice of Mr Sakamoto. Having returned to Perth and following her friend's passing, Alice determines to call his daughter, Haruko, in Japan, only to have the answering machine switch on when no one picks up the telephone. The voice she hears is Mr Sakamoto's. While Alice cannot understand what are presumably his greetings in Japanese, she calls three times to listen to their sounds. Her insistent calling mimics, or mirrors, the repeatability of the recorded voice, to which she addresses her grief: "Ah, Mr Sakamoto, I have so much to tell you" (213). In so far as the technology preserves and replays the voice it separates from the body, the recording is a testament to Mr Sakamoto's existence in the modern world where these technologies defeat not only distance but perhaps even time. With this recording, Mr Sakamoto is afforded a version of eternity that he and Alice first recognised together when they heard the John Lennon song on the train.

If this technologically mediated afterlife is granted, it is of little immediate consolation to Alice, however. The voice recording prompts Alice to speak of all that is now lost, and her apostrophe, signalled by a colloquial rendering of the poetic vocative exclamation "O" – "Ah" – underscores the force of his absence, which is the subject of her mournful address. It is not that Alice fancifully mistakes the voice for

---

52 Pei Xing in *Five Bells* has other ideas. She is moved that a nurse should call to say that "she had left her plastic rice container behind, and would she like them to hold it for a week or post it in the mail?" (192). Pei Xing is alive to the idea that everyday interactions, facilitated by the commonplace technologies that Mr Sakamoto and Alice seek to make unfamiliar, might also have affective dimensions.

Mr Sakamoto; it is the very presence of the voice in this mediated form that signals his absence and has her consciously contemplate the notion of sympathetic vibration – "like the pianos you told me about, a vibration that I took to be the sound we had established between us …" (213) – and which the friends sensed in the airport scene earlier in the novel. It is this notion of sympathetic vibration that the novel offers not as solace but as a model and ethics of sensorial modernity.

The barcode – a derisory invention in *Dreams of Speaking* – cannot compute the affective and perception ranges of modernity with which Jones' writing grapples, and represents. Jones' novels suggest instead that fictional narrative might go some way to imagining the sensorial complexities, contradictions and possibilities of modernity, as well as admitting the atrocities and violence conducted in its name, and in its times.

Conclusions

To conclude this book, as convention dictates, is a fraught task. The readings presented here have by no means sought to offer a definitive account of Gail Jones' writing, so the conceit of presenting the final word on the subject, as conclusions often do, is neither suitable nor desirable. Also, when the idea for this book was first entertained, *The Death of Noah Glass* was yet to be released. Jones might well be preparing further additions to her *oeuvre*, which means that any conclusions that might tentatively be drawn here about her body of work are limited, and certainly open to future modification and refutation if and when new texts are available. Further, and most interestingly, Jones' writing does not itself offer conclusions, at least in the conventional sense of tying up loose ends. More often than not, Jones' conclusions do not occur at the ending of the stories at all.

In *Sixty Lights*, Lucy Strange enacts this narrative disposition as she awaits her coming death. She privately rearranges the plotline of Wilkie Collins' *The Woman in White* (1860), so that the recognised beginning of the novel becomes its end: "The mysterious encounter with the woman in white, an enigma drifting out of the darkness with no identity and purpose, seemed to her especially poignant and compelling, and the end, not the beginning of any story."[1] In imaginatively restructuring the novel, Lucy sets herself apart from her closest confidantes, Mrs Minchin and her sister-in-law Violet, who "sank agreeably into the fakery and mischief of made-up people, the rigmarole of mean and devious motivation, the scheming against love" (242). Lucy "was charmed that her sister-in-law was so entranced by art" (243), although she herself "had requested Keats" in the first instance – only to be rebuffed by Violet who "thought that morbid" (242). Her reassembling of the Collins novel is an act of quiet resistance, which also calls forth her own private spectres.

---

1 Gail Jones, *Sixty Lights* (London: Harvill Press, 2004), 243. All subsequent references are to this edition and appear in parentheses in the text.

If Lucy upholds enigma and ambiguity as the best means to conclude any narrative, then Jones' novels certainly misplace their endings, as the telling of the future death of Victoria Morrell in *Black Mirror* suggests. It is said of the Surrealist artist, more or less at the centre of the book, that she will

> carry to her grave only a generic and incomplete entrance hall, a cinematic compilation of columns, chairs and a chequered floor; together with the simple phrase *flame tree* drifting inexplicably within it. There will be no resolution to the mystery of these words. Victoria will greet her death still waiting for meaning as a bride awaits her lover.[2]

This flashforward to Victoria's death, which both she and her biographer are anticipating from the novel's opening pages – although the next paragraph reverses that temporal trajectory and recalls the artist's "first complete memory" (167), only to return to the present of Anna and Victoria's encounter – withholds any promise of final explanation or total understanding. Pei Xing suggests as much in *Five Bells* when she reflects that "In the unresolvable story she had been given to live there was no guarantee that everything finally and securely would repair".[3] This conviction is enacted by the narrative in which these meditations take place; the disappearance of a young girl is left unresolved.

That is not to say that Jones' novels and short stories leave a reader suspended, frustrated even, with cliff-hanger-like moments, or that the design of her stories is wilfully negligent or artless. Nor are they blissfully unaware of narrative conventions and the tutored desire of many readers for resolution and closure. But they are not of the order of the movies Victoria attends as a young girl in *Black Mirror*, wherein "Life was racy. Middles were disastrous. Endings were happy. The women were all gorgeous and the men all handsome" (194). This is so even as that novel acknowledges the playful pleasures and solidarities these representations and the narrative forms that contain them can afford:

> At home Victoria replayed the pictures. She was always the star, and everyone fell in love with her. Ruby was given only minor roles – she was after all still little and easy to boss – and together they walked around in accelerated fashion and practised virtually their own version of cinema-melodrama. (194)

Jones' work is alert to how the organisation of story has a significant part to play in what can be told and known, and indeed not known. The commencement of *A Guide to Berlin* with a scene that sees a shocked and bereaved group huddling in the snow while a character delivers what seems to be an impromptu eulogy,

---

2   Gail Jones, *Black Mirror* (Sydney: Picador, 2002), 166. All subsequent references are to this edition and appear in parentheses in the text.
3   Gail Jones, *Five Bells* (London: Harvill Secker, 2011), 197.

anticipates what turns out to be the text's near-ending. This moment out of time not only reveals at the novel's beginning what a linearly ordered narrative might be resolutely directed towards – a climax – but also draws subtle attention to narrative form itself. It is also within this novel that one of its characters, Gino, proposes to write his own version of Vladimir Nabokov's short story "A Guide to Berlin" (1925), calling it "The Book of Conclusions" because, his friend Marco insists, "Conclusions are everything. In the Nabokov story, what matters is that the guide is one-armed and scarred."[4] Cass Turner privately disagrees as "[i]n her discussions with Victor, they had never spoken of the ending" (143).

Similarly, *The Death of Noah Glass* begins more or less where it ends, with the moment of Noah Glass' passing. Or, at least one narrative strand does. The art-heist detective narrative that Noah's death initiates, and which partly draws in the art historian's surviving children, runs parallel to (or entwines with) the telling of moments that close with Noah's death. And the story "ends" not with the case solved and the status quo restored, but rather on an uncertain note, with Evie Glass repeating "I don't know" to a question posed by her brother and to which the reader is not given access.[5] *Five Bells* not only leaves unanswered the disappearance of a young girl; Ellie's silent determination at the novel's end that she must telephone her former lover, James (whom she has met up with again earlier that day for the first time in years and who, unbeknown to her, will take his own life before she has the chance to call), is concluded by an ellipsis. It is a sign, perhaps, of unmet desire as well as omission that anticipates the silence her future action would receive.

Of course, all kinds of reasons might be given as to why Jones' narratives rest on inconclusive conclusions. One explanation, or at least an interpretation, might lie with the short story "Resuscitating Proust" in *Fetish Lives*. In this story, the narrator dreams of Marcel Proust, "French novelist *extraordinaire* of dilatory and arduous prose, French novelist of idiosyncratic and omniretrievable memory, of transposed sensations, of multi-dimensional desirings, of a neuroticism fanned open – flick! see its design! – into fluttering ostentation", and who travels (as did the historical Proust) to Venice with a volume of John Ruskin's writing tucked in his luggage.[6]

The story begins with an image that is "eidetic, of a body suspended in water" (71), and what follows is hardly a faithful rendering of Proust's biography. Rather, the story moves between and through this watery dream-vision, the bedroom in which the author is said in effect to have entombed himself to write, Proust's travels in Venice, his relationship with Alfred Agostinelli, and the pages of his magnus opus *Remembrance of Things Past* (1913–27). The story is less about Proust than a meditation on the imaginative capacity of writing to bring into being

---

4 Gail Jones, *A Guide to Berlin* (North Sydney: Vintage, 2015), 143. All subsequent references are to this edition and appear in parentheses in the text.
5 Gail Jones, *The Death of Noah Glass* (Melbourne: Text, 2018), 313, 314.
6 Gail Jones, "Resuscitating Proust", *Fetish Lives* (Fremantle: Fremantle Arts Centre Press, 1997), 71–2. All subsequent references are to this edition and appear in parentheses in the text.

the dead, the past and that which is otherwise impossible or imperceptible. In this way, the story can presume to tell of a dream that Proust is said to have forgotten immediately upon waking.

That story also takes its cue, and limits, from its ostensible subject. The first-person narrator-dreamer of the story grants that like Proust, who was famously suspicious of the stillness of photography, "the face I am seeking is in the end unfixable … Even the dead are not immobile, and dreams pay no homage to the absurd waking-myth of fixity" (82). It is this myth of fixity (of knowledge, identity, the past, time) that Jones' reluctant conclusions recall and resist as part of her writerly enquiry and ethical openness to unknown futures.

Works Cited

Abraham, Nicholas, and Maria Torok. *The Wolf Man's Magic Word: A Cryptonomy*. Translated by Nicholas Rand. Minneapolis: University of Minnesota Press, 1986.
Adamson, Jane. "Against Tidiness: Literature and/versus Moral Philosophy." In *Renegotiating Ethics in Literature, Philosophy and Theory*, edited by Jane Adamson, Richard Freadman and David Parker, 84–110. Cambridge: Cambridge University Press, 1998.
Adorno, Theodor. *Prisms*. Translated by Samuel and Shierry Weber. Cambridge, MA: MIT Press, 1967.
Aguiar, Marian. *Tracking Modernity: India's Railway and the Culture of Mobility*. Minneapolis: University of Minnesota Press, 2011.
Alperson, Philip. "'Musical Time' and Music as an 'Art of Time.'" *Journal of Aesthetics and Art Criticism* 38 (1980): 407–17.
Appadurai, Arjun. *Modernity at Large: Cultural Dimensions of Globalization*. Minneapolis: University of Minnesota Press, 1996.
Apter, Emily. *Against World Literature: On the Politics of Untranslatability*. London: Verso, 2013.
Attridge, Derek. *The Singularity of Literature*. London: Routledge, 2004.
Barthes, Roland. *Camera Lucida: Reflections on Photography*. Translated by Richard Howard. New York: Hill & Wang, 1981.
—— *The Grain of the Voice: Interviews 1962–1980*. Translated by Linda Coverdale. Berkeley: University of California Press, 1991.
Beaumont, Matthew and Michael Freeman, eds. *The Railway and Modernity: Time, Space, and the Machine Ensemble*. Bern: Peter Lang, 2007.
Belleflamme, Valérie-Anne. "'Shakespeare was Wrong': Counter-Discursive Intertextuality in Gail Jones' *Sorry*." *Journal of Postcolonial Writing* 51 no. 6 (2015): 661–71.
Ben-Hur. Directed by William Wyler. Metro-Goldwyn-Mayer, 1959.
Benjamin, Walter. "A Short History of Photography." 1931. Translated by Stanley Mitchell. *Screen* 13 no. 1 (1972): 5–26.
—— *Berlin Childhood Around 1900*. Translated by Howard Eiland. Cambridge, MA: The Belknap Press, 2006.
—— *Illuminations*. Translated by Harry Zorn. Edited by Hannah Arendt. 1968. London: Pimlico, 1999.
—— *The Arcades Project*. Translated by Howard Eiland and Kevin McLaughlin. Edited by Rolf Tiedemann. Cambridge, MA: Harvard University Press, 1999.
—— *The Origin of German Tragic Drama*. Translated by John Osborne. London: Verso, 2003.

Blanchot, Maurice. *Friendship*. Translated by Elizabeth Rottenber. Stanford: Stanford University Press, 1997.
—— *The Writing of the Disaster*. Translated by Ann Smock. Lincoln: University of Nebraska Press, 1986.
Blue. Directed by Derek Jarman. Tate Gallery, 1993.
Born, Georgina. "Making Time: Temporality, History, and the Cultural Object." *New Literary History* 46 no. 3 (2015): 361–86.
Bradley, James. "On *Five Bells*". *Griffith Review* (2011): https://griffithreview.com/five-bells-gail-jones/
Bringing Them Home: Report of the National Inquiry into the Separation of Aboriginal and Torres Strait Islander Children from their Families. Ronald Wilson, Commissioner. Sydney: Human Rights and Equal Opportunity Commission, 1997.
Brontë, Charlotte [Currer Bell]. *Jane Eyre: An Autobiography*. London: Smith, Elder & Co., 1847.
Brydon, Diana. "'Difficult Forms of Knowing: Enquiry, Injury and Translocated Relations of Postcolonial Responsibility." In *Postcolonial Translocations: Cultural Representation and Critical Ppatial Thinking*, edited by Marga Munkelt, Markus Schmitz, Mark Stein and Silke Stroh, 3–28. New York: Rodopi, 2013.
Bulwer-Lytton, Edward. *Paul Clifford*. London: G. Routledge, 1848.
Butler, Judith. "Giving an Account of Oneself." *Diacritics* 31 no. 4 (2001): 22–40.
Cadava, Eduardo. "*Lapsus Imaginis*: The Image in Ruins." *October* 96 (2001): 35–60.
—— *Words of Light: Theses on the Photography of History*. Princeton, NJ: Princeton University Press, 1997.
Caruth, Cathy. "Trauma and Experience: Introduction." In *Trauma: Explorations in Memory*. Edited by Cathy Caruth, 3–12. Baltimore: Johns Hopkins University Press, 1995.
Celan, Paul. *Die Niemandrose*. Frankfurt am Main: S. Fischer, 1963.
Chatterjee, Partha. *Our Modernity*. Sephis-Codestria Lecture No. 1. Dakar: South – South Exchange Programme for Research on the History of Development and the Council for the Development of Social Science Research in Africa, 1997.
Chee Dimock, Wai. "Weak Theory: Henry James, Colm Tóibín, and W. B. Yeats." *Critical Inquiry* 39 no. 4 (2013): 732–53.
Classen, Constance. *The Color of Angels: Cosmology, Gender and the Aesthetic Imagination*. London: Routledge, 1998.
Collins, Wilkie. *The Woman in White*. London: Sampson, Low, 1860.
Connor, Steven. "Incidents of the Breath: In Pneumatic and Electric Ventriloquisms." In *Articulate Objects: Voice, Sculpture and Performance*, edited by Aura Satz and Jon Wood, 63–80. London: Peter Lang, 2009.
—— "Introduction." In *The Five Senses: A Philosophy of Mingled Bodies* by Michel Serres. Translated by Margaret Sankey and Peter Cowley, 1–16. London: Continuum, 2008.
—— "Literature, Technology and the Senses." In *The Cambridge Companion to the Body in Literature*, edited by David Hillman and Ulrika Maude, 177–96. Cambridge: Cambridge University Press, 2015.
—— "Topologies: Michel Serres and the Shapes of Thought." *Anglistik* 15 (2004): 105–17.
Crary, Jonathan. *Suspensions of Perception: Attention, Spectacle and Modern Culture*. Cambridge, MA: MIT Press, 2000.
Critchley, Simon. *The Ethics of Deconstruction: Derrida and Levinas*. Oxford: Blackwell, 1992.
Dale, Leigh. "No more boomerang? 'Nigger's Leap' and 'Five Bells.'" *Journal of Australian Studies* 37 no. 1 (2013): 48–61.
de Man, Paul. *Allegories of Reading: Figural Language in Rousseau, Nietzsche, Rilke and Proust*. New Haven, CT: Yale University Press, 1979.
Deleuze, Gilles. *Cinema 2: The Time-Image*. Translated by Hugh Tomlinson and Robert Galeta. Minneapolis: University of Minnesota Press, 1989.

Works Cited

Derrida, Jacques. *Politics of Friendship*. Translated by George Collins. London: Verso, 1997.
—— *Spectres of Marx: The State of the Debt, The Work of Mourning and the New International*. Translated by Peggy Kamuf. London: Routledge, 1994.
—— *The Ear of the Other: Otobiography, Transference, Translation*. Translated by Peggy Kamuf. Edited by Christie McDonald. Lincoln: University of Nebraska Press, 1985.
—— *The Work of Mourning*. Edited by Pascale-Anne Brault and Michael Naas. Chicago: University of Chicago Press, 2001.
Diamond, Cora. "Martha Nussbaum and the Need for Novels." In *Renegotiating Ethics in Literature, Philosophy and Theory*, edited by Jane Adamson, Richard Freadman and David Parker, 39–64. Cambridge: Cambridge University Press, 1998.
Dickens, Charles. *Great Expectations*. London: Chapman and Hall, 1861.
Dixon, Robert. "Cosmopolitan Australians and Colonial Modernity: Alex Miller's *Conditions of Faith*, Gail Jones' *Black Mirror* and A.L. McCann's *The White Body of Evening*." *Westerly* 49 (2004): 122–37.
—— "Figures in Geometry: *The Death of Noah Glass* by Gail Jones." *Sydney Review of Books* 7 September 2018, https://sydneyreviewofbooks.com/death-noah-glass-jones/.
—— "Ghosts in the Machine: Modernity and the Unmodern in Gail Jones' *Dreams of Speaking*." *JASAL: Journal of the Association for the Study of Australian Literature* 8 (2008): 121–37.
—— "Invitation to the Voyage: Reading Gail Jones' *Five Bells*." *JASAL: Journal of the Association for the Study of Australian Literature* 12 no. 3 (2012): 1–17.
Dow, Steve. "Gail Jones and the Art of Words." *The Saturday Paper*, 10–16 March 2018, https://www.thesaturdaypaper.com.au/2018/03/10/gail-jones-and-the-art-words/15206004005912.
Duthie, Fiona. "From Innocent to Evil: The Representation of the Child in the Works of Gail Jones." *Westerly* 58 no. 1 (2013): 126–47.
Eagle, Christopher. "'Angry Because She Stutters': Stuttering, Violence and the Politics of Voice in *American Pastoral* and *Sorry*." *Philip Roth Studies* 8 no. 1 (2012): 17–30.
Eaglestone, Robert. *Ethical Criticism: Reading after Levinas*. Edinburgh: Edinburgh University Press, 1997.
Eakin, Paul John, ed. *The Ethics of Life-Writing*. Ithaca, NY: Cornell University Press, 2004.
Elliot, Jane and Derek Attridge, eds. *Theory After Theory*. London: Routledge, 2011.
Fabian, Johannes. *Time and the Other: How Anthropology Makes its Object*. New York: Columbia University Press, 1983.
Felski, Rita. *The Gender of Modernity*. Cambridge, MA: Harvard University Press, 1995.
—— *Uses of Literature*. Oxford: Blackwell, 2008.
Flaubert, Gustave. *Madame Bovary*. Translated by Eleanor Marx-Aveling. 1856. London: Dent, 1928.
Flint, Kate. *Flash!: Photography, Writing and Surprising Illumination*. Oxford: Oxford University Press, 2017.
Freud, Sigmund. "Mourning and Melancholia." 1917. *The Standard Edition of the Complete Psychological Works of Sigmund Freud*, vol. 14. Translated by James Strachey, 243–58. London: Hogarth Press, 1957.
—— "The Ego and the Id." 1923. *The Standard Edition of the Complete Psychological Works of Sigmund Freud*, vol. 19. Translated by James Strachey, 12–66. London: Hogarth Press, 1961.
Friedman, Marilyn. *What are Friends For?: Feminist Perspectives on Personal Relationships and Moral Theory*. Ithaca: Cornell University Press, 1993.
Frow, John. "The Politics of Stolen Time." *Australian Humanities Review* 9 (1998), http://australianhumanitiesreview.org/1998/02/01/a-politics-of-stolen-time/.
Genette, Gérard. "Boundaries of Narrative." Translated by Ann Levonas. *New Literary History* 8 no. 1 (1976): 1–13.

Genoni, Paul. ""Art is the Windowpane": Novels of Australian Women and Modernism in Inter-War Europe." *JASAL: Journal of the Association for the Study of Australian Literature* 3 (2004): 159–72.
Goethe, Johann Wolfgang von. *Theory of Colours*. 1810. Translated by Charles Lock Eastlake. London: Routledge, 2019.
Green-Lewis, Jennifer. *Framing the Victorians: Photography and the Culture of Realism*. Ithaca: Cornell University Press, 1996.
Hales, Dorothy. "Aesthetics and the New Ethics: Theorizing the Novel in the Twenty-first Century." *PMLA* 124 no. 3 (2009): 896–905.
Hecq, Dominique. "Autofrictions: The Fictopoet, the Critic and the Teacher." *Cultural Studies Review* 11 no. 2 (2005): 183–8.
Herrero, Dolores. "The Australian Apology and Postcolonial Defamiliarization: Gail Jones' *Sorry*." *Journal of Postcolonial Writing* 47 no. 3 (2011): 283–95.
Hillis Miller, J. "Time in Literature." *Daedalus* 132 no. 2 (Spring 2003): 86–97.
Hirsch, Marianne. *Family Frames: Photography, Narrative and Postmemory*. Cambridge, MA: Harvard University Press, 1997.
—— *The Generation of Postmemory: Writing and Visual Culture After the Holocaust*. New York: Columba University Press, 2012.
Jackson, Noel. *Science and Sensation in Romantic Poetry*. Cambridge: Cambridge University Press, 2008.
Jacobs, Lyn. "Gail Jones' 'Light Writing': Memory and the Photo-graph." *JASAL: Journal of the Association for the Study of Australian Literature* 5 (2006): 191–208.
James, Henry. *The Portrait of a Lady*. Boston: Houghton Mifflin, 1881.
Jay, Martin. *Downcast Eyes: The Denigration of Vision in Twentieth-Century French Thought*. Berkeley: University of California Press, 1993.
Jones, Gail. "A Dreaming, A Sauntering: Re-imagining Critical Paradigms." *JASAL: Journal of the Association for the Study of Australian Literature* 5 (2006): 11–24.
—— *A Guide to Berlin*. North Sydney: Vintage, 2015.
—— "A Poetics of Sense: Michael Ondaatje's *In the Skin of a Lion*." *Moving Worlds* 10 no. 2 (2010): 57–67.
—— "Artistic Light into the Future." Interview by Bron Sibree. *The West Australian Weekend Extra*, 28 August 2004.
—— *Black Mirror*. Sydney: Picador, 2002.
—— "Celebrating our Far Western City of Contradictions: CITIES." *The Age*, 1 March 2014.
—— "Dark Places: The Movement of the Image (Thoughts on the Work of Veronica Brady)." *Coolabah* 22 (2017): 10–18.
—— "Desolation." *The Kenyon Review* 25 no. 1 (2003): 13–17.
—— "Desperate, Marvellous, Shuttling: White's Ambivalent Modernism." In *Patrick White Beyond the Grave: New Critical Perspectives*, edited by Ian Henderson and Anouk Lang, 155–62. New York: Anthem Press, 2015.
—— *Dreams of Speaking*. Milsons Point, NSW: Vintage, 2006.
—— *Fetish Lives*. Fremantle: Fremantle Arts Centre Press, 1997.
—— *Five Bells*. London: Harvill Secker, 2011.
—— "Five Meditations on a Moonlit Night." *Le Simplegadi* 14 no. 16 (2016): 16–24.
—— "Imaginative Excursions: About *The House of Breathing*." Interviewed by Peter Holland and Pippa Tandy. *Fremantle Arts Review* 7 no. 12 & 8 no. 1 (1992-3): 4–7.
—— "In the Darkness, Words to the Rescue." *The Australian Literary Review*, 5 May 2010.
—— "Interview." Interviewed by Susan Wyndham. *The Age*, 8 August 2015.
—— "Introduction." In *The Cockatoos* by Patrick White, vii–xvi. Melbourne: Text, 2019.
—— "My Favourite Novel: Swooning to Ondaatje's roar." *The Australian*, 6 August 2011.
—— "On a Library of Memories." *The Weekend Australian*, 23 February 2008.

—— "On Small Things." *The Weekend Australian Review*, 8–9 January 2005.
—— "Open Page." *Australian Book Review* no. 329 (March 2011): 68.
—— *Sixty Lights*. London: Harvill Press, 2004.
—— "Skulls, Fontanelle and the Spaces Between." *The UTS Review* 1 no. 2 (1995): 170–79.
—— *Sorry*. North Sydney: Vintage, 2007.
—— "Sorry-in-the-Sky: Empathetic Unsettlement, Mourning and the Stolen Generations." In *Imagining Australia: Literature and Culture in the New, New World*, edited by Judith Ryan and Chris Wallace-Crabbe, 159–71. Cambridge, MA: Harvard University Press, 2004.
—— "Speaking Shadows: Justice and the Poetic." In *Just Words? Australian Authors Writing for Justice*, edited by Bernadette Brennan, 76–86. St Lucia: University of Queensland Press, 2008.
—— "Spiral Time, Biscuit Tins, Butterflies: How Nabokov Enlivens Us." *Sydney Writers' Festival*, 22 May 2016. Podcast.
—— "Supporting Justice and the Power of the Individual Voice." Interviewed by Anon. *Sydney PEN Magazine*, November 2011.
—— "Surviving a Bootprint on the Page." *The Australian Literary Review*, 2 May 2007.
—— *The Death of Noah Glass*. Melbourne: Text, 2018.
—— "The Heart Beating Across the Room (on Possessing Someone Else's Photographs)." *Australian Book Review* no. 173 (August 1995): 36–41.
—— *The House of Breathing*. Fremantle: Fremantle Arts Centre Press, 1992.
—— "The Interview." Interviewed by Michele McCrea. *Wet Ink* 3 (2006): 26–9.
—— "The January Interview." Interviewed by Summer Block. *January Magazine*, 2008, https://www.januarymagazine.com/profiles/gailjones.html.
—— "The Legend of Jandamarra." *The Monthly*, October, 2011.
—— "The Ocean." In *A Country Too Far: Writings on Asylum Seekers*, edited by Rosie Scott and Tom Keneally, 103–9. Melbourne: Viking, 2013.
—— *The Piano*. Sydney: Currency Press, 2007.
—— "The Pleasure of Language Itself: An Interview with Gail Jones." Interviewed by Robert Wood. *Los Angeles Review of Books*, 4 May 2018, https://blog.lareviewofbooks.org/interviews/pleasure-language-interview-gail-jones/
—— "Turnings and Over-Turnings in Glebe." *Sydney Review of Books*, 9 February 2018, https://sydneyreviewofbooks.com/turnings-and-over-turnings-in-glebe/.
—— "Without Stars: A Small Essay on Grief." *HEAT* no. 7 (1998): 138–50.
Joyce, James. "The Dead." In *Dubliners*, 159–227. 1914. London: Vintage, 2012.
Jütte, Robert. *A History of the Senses from Antiquity to Cyberspace*. London: Polity Press, 2005.
Kazuo Steains, Timothy. "The Mixed Temporalities of Transnationalism in *Dreams of Speaking*." *Journal of Australian Studies* 41 no. 1 (2017): 32–46.
Kennedy, Roseanne. "Australian Trials of Trauma: the Stolen Generations in Human Rights, Law and Literature." *Comparative Literature Studies* 48 no. 3 (2011): 333–55.
Kern, Stephen. *The Culture of Time and Space*. Cambridge, MA: Harvard University Press, 2003.
Kossew, Sue. "Saying Sorry: The Politics of Apology and Reconciliation in Recent Australian Fiction." In *Locating Postcolonial Narrative Genres*, edited by Walter Goebel and Saskia Schablo, 171–83. New York: Routledge, 2011.
Krauss, Rosalind. *The Optical Unconscious*. Cambridge, MA: MIT Press, 1993.
Kumar, Amitava. *Passport Photos*. Berkeley: University of California Press, 2000.
LaCapra, Dominick. "Trauma, Absence, Loss." *Critical Inquiry* 25, no. 4 (1999): 696–727.
—— *Writing History, Writing Trauma*. Baltimore: Johns Hopkins University Press, 2001.
Latour, Bruno. "How to be Iconophilic in Art, Science and Religion" In *Picturing Science, Producing Art*, edited by Caroline A. Jones and Peter Galison, 418–40. London: Routledge, 1998.
—— *We Have Never Been Modern*. Cambridge: Harvard University Press, 1993.
Leslie, Esther. "Snow Shaker." In *The Object Reader*, edited by Fiona Candlin and Raiford Guins, 516–18. New York: Routledge, 2009.

Levinas, Emmanuel. *Humanism of the Other*. Translated by Nidra Poller. Urbana: University of Illinois Press, 2006.
—— *Otherwise Than Being; or, Beyond Essence*. Translated by Alphonso Lingis. Pittsburgh: Duquesne University Press, 1998.
Lukács, Georg. *Theory of the Novel: A Historico-Philosophical Essay on the Forms of Great Epic Literature*. Translated by Anna Bostock. Cambridge, MA: MIT Press, 1971.
Lyotard, Jean-François and Jean-Loup Thebaud. *Just Gaming*. Translated by Brian Massumi and Samuel Weber. Minneapolis: University of Minnesota Press, 1985.
Marnie. Directed by Alfred Hitchcock. Universal Pictures, 1964.
Marx, Karl. *Capital*, Vols. 1 and 2. Translated by Ben Fowkes. New York: Vintage, 1977.
—— *Economic and Philosophic Manuscripts of 1844*. Translated by Martin Milligan. Edited by Dirk J. Struik. New York: International Publishers, 1964.
McCredden, Lyn. "Saying Sorry: the Apology." In *Telling Stories: Australian Life and Literature, 1935–2012*, edited by Tanya Dalziell and Paul Genoni, 559–65. Clayton: Monash University Press, 2013.
McGonegal, Julie. "The Great Canadian (and Australian) Secret: The Limits of Non-Indigenous Knowledge and Representation." *ESC* 35 no. 1 (2009): 67–83.
Merleau-Ponty, Maurice. "Eye and Mind." In *The Primacy of Perception*. Translated by Carleton Dallery. Edited by James E. Edie, 159–90. Evanston, IL: Northwestern University Press, 1964.
—— *Phenomenology of Perception*. Translated by Colin Smith. London: Routledge, 1962.
Midalia, Susan. "The Idea of Place: Reading for Pleasure and the Workings of Power." *English in Australia* 47 no. 3 (2012): 44–51.
Mitchell, Kate. "Ghostly Histories and Embodied Memories: Photography, Spectrality and Historical Fiction in *Afterimage* and *Sixty Lights*." *Neo-Victorian Studies* 1 no. 1 (2008): 81–109.
—— *History and Cultural Memory in Neo-Victorian Fiction: Victorian Afterimages*. London: Palgrave, 2010.
Mitchell, W.J.T. *Picture Theory: Essays on Verbal and Visual Representations*. Chicago: University of Chicago Press, 1995.
Mudie, Ella. "The Synchronous City: Aural Geographies in Gail Jones' *Five Bells*." *New Scholar: An International Journal of the Humanities, Creative Arts and Social Sciences* 3 no. 2 (2014): 11–22.
Nabokov, Vladimir. *Lolita*. 1955. New York: Phaedra, 1967.
—— *Speak, Memory: An Autobiography Revisited*. 1951. London: Penguin, 2000.
—— *The Stories of Vladimir Nabokov*. New York: Random House, 1997.
Nead, Lynda. *Victorian Babylon: People, Streets and Images in Nineteenth Century London*. New Haven, CT: Yale University Press, 2000.
Newton, Isaac. *The Principia: Mathematical Principles of Natural Philosophy*. Trans. I. Bernard Cohen and Anne Whitman. 1687. Berkeley: University of California Press, 1999.
—— *Opticks; or, A Treatise of the Reflections, Refractions, Inflections and Colours of Light*. 1704. London: G. Bell & Sons Ltd, 1931.
Ninotchka. Directed by Ernst Lubitsch. Metro-Goldwyn-Mayer, 1939.
Nussbaum, Martha. *Love's Knowledge: Essays on Philosophy and Literature*. Oxford: Oxford University Press, 1990.
—— *The Fragility of Goodness: Luck and Ethics in Greek Tragedy and Philosophy*. Cambridge: Cambridge University Press, 1986.
Olalquiaga, Celeste. *The Artificial Kingdom: A Treasury of Kitsch Experience*. New York: Pantheon, 1998.
Ondaatje, Michael. *In the Skin of a Lion*. New York: Knopf, 1987.
—— *The English Patient*. New York: Knopf, 1992.
Onley, James. *Memory and Narrative: The Weave of Life-Writing*. Chicago: University of Chicago Press, 1998.

Orb, Naomi. "Mirroring, Depth and Inversion: Holding Gail Jones' *Black Mirror* Against Contemporary Australia." *Sydney Studies in English* 35 (2009): 112–27.

Palumbo-Liu, David. *The Deliverance of Others: Reading in a Global Age*. Durham, NC: Duke University Press, 2012.

Pasternak, Boris. *Doctor Zhivago*. Translated by Richard Pevear and Larissa Volokhonsky. 1957. London: Vintage, 2011.

Pessoa, Fernando. *The Book of Disquiet*. Translated by Richard Zenith. London: Penguin, 2015.

Pilar Royo Grasa, Maria del. "In Conversation with Gail Jones." *JASAL: Journal of the Association for the Study of Australian Literature* 12 no. 3 (2013): 1–12.

—— "Looking for Othello's Pearl in Gail Jones's *Sorry* (2007): Symbolic and Intertextual Questioning of the Notion of 'Settler Envy.'" *Journal of Postcolonial Writing* 54 (2018): 200–13.

Pound, Ezra. "In a Station of the Metro." *Poetry* 2 no. 1 (1913): 12.

Presner, Todd S. *Mobile Modernity: Germans, Jews, Trains*. New York: Columbia University Press, 2007.

Proust, Marcel. *Remembrance of Things Past*. Translated by C.K. Scott Moncrieff. 1913–27. London: Chatto & Windus, 1922–31.

Rancière, Jacques. *Aisthesis: Scenes from the Aesthetic Regime of Art*. Translated by Zakir Paul. London: Verso, 2013.

Rebecca. Directed by Alfred Hitchcock. United Artists, 1940.

Reed, Arden. *Romantic Weather: The Climates of Coleridge and Baudelaire*. Hanover, NH: University Press of New England, 1983.

Ricciardi, Alessia. *The Ends of Mourning: Psychoanalysis, Literature, Film*. Stanford: Stanford University Press, 2003.

Richards, Edward Graham. *Mapping Time: The Calendar and its History*. Oxford: Oxford University Press, 1999.

Ricoeur, Paul. "Narrative Time." *Critical Inquiry* 7 no. 1 Autumn (1980): 169–90.

Rothberg, Michael. *Multidirectional Memory: Remembering the Holocaust in the Age of Decolonization*. Stanford: Stanford University Press, 2009.

Roughley, Fiona. "Spatialising Experience: Gail Jones' *Black Mirror* and the contending of postmodern space." *Australian Literary Studies* 23 no. 2 (2007): 58–73.

Saadi Nikro, Norman. "Paratactic Stammers: temporality in the novels of Gail Jones." *JASAL: Journal of the Association for the Study of Australian Literature* 16 no. 1 (2016): 1–16.

Sachs, Mendel. "Changes in concepts of time from Aristotle to Einstein." *Astrophysics and Space Science* 224 no. 1–2 (1996): 269–81.

Sanders, Mark. "Introduction: ethics and interdisciplinarity in philosophy and literary theory." *Diacritics* 32 no. 3–4 (2002): 2–16.

Schivelbusch, Wolfgang. *The Railway Journey: Trains and Travel in the Nineteenth Century*. Translated by Anselm Hollo. New York: Urizen, 1979.

Scott, Rosie. "Introduction." In *A Country Too Far: Writings on Asylum Seekers*, edited by Rosie Scott and Tom Keneally, 1–4. Melbourne: Viking, 2013.

Sebald, W.G. *The Emigrants*. Translated by Michael Hulse. London: Vintage, 2002.

Serres, Michel. *Hominescence*. Translated by Randolph Burks. London: Bloomsbury, 2019.

—— *The Five Senses: A Philosophy of Mingled Bodies*. Translated by Margaret Sankey and Peter Cowley. London: Continuum, 2008.

Slessor, Kenneth. *Five Bells: XX Poems*. Sydney: Frank Johnson, 1939.

Sontag, Susan. *On Photography*. New York: Farrar, Straus & Giroux, 1977.

—— *Regarding the Pain of Others*. New York: Farrar, Straus & Giroux, 2003.

Sterne, James. *The Audible Past: Cultural Origins of Sound Reproduction*. Durham, NC: Duke University Press, 2003.

Tarkovsky, Andrei. *Sculpting in Time: Reflections on the Cinema*. Translated by Kitty Hunter-Blair. London: Bodley Head, 1986.

The Godfather. Directed by Francis Ford Coppola. Paramount Pictures, 1972.
Trexler, Adam. *Anthropocene Fictions: The Novel in a Time of Climate Change*. Charlottesville: University of Virginia Press, 2015.
Trower, Shelley. "Editorial: Vibratory Movements." *The Senses and Society* 3 no. 2 (2008): 133–5.
Uluru Statement From the Heart. Final Report of the Referendum Council. 30 June 2017, https://www.referendumcouncil.org.au/sites/default/files/report_attachments/Referendum_Council_Final_Report.pdf
Virilio, Paul. *War and Cinema: The Logistics of Perception*. Translated by Patrick Camiller. New York: Verso, 1989.
Wade, Nicholas J. and Josef Brožek, in collaboration with Jiří Hoskovec. *Purkinje's Vision: The Dawning of Neuroscience*. Mahwah, NJ: Lawrence Erlbaum Associates, 2001.
Watkins, Beth. *Reluctant Theologians: Franz Kafka, Paul Celan, Edmond Jabès*. New York: Fordham University Press, 2002.
—— "The Washing of the Word, the Washing of the World: Paul Celan and the Language of Sanctification." *Shofar: An Interdisciplinary Journal of Jewish Studies* 20 no. 4 (2002): 36–63.
West-Pavlov, Russell. "Shakespeare Among the Nyoongar: Post-Colonial Texts, Colonial Intertexts and Their Imbrications – *Macbeth* in Gail Jones' *Sorry*." *ZAA* 63 no. 4 (2015): 391–410.
Wevers, Lydia. "Fold in the Map: Figuring Modernity in Gail Jones' *Dreams of Speaking* and Elizabeth Knox's *Dreamhunter*." *Australian Literary Studies* 23 no. 2 (2007): 187–98.
Woman of the Dunes. Directed by Hiroshi Teshigahara. Teshigahara Productions, 1964.
Woolf, Virginia. *A Woman's Essays*. Edited by Rachel Bowlby, 69–87. London: Penguin, 1992.
—— *Moments of Being: Autobiographical Writings*. Edited by Jeanne Schulkind. London: Pimlico, 2002.
—— *Mrs Dalloway*. London: Hogarth Press, 1925.
—— *The Common Reader*, vol. 1. Edited by Andrew McNeillie. London: Vintage, 2003.
—— *The Essays of Virginia Woolf*, vol. 6 1933–41. Edited by Stuart N. Clarke. London: Hogarth Press, 2011.
—— *The Waves*. 1931. London: Penguin, 1992.
—— *To the Lighthouse*. London: Hogarth Press, 1927.
Zavaglia, Liliana. *White Apology and Apologia: Australian Novels of Reconciliation*. Amherst, NY: Cambria, 2016.

Index

acheiropoieta 81, 127
Adamson, Jane 3
Adorno, Theodor 30, 161
aeroplanes 7, 142, 158–159
aesthetic 12, 13–15, 40, 46, 63, 75, 89, 91, 94, 116–117, 122, 124, 142, 144–145, 163
Agamben, Giorgio 2
Aguiar, Marian 152
airport 68, 151, 158, 159, 167
aisthesis 144
alienation 22, 66, 143, 153
answering machine 166
anthropology 33, 34, 35, 55, 144
Appadurai, Arjun 151
Apter, Emily 151
Aristotle 50
art 8, 11, 13, 96, 101, 107–109, 116, 117, 119–120, 125–128, 131, 134–135
  heist 127, 129, 171
  history 108, 119, 120, 171
  iconography 132
  visual 16, 107, 108, 114–115, 122, 132, 142, 143
  written 3, 13
astronaut 147, 157, 162, 166
asylum seekers 4
atomic bomb 9, 162
Atomic Bomb Museum (Nagasaki) 94, 162, 163
Attridge, Derek 3
Australia 4, 9–11, 32, 33, 37, 104, 131, 150

Bach, Johann Sebastian 44
Badiou, Alain 2
Balbuk, Fanny 6
barcode 151, 167

Barthes, Roland 18, 22
Beatles, The 64; *see also* Lennon, John
Beaumont, Matthew 152
Bebelplatz 80
Bell, Alexander Graham 9, 95, 151, 160, 164, 165
Belleflamme, Valérie-Anne 19
Ben-Hur 68, 131
Benjamin, Walter 12, 29–32, 42, 73, 86
  Berlin 30, 31
  Berlin Childhood 31
  childhood 30
  photography 30, 112
  snow flurries 32
  snow globes 30
  "Unpacking My Library" 86
  weather 29–31
  "Work of Art in the Age of Mechanical Reproduction, The" 12, 138
Berlin 11, 16, 23, 30, 41, 44–45, 80, 109, 154
Berlin Aquarium 45
biographies 8, 9, 81, 82, 96–100, 115, 120, 121, 150, 152
bioluminescence 75, 134
Blanchot, Maurice 15
blindness 30, 73, 104, 108, 129, 143, 160
blue (colour) 19, 23, 33, 35, 71, 99, 158, 164
Bologna 162
Bombay 16, 73, 75, 134
borders 15, 151
Born, Georgia 62
Bowie, David 44
Bradley, James 16
Brady, Veronica 132
Brahe, Tycho 57

Brando, Marlon 128
Breton, André 116
Bringing Them Home (report) 5
Brontë, Charlotte 83
    Jane Eyre 83, 87, 89
Broome 7, 93
brothers *see* siblings
Brožek, Josef 130
Brydon, Diana 33
Bulwer-Lytton, Edward 27
    Paul Clifford 27
Bunuba country 6
Bunuba people 6
Butler, Judith 103
butterflies 42
butterfly powder 43

Cadava, Eduardo 18, 112
Campion, Jane 4
    Piano, The 4, 20–21
capitalism 61, 64, 104, 148, 152, 153, 156
Caravaggio, Michelangelo Merisi da 128
    Crucifixion of St Peter, The 127
Carrington, Leonora 160
Caruth, Cathy 102
Celan, Paul 5, 44
Chatterjee, Partha 146
Chee Dimock, Wai 21
Chekhov, Anton 8, 36
chewing gum 152
childhood 4, 6, 28, 31, 45, 45, 91, 96, 120, 157;
    see also Jones, Gail: childhood of
chronophotography 69
cinema 1–2, 50, 69, 106–110, 128, 143, 153, 163;
    see also film
Circular Quay 10, 16, 19, 58, 60, 62, 65
class 42, 73, 88, 120, 132
Classen, Constance 160
clepsydra 57–59, 60, 65, 67
cli-fi 27
clocks 51, 55, 56, 63, 67, 77, 162
clouds 25, 29, 71, 122
cochlear implants 143
Coldplay
    "Clocks" 64
Collins, Wilkie
    Woman in White, The 169
colonialism 4, 9, 15, 33, 37, 97, 104, 134, 148
colour 28, 40, 54, 80, 130, 131
Connor, Steven 145, 165
convulsive beauty 117, 142

Crary, Jonathan 145
Critchley, Simon 3
Cultural Revolution 14, 15, 90, 113

Dale, Leigh 19, 63
Dalí, Salvador 60, 101
deafness 28, 143, 160
death 8, 12, 15, 19, 33, 34, 45–48, 52, 60, 66–70,
    74, 90, 92, 96–101, 108, 112, 134–138, 162,
    170, 171
Deleuze, Gilles 50
Derrida, Jacques 2, 97, 100
desire 13, 14, 40, 43, 59, 69, 110, 171
    sexual 20, 87, 124
Desnos, Robert 116, 123
Diamond, Cora 3
Dickens, Charles 83, 87
    Great Expectations 52, 83, 88
didgeridoo 19, 65, 66
Dixon, Robert 18, 62, 94, 116
dreams 7–8, 29, 32, 34–37, 39, 51, 54, 63, 71,
    101, 117, 123, 139, 162, 171
Duchamp, Marcel
    Nude Descending a Staircase 69
Duthie, Fiona 4
Dylan, Bob 66

Eagle, Christopher 35
Eaglestone, Robert 3
Eakin, Paul John 98
Edinburgh 94, 156
Einstein, Albert 55
ekphrasis 123
electricity 130, 149
Eliot, George 87
Elliot, Jane 20
Enlightenment, The 28, 145
Ernst, Max 116, 119
ethics 2–6, 10, 11, 14, 16, 43, 81–82, 90,
    98–100, 101, 102–104, 111, 133, 144, 146,
    148, 156, 160–161, 166, 167

Fabian, Johannes 56
Facebook 44
family 43, 92, 114, 121–123, 138, 162–163
Fang, Liu 64
fathers 11, 16, 28, 31, 45–46, 49, 56, 67–73,
    89–90, 100, 103, 107, 113, 121–127, 130, 133,
    138, 148, 162
    death of 35–36, 39, 67, 84, 118
Felski, Rita 146

film 1, 20, 21, 26, 50, 73, 106–107, 109–111, 122, 130, 132, 154, 161; *see also* cinema
Flaubert, Gustave 22
  Madame Bovary 13, 87
Flint, Kate 30
Foucault, Michel 2
fragment 16, 82
Francesca, Piero della 16, 32, 68, 72, 108, 126, 131, 143
  Baptism of Christ, The 72
  Flagellation of Christ, The 114
  Legend of the True Cross, The 72
  Madonna del Parto 69
  Nativity, The 131
Freeman, Michael 152
Freud, Sigmund 8, 97
Friedman, Marilyn 100
friendships 9, 43, 88, 97, 100, 134, 148, 156–157, 161, 163
Frow, John 10
Futurists 63, 69

Galilei, Galileo 57
Garbo, Greta 106, 110
gaze 77, 115, 121, 129, 142, 157, 158
Genette, Gérard 50
Genoni, Paul 115
giallo 11
Glebe 16
Godfather, The 128
von Goethe, Wolfgang
Green-Lewis, Jennifer 75
Guerin, Veronica 94

Hales, Dorothy 2
hands 28, 73–74, 83, 124, 160
Hari, Mata (Magaretha Geertruida Zelle) 8, 105–107
Hecq, Dominique 4
Herrero, Dolores 10
Heston, Charlton 131
Hillis Miller, J. 53
Hirsch, Marianne 43, 121
Hitchcock, Alfred 73
  Marnie 129
  Rebecca 109
Holocaust 5, 100, 161

Indigenous cultures 4, 149
Indigenous identities 4, 6, 36
industrialisation 124, 153

insomnia 60, 71, 158
internet 94, 147

Jackson, Noel 146
Jacobs, Lyn 18, 113
James, Henry 4
  Portrait of a Lady, The 94
Jandamarra 6
Japan 151, 159
Jarman, Derek
  Blue 130
Jay, Martin 145
Jewish identity 42, 43, 150
Jones, Gail
  and the apology 9, 15, 38
  awards (literary) of 2, 7
  childhood of 4, 5, 91
  father 7
  interviews 2, 8, 15, 50, 52, 69, 108
  on activism 2
  on mourning 6, 54, 97
  on writing 2, 4, 7, 15, 50, 81–83, 93, 106, 108, 133
Jones, Gail (works)
  Black Mirror 9, 26, 36, 51, 69, 81, 96–98, 100, 101–103, 108, 110, 113–116, 119, 123, 125, 125, 142, 148, 149, 152, 158, 160, 170
  Death of Noah Glass, The 11, 13, 16, 18, 24–25, 27, 28, 31, 46, 49, 55, 67–68, 108, 114, 126, 143, 147, 171
  Dreams of Speaking 5, 9, 16–17, 24, 25, 27, 28, 31, 45, 51, 53, 69, 81, 91, 92, 94, 96, 110, 118, 137, 142, 146–149, 153, 155, 161, 164
  Fetish Lives 8, 13, 36, 43, 51, 74, 81, 91, 105, 107, 143, 171
  Five Bells 10, 14, 15, 18–19, 24, 25, 28, 31, 55–59, 62, 63, 82, 89, 93, 94, 112, 116, 128, 131, 142, 154, 165, 170
  Guide to Berlin, A 11, 14, 19, 23, 26, 28–30, 32, 40, 43–46, 52, 79–82, 84–86, 87, 109, 154, 162, 170
  House of Breathing, The 1, 8–9, 11, 14, 53, 93, 109
  Piano, The 20, 21–22
  Sixty Lights 9, 12, 18, 29, 30, 51, 54–55, 81, 83, 87, 108, 117, 123, 134, 141, 146, 152, 163, 169
  Sorry 7, 9–10, 15, 19, 24, 29, 32, 33, 35, 37–40, 46, 53, 55, 67, 83, 92, 94, 109, 111, 163
Joyce, James
  "Dead, The" 10, 24, 62, 67

justice 2, 37
Jütte, Robert 144

Kalgoorlie 5
kangaroo 6, 151
Kazuo Steains, Timothy 162
Keats, John 169
Kennedy, Roseanne 33
Kern, Stephen 55
Kimberley 6
kitsch 34, 101, 128
Klee, Paul
  Angelus Novus 86
Kossew, Sue 10
Krauss, Rosalind 145
Kristel, Sylvia 106
Kumar, Amitava 151

LaCapra, Dominick 43, 102
Latour, Bruno 132, 146
law 37, 38, 58, 67, 97
Lennon, John 155–156, 166; *see also* Beatles, The
  Instant Karma 155
Leslie, Esther 34
Levinas, Emmanuel 2
libraries 86–87, 117, 121
lightning 30
London 16, 27, 73, 76, 83, 96, 109, 111, 113, 115–119, 131, 141, 148
  Underground 152–153
loss 10, 14, 32, 34, 82, 91, 97–104, 107, 112–114, 118, 122, 161
love 13, 40, 43, 45, 52, 67, 72, 94, 107, 113–114, 117, 118, 121, 137, 139, 166
  of books 95
Lukács, Georg 53
Lyotard, Jean-François 3

Maar, Dora 119
maculate 12, 74, 76, 77
Maduwongga 149
magic lantern 76, 111
Maisky, Mischa 44
Mao Zedong 56, 91
Maoism 14
Marey, Étienne-Jules 69
Marx, Eleanor 8, 13, 22, 87
Marx, Karl 142, 146
McCredden, Lyn 10
McGonegal, Julie 35
Melbourne 127, 130

memory 5, 6, 18, 29, 36, 43, 45, 47, 51, 54, 58, 62, 72, 75, 82, 85, 89, 91, 102, 103, 113, 122, 125, 133, 154, 161; *see also* speak-memories
multidimensional memory 5, 161
Merleau-Ponty, Maurice 145
Midalia, Susan 10
mining 31, 96, 100, 104, 124, 148, 153
Mitchell, Kate 18, 83
Mitchell, W.J.T. 108
modernism 12, 115
Monet, Claude 125
Monreale Cathedral 72
Moreau, Jeanne 106
Morrison, Toni 19
mothers 33, 34, 35–38, 43, 60, 71, 77, 84, 87, 90, 113, 118, 122–127
  removal from 92, 97
mourning 11, 53, 67, 69, 95, 97, 100, 112
Mozart, Wolfgang Amadeus
  Marriage of Figaro, The 64
Mudie, Ella 62
Mumbai *see* Bombay
music 28, 62–67, 145
Muybridge, Eadweard 69

Nabokov, Vladimir 11, 19, 30, 42, 52, 85, 101
  "First Love" 83
  Guide to Berlin, A 29, 171
  Lolita 14
  Speak, Memory 42, 52, 82
Nagasaki 94, 159, 161, 162
narrative theory 50
Nead, Lynda 147
neo-Victorian fiction 18
Newton, Isaac 54, 75, 134
  Opticks 130
Ninotchka 110
Nirvana 64
  Tourette 66
Nussbaum, Martha 2–3, 98
Nyoongar 67

Olalquiaga, Celeste 44
Ondaatje, Michael 146
  English Patient, The 144
  In the Skin of a Lion 11, 143
Onley, James 98
Orb, Naomi 36

painting 13, 60, 72, 101, 108–109, 114, 117, 119, 124–127, 131, 131

Index

Palermo 11, 16, 70, 72, 128, 132, 133
Palumbo-Liu, David 3
paperweight 35
Paris 9, 16, 24, 27, 94, 103, 110, 142, 149, 164, 165
passport 151
Pasternak, Boris 90
  Doctor Zhivago 28, 90
Perth 16, 24, 95, 164
Pessoa, Fernando 5
photography 18, 30, 52, 54, 73–77, 107, 108, 112–114, 117–119, 120–122, 124, 135–137, 147, 162, 163
Picasso, Pablo 119
pictograms 123, 125
Pilar Royo Grasa, Maria del 13, 19
Pliny the Elder 27
poetry 5, 13, 19, 93, 125, 156, 161
postmemory 43
Pound, Ezra 123
Presley, Elvis 8
Presner, Todd S. 161
prison 14, 93
prolepsis 52, 74
proleptic mourning 97, 100
Proust, Marcel 8, 171–172
psychoanalysis 20
Purkyně, Jan Evangelista 130

race 6, 33, 35, 37, 56, 73, 92, 130
Ragusa, Eleanor (Kiyohara Tama) 68, 71
rain 24–27, 31, 33, 38, 60, 66, 115
Rancière, Jacques 146
Ray, Man 116
Reed, Arden 28
refugees 7, 44, 150
religion 41, 73, 132, 134
Ricciardi, Alessia 97
Richards, Edward Graham 58
Ricoeur, Paul 50
Ritter, Johann Wilhelm 130
Rolling Stones, The 64
Romantic poets 27, 29, 74, 146
Rothberg, Michael 5, 161
Roughley, Fiona 51

Saadi Nikro, Norman 18
Sachs, Mendel 55
Sanders, Mark 2
Schivelbusch, Wolfgang 152
Scott, Rosie 150

Sebald, W.G
  Emigrants, The 49
Second World War 7
senses *see* blindness, deafness, sight, sound, taste
Serres, Michel 144–146
shadows 5, 43–44, 59, 74, 77, 118, 162, 163
Shakespeare, William 19, 83, 100
  Hamlet 83
  King Lear 8
  Macbeth 19, 35, 37
  Winter's Tale, The 37
shame 11, 39, 45, 46, 130
Shelley, Percy Bysshe 93
shock 25, 47, 109, 141–142
siblings 45–47, 49, 70, 71, 96, 150, 162
sight 129–130, 145, 150; *see also* blindness
silence 6, 39, 46, 58, 66, 103, 128, 157
sisters *see* siblings
Skype 70, 129, 147
sleep 60, 70, 71, 99, 123, 158, 162
Slessor, Kenneth 19
  Five Bells 19, 58
snow 14, 23–24, 28–30, 31–32, 34–37, 39–45, 47–48, 62, 85
snow globe 29, 34, 39–40, 60
Sontag, Susan 133
sound 13, 62–67, 130, 143, 166
speak-memories 42, 43, 44–47, 80, 81, 86; *see also* memory
speed 118, 141, 152, 153, 155, 156
stereotypes 157
Sterne, James 160
Stolpersteine 45, 79
storm 25, 28, 37, 45–46
summer 24, 60, 63
Surrealism 9, 60, 101, 114–118, 123, 124, 142, 153, 160
Swan River 16, 24
Sydney 10–11, 16, 19, 24, 25, 31, 58–59, 69, 70, 109, 128, 155, 156
Sydney Opera House 16, 63, 67
Sydney PEN 2

Tama, Kiyohara (Eleanor Ragusa) *see* Ragusa, Eleanor (Kiyohara Tama)
Tarkovsky, Andrei 50
taste 91, 126, 144, 145, 152
telephone 9, 142, 147–148, 149, 150, 160, 164–166, 171
Thackeray, William 87
Thebaud, Jean-Loup 3

time traveller 51, 74, 75, 77
Tokyo 16, 68, 142, 159
tourism 128, 149, 156
trains 26, 69, 152–156, 161
trauma 5, 10, 15, 28, 33, 43, 90, 97, 100, 102–104, 160, 161
travel 9, 11, 26, 32, 41, 87, 93, 109, 134, 149, 151, 154, 158, 171; *see also* trains
travel photography 133
Trexler, Adam 27
Triffids, The 66
Trower, Shelley 160
Truffaut, Francois 106
Tussaud, Madame 8, 107
Twitter 44

Ullman, Micha 80
Uluru Statement from the Heart 9
umbrellas 25, 44, 52, 96, 115
Underground *see* London: Underground

value 5, 11, 20, 25, 62, 80, 85, 87, 131
violence 6, 9, 10, 20, 25, 85, 91, 94, 122, 128, 132, 133, 136
  family 37, 129
  sexual 35, 100
Virilio, Paul 163
Vivaldi, Antonio 64
  Four Seasons 64
votive 128

Wade, Nicholas J. 130
Walker, Brenda 81
Walmajarri 9, 35, 92
war 7, 23, 36, 76, 107, 111, 150, 160–163
watches 57, 61, 117
Watkins, Beth 5
West-Pavlov, Russell 19
Western Sydney University 16, 21
Wevers, Lydia 163
White, Patrick 12
whiteness 23, 36, 37, 54, 121
Whitman, Walt 8, 51, 143
wind 24, 27–29, 29, 38, 40, 45, 106, 141, 164
Windjana Gorge 6
windsurfing 24, 164
winter 11, 23, 32, 38, 43, 48
Wish-Wilson, David 16
Wollstonecraft, Mary 8, 11
Woman of the Dunes 128
Woolf, Virginia 8, 12, 15, 42, 54
  "Art of Biography, The" 12
  "Modern Fiction" 54, 74
  "Mr Bennett and Mrs Brown" 54
  Mrs Dalloway 19
  The Waves 15, 43
  To the Lighthouse 29

x-ray 74, 118

Zavaglia, Liliana 10, 19

www.ingramcontent.com/pod-product-compliance
Lightning Source LLC
Chambersburg PA
CBHW081023240426
43668CB00031B/2388